SCRAPING HEAVEN

SCRAPING HEAVEN

HEAVEN

A Family's Journey Along the Continental Divide

CINDY ROSS

RAGGED MOUNTAIN PRESS / McGRAW-HILL

Camden, Maine · New York · Chicago · San Francisco · Lisbon · London · Madrid
Mexico City · Mi   ngapore · Sydney · Toronto

The **McGraw·Hill** Companies

2 4 6 8 10 9 7 5 3 1 DOC
Copyright © 2003 Cynthia L. Ross

LIBRARY OF CONGRESS CATALOGING-IN-PUBLICATION DATA
Ross, Cindy.
Scraping heaven : a family's journey along the Continental Divide /
Cindy Ross.
    p.   cm.
ISBN 0-07-137360-8 (hardcover : alk. paper)
1. Continental Divide National Scenic Trail—Description and travel.
2. Hiking—Continental Divide National Scenic Trail. 3. Llama pack
camping—Continental Divide National Scenic Trail. 4. Ross,
Cindy—Journeys—Continental Divide National Scenic Trail. 5. Ross,
Cindy—Family. I. Title.
  F721 .R75 2002
  917.8—dc2   2002006361

MAPS BY Todd Gladfelter and Cindy Ross

Dedication

To Bob Riley,
Trail Angel Magnifico,
and
To Todd, my husband,
my hero in all of life

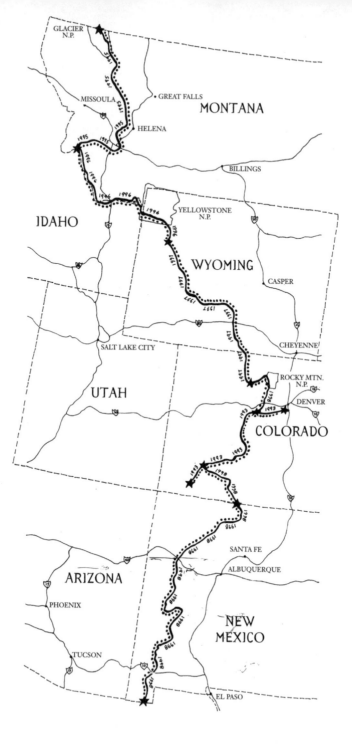

Contents

PART FOUR

THE CONTINENTAL DIVIDE TRAIL
THROUGH WYOMING, 1997

PART FIVE

THE CONTINENTAL DIVIDE TRAIL
TO MEXICO, 1998

Prologue
MONTANA, JULY 1995

WE ARE walking along the Continental Divide—the backbone of the continent, where the wind blows with a vengeance. On this day it feels serious. It steals our hats and sends us chasing down the mountainside after them, hair whipping across our faces. It sucks our mouths dry of saliva when we yell to one another. It makes us want to make our bodies small and huddle close to the ground. This wind makes my husband, Todd, and me anxious, because we are on the edge. This we can handle, but barely. More, we aren't sure about.

My forehead wrinkles, and I gnaw my lower lip. "The wind won't let me breathe, Mommy!" gasps Bryce. At three years old, he is light enough to be blown off the llama he is riding.

1

"Daddy's going to put you in the backpack," Todd reassures him.

Five-year-old Sierra is perceptive enough to realize she isn't much heavier than her brother. I tell her we're going to descend now—that maybe the wind will die down once we lose elevation. But that isn't what happens. The lower we drop into the saddle of land between the two peaks, the worse conditions become.

"Sierra, hold Mommy's hands," I yell, placing her in front of my body so my bulk can support her.

The saddle, bathed in sunlight, is deceptively inviting. But it acts as a wind tunnel, gathering up air from the valley and blasting it over the Divide. We take each step slowly, planting one foot at a time, knees locked and spines braced. No matter. A gust hits us broadside and knocks us to the ground. I lie there in the dirt, Sierra clutched in my arms, and grip the llama's lead rope. The beast is thrashing wildly because his saddle and panniers have been blown off and the whole mess dangles under his belly. He stomps, stepping on Sierra. We scream, hoping Todd can help.

Todd is just ten yards away, but it might as well be ten miles. He and Bryce have been blown down too. The roar of the wind drowns out our cries.

I look down into my daughter's wide brown eyes. "Are we going to be OK, Mommy?"

PART ONE

THE COLORADO
TRAIL
1992–93

WYOMING

MT. ZIRKEL
WILDERNESS

ROCKY MOUNTAIN N.P.

CHEYENNE

MASONVILLE

DENVER

76

70

WATERTON

TEN MILE RANGE

BRECKENRIDGE

SOUTH PLATTE

LEADVILLE

KENOSHA
PASS

HOPE PASS

COLLEGIATE PEAKS

COLORADO

BUENA VISTA

COCHETOPA HILLS

SAN LUIS
PEAK

CONEY
SUMMIT

SILVERTON

LA GARITA
WILDERNESS

MOLAS PASS

WEMINUCHE
WILDERNESS

INDIAN RIDGE
TRAIL

DURANGO

SOUTH SAN JUAN
WILDERNESS

25

CUMBRES PASS

NEW MEXICO

CHAMA

1

A Dream Takes Root
SEPTEMBER 1992

Life is either a daring adventure or nothing at all.
—HELEN KELLER

IT's THE kind of adult party where children are tolerated, not welcomed. Our two-and-a-half-year-old daughter, Sierra, is being antisocial and refuses to acknowledge anyone who speaks to her or smiles at her, while I use that age-old mother's excuse, "She's tired." Meanwhile we are working hard to keep ten-month-old Bryce out of the hostess's manicured English herb garden, obviously rushed to completion for this event. Rocks are strategically placed among the meticulously planted vegetation to control traffic. But an inquisitive child who loves the outdoors knows no boundaries to exploring. My husband, Todd, and I are beginning to wonder what possessed us to come when we spot the couple on the other side of the flag-stone patio.

A braid of yellow hair falls to her waist—it's the color children use to paint the sun. Her face is scrubbed and beautiful. She wears an Australian herder's oilskin coat with its short cape attached at the shoulders.

The man's gray-streaked hair falls softly over his ears and down the back of his neck. He wears one tiny earring. His gray beard and moustache are framed by the Australian hat pulled low over his warm eyes. He is handsome in a way that attracts you, even if you're a much younger woman and not even faintly interested in "older men."

I wonder who they are and how they came to be at this party, for it's obvious they are not from this little corner of Pennsylvania German farm country, where the folks are conservative, slow to change, and wary of outsiders.

A few minutes later Todd and I are complaining a bit to some friends who have asked if we have any big adventures planned. They know our histories. How we both hiked the entire 2,100-mile Appalachian Trail at a young age and then went on to hike the 2,600-mile Pacific Crest Trail. How we each have over 6,000 long-distance miles on our legs. They know we are in love with long-distance hiking, perhaps to the point of obsession.

"It's going to be about seven years before we can get out on the trail for any length of time," we pout. "Until our kids can walk a decent day under their own steam."

"With llamas, you can get back on the trail *right now!*" a voice says from behind us. I turn to see the couple I had admired. "Forgive us for overhearing, but if you use llamas to carry your children and their diapers and your gear, you needn't wait seven years."

Wally White is a llama breeder from Durango, Colorado. He and his wife, Katy, are in our neck of the woods while Wally temporarily manages another breeder's herd. He tells us he raised his two daughters in the Rocky Mountains, on the trails, on the backs of the llamas. "They are so gentle and calm a two-year-old can lead one."

The more we talk, the more we reveal to each other. He learns that I am a writer. I learn he helped build the new Colorado Trail that stretches five hundred miles across the Rockies, from Denver to Durango.

"I bought Todd a guidebook on that for Christmas before we conceived," I tell him. "If not for that, we would have hiked that trail. It's going to be our first journey once we get back to long-distance hiking."

"With llamas, you can do it *now*," Wally repeats.

"Sounds great," we say, "but we don't have any llamas, and we can't afford to buy any or even rent them for the summer."

"I have some contacts out there," Wally says. "Let me make some phone calls. I've got connections with people at the Rocky Mountain Llama and Alpaca Association (RMLA), and they are very interested in promoting llamas. Let me see if I can get you some sponsors." We exchange phone numbers and call it a night.

Thank goodness the children sleep on the drive home so I can go off talking about this fabulous new possibility. I get excited over "coincidental" meetings like these. They seem a little too strange to be chance. It feels as if a door has been flung open, showing me a new path I might take. "What if," I say to Todd.

"What if this really happens? What if we get to take our little babes five hundred miles across the rooftops of Colorado with llamas? Oh, my God!" I really believe we were meant to be at that party, that our paths were supposed to cross Wally's. We have been presented with an opportunity. What we choose to do with it is up to us. I look over at my husband's face, illuminated by the farm spotlights we pass under. He sports a small smile as he carefully maneuvers the curving country road. Unlike me, he approaches nearly everything in life cautiously, especially new ideas and dreams.

"Why would the llama association people want to do all that for us?" he asks. "They don't even know us."

"We can help one another," I say. "I can write about it. People will learn how wonderful llamas are. Why *wouldn't* it work? Why *wouldn't* it happen?" I decide to sidestep my skeptical husband, and as soon as we carry the babies to their beds, I run up to my office to gather materials to send to Wally—my book jackets, my publication list, some magazine clippings I've written, a list of the places where I've lectured over the years, and a letter telling what I could do for RMLA and the llama industry. When I come downstairs ready to go to bed, sealed manila envelope in hand, I find my husband sitting in the easy chair by the woodstove, quietly examining the Colorado Trail guidebook.

TODD AND I have been married almost ten years. We have covered many thousands of miles together. We both loved long-distance hiking even before we met, and we probably came of age on the Appalachian Trail. After hiking the trail in 1979 at age twenty-four, I moved to a farmhouse by the trail in Pennsylvania, where I could write and paint. Occasionally I would cruise down to town where the trail crossed to see if any hikers were passing through. When I felt like having company, I would bring them home to share my home-cooked dinner. When I brought Todd home in 1980, he had just turned nineteen and was shy and boyish. He hardly spoke all evening, but his dark, expressive eyes spoke for him.

Two years later, we both happened to be on the Pacific Crest Trail at the same time, though our paths never crossed. A broken foot cut his journey short, and he came back home to attend a hiking conference, where we met again. Every hiker there was wrapped up in the Appalachian Trail, but the two of us couldn't keep our minds off the trail out west. Since we lived fairly close to each other, we decided that when his foot mended a hike was in order so we could reminisce some more.

After our hike I said to my mother, "That's the kind of guy I ought to marry. He loves the mountains, he loves to hike, and he's kind and sweet."

"Well, what's wrong with him?" she asked.

"He's too young, and he doesn't talk much."

"He'll get older," she said, "and he'll learn to talk."

We spent our honeymoon traversing 1,400 miles through the Cascade Mountains. Living together twenty-four hours a day for four months was an intense initiation. We couldn't escape to a job when we argued. We were forced to work things out. We couldn't run to friends or mothers. We had only each other. On the trail, we experienced everything together. We watched the same breathtaking sunsets and battled through the same lightning storms. We crawled into our sleeping bags feeling the same exhaustion, and we felt the same joy at diving into a refreshing mountain lake. In those four months of hiking we bonded so we never wanted anything to come between us, and we grew to believe there was little we could dream about that couldn't come true.

When our daughter, Sierra, was born in 1990, I expected her to change my life. Every mother I knew told me I would have to give up many of the things I'd done when I was childless. But there were some things, like hiking, that I was determined not to part with. I would adapt, but I wouldn't abandon my passion.

Our first try was the sixty-mile Loyalsock Trail in north-central Pennsylvania, when Sierra was three months old. In case we needed to bail out, we picked a trail that had road crossings every five to ten miles. Bad weather or any sign of fever or gross unhappiness from Sierra would be reason not to continue.

We had to learn to deal with diapers on the trail, live without high chairs for mealtimes and rocking chairs for restless nights, learn to nurse on the trail and in a tent at night. We took a well-stocked first-aid kit including children's Tylenol and plenty of diaper rash ointment and hoped for the best.

Our pace slowed and the workload increased, but we watched our baby's senses open wide to all nature has to offer. We saw her mesmerized by sparkling sunlight on a lake. We watched her listen to singing brooks and follow the wind as it raked through trees and fluttered the leaves. We listened to her caw to ravens and saw her delight when they answered. We knew she was happy out there.

Then Bryce was born. Since then, we've been camping extensively and doing short hikes, but nothing of any great magnitude. Todd and I miss the long haul, the extended trip in the mountains, that has always pulled hardest at our heartstrings. We're lucky that we can take time off from our "normal" lives to hike. Todd, besides crafting furniture in his basement shop, helps a friend paint houses a few days a week. His "boss" takes a few weeks off a year and walks long distances to raise money for juvenile diabetes, so he doesn't mind if Todd takes a week or even a few months off to hike. As long as we can save up the bucks, we are free to seek adventures.

Especially to me, hiking has become more than a sport or a pastime. It's my job, my livelihood, and also my life force. Next to my family, it's my reason to live. Todd and I had an interesting life before we had children. If this llama deal promises a way of getting back into the wilderness with my family for long periods, you'd better believe I'm going to run with the ball.

AFTER A FEW WEEKS we get a phone call from Wally. He says we need to talk, so we invite him and Katy for dinner and a Finnish sauna.

Their eyes well up with tears when they enter our beautiful handmade log home. We stripped its massive logs with our own hands and fitted them with a scribed cut, just as they do in the West and the Far North. Our home is adorned with stained glass, carvings, paintings, and unique recycled materials, by-products of our artistic leanings.

"I didn't realize how much I missed Colorado until I walked into your home," Wally says softly. During a venison dinner and the penetrating heat of our sauna, our friendship takes root. He tells us the RMLA wants to work with us and that, incredibly, all the details can be ironed out. He has found a commercial llama packer who is willing to lend llamas for the hike. He has found a llama gear manufacturer who is willing to donate the saddles, panniers, and all the other equipment we need. And Dee Goodman, the president of RMLA, will coordinate our resupply points and make sure we get support. I'm flying high, totally confident it will happen.

If Todd is excited after that evening, he doesn't say anything, but I find him poring over the llama books Wally brought every chance he gets. Any time we're in the car together, he asks me to drive so he can study.

We saw llama trekkers on the Pacific Crest Trail when we through-hiked from Mexico to Canada. They struck us as epicurean intruders, these hikers who had their gourmet picnic lunches carried up for them, complete with microbrewed beer and wine in crystal glasses. With llamas to carry the gear, you can deviate from the normal hiker's diet of jerky, dried fruit, instant oatmeal, and macaroni and cheese. We were reluctant then to share the wilderness with them, as if carrying our own packs made us better or more deserving to be there. We're a little sheepish about those smug feelings now that we're considering using the animals.

But things change. Our family now includes two small children, whose gear could include up to forty pounds of wet cotton diapers. It's impossible for us to go into the backcountry for any length of time without the aid of stock. We think of our die-hard long-distance-hiking friends. Some may say we'd be selling our souls. But if it makes sense, who cares?

And so we learn. Llamas' two-toed padded feet make them very surefooted in the most rugged terrain. With their 300 to 350 pounds distributed over four feet, they have about the same environmental impact as a Vibram-soled backpacker. All the world is a salad bar to llamas, and they usually can meet their nutritional needs from what grows alongside the trail, dried pine needles included. They browse throughout the day, nibbling and sampling as they go. Their droppings are small pellets similar to an elk's that can easily be kicked off the trail by the last person in the group. Since they are cousins to the camel, they don't require a lot of water, usually a gallon a day, which includes the moisture in their food.

Although llamas are considered exotics by some, they originated on the North American plains, then migrated down the land bridge to South America, where they have been used for over five thousand years to transport goods. In some remote villages of Peru, these "trucks of the Andes" are still the only means some families have of carrying their potatoes and other goods many miles to the marketplace. Llamas are just now returning to their land of origin, where they are being rediscovered as wonderful pack animals.

Perhaps the most important thing to us is that they are extremely gentle creatures. A well-trained pack llama on a lead rope will follow nearly anywhere, even where a two-year-old child wants to lead it. They aren't skittish like horses, and the ones trained for riders will safely carry a child who is old enough to sit upright. If we decide to hike the Colorado Trail, three-year-old Sierra will ride a llama most of the trail, and one-year-old Bryce will travel in a backpack child carrier.

Todd and I have never been afraid of hard work. We have perhaps been afraid of not having control over how we spend our time. We rather enjoy the challenge. We know what planning a long hike entails, but throwing in babes and beasts complicates it tremendously. Fortunately the Colorado Trail was designed to make this part easy.

The five hundred miles of continuous nonmotorized recreational trail passes through seven national forests and six wilderness areas as it makes its way from Denver to Durango. It was created through a massive volunteer effort involving thousands of people. Gudy Gaskill, "the Mother" and moving force behind the volunteer building of the CT, wanted to create something different from the Continental Divide Trail, the other long trail through this mountainous state. The CDT hugs the Divide as much as possible, making it very high, exposed, and remote nearly all the way. Great care was taken when laying out the Colorado Trail to dip it into the timber to reduce the long stretches of altitude exposure. Most of the trail is still very high—above 10,000 feet, with the highest point at 13,334 feet—but you can get to the safety of trees every night. You also cross roads nearly every day, making it easier to get out should an emergency arise and making logistical planning easier.

AS OUR ROUTE PLANNER, Todd knows the tremendous workload that awaits him if we decide to go ahead with this undertaking the following June. He'll need to order all the trail's Forest Service maps and spend hours on the floor with his highlighter. To find our resupply points, he'll look for road crossings that lead to towns close to the trail. He'll aim for six to seven days between stops but might sometimes have to go as long as fourteen in a particularly remote area. We are told by a commercial llama packer that we should expect to cover just five or six miles a day, but we find this difficult to believe. Todd feels he'll need to work out two schedules, a fast one at ten miles a day and a slow one at eight miles. The next step will be typing up both schedules and mailing them to the president of RMLA, who will publish it in the newsletter with the request that members who live near our resupply points volunteer to help us.

As an independent backpacker, you can just walk to the road and hitchhike into town, but that's impossible with a family of four and a pack string of four llamas. Animals and children make things incredibly complicated. We'll need people with stock trailers who will take the llamas to their ranches while we do our laundry and wash diapers and buy and repack food and supplies. But RMLA's president, Dee Goodman, is excited about this adventure and feels confident that everything can be worked out.

"How would we coordinate meeting at the designated road crossing without communicating for over a week?" Todd asks. "We could get behind schedule for tons of reasons, and then that stranger is left sitting on the road wondering what happened to us." Questions like this illustrate how challenging a trip this could be.

If we decide to go ahead, I will have to send information packets to equipment manufacturers telling about our endeavors past and future and asking them to sponsor us with gear. I'll hit the essentials first, then make out a list of luxuries, like collapsible camp chairs, to write for later if time permits. We have to locate and buy a ton of small gear like children's sunglasses, wool mittens, and balaclavas, which are difficult to find once winter is over and inventories are low. And many manufacturers' sizes don't go small enough for a one-year-old.

And then there's food. When I see what my children eat at their ages, I hate to think about adolescence. Even now, besides quantity, we'll need high quality. Because the children are growing so quickly, they need vast quantities of protein and calcium; dry milk, although a good source for these on the trail, is not considered a treat by people of any age, especially young ones. We'll need to get a home food dehydrator that can dry liquids on solid trays so we can mix fruit preserves into our homemade yogurt and dry it into leathers, which taste like saltwater taffy. Since our children love meat, we'll have to make venison jerky, leaving out the harmful additives that lace most commercial jerky. We'll make trips to the farmers' market and buy half bushels of apple seconds to slice and dry, and ripe bananas by the bagful to dry into chips.

Once we dehydrate as much food as we can and collect cases of freeze-dried dinners and energy bars from sponsors, we will still need to buy more food to add to our resupply boxes. We like to supplement our supplies with fresh food from grocery stores along the way, but there are some health foods and items in bulk that we'll have to buy ahead of time.

"Logistics king" Todd will then need to make a close estimate of how much *all* our gear will weigh, so he can tell our llama supplier how many animals we'll need. In a span of only a few months, we'll have to decide everything we are bringing—including which toys and books for the kids, how many diapers for Bryce—and pack and weigh the whole pile.

Since we have no idea how quickly Bryce might go through his stash of a hundred diapers, we'll bring them all. If we still run out of clean diapers before a town stop, we'll have to air-dry the wet ones and sandwich them between clean layers.

The kids will need some new toys. For Bryce, a Matchbox dump truck and bulldozer for playing in the dirt, and a tractor and wagon with small vinyl farm animals. For Sierra, a zippered plastic bag with two Barbie dolls (a mom and a daughter) and half a dozen out-fits. Paperback books that are thin and light, balloons for tent fun, finger puppets, crayons, paper and scissors, card games—the list goes on. It would be a good idea to buy some paperbacks and small toys for each town stop, wrap them, and use them as rewards for successfully completing another stretch and to keep the kids occupied while Todd and I do chores in town.

I'll need to buy camera film in bulk and set up an account with the photography store I'll be mailing the exposed film to. They'll mail the slides to our friends Frank and Lila Fretz, artists with an eye for photography, who can critique them for us along the way.

If we go, we'll drive our resupply boxes across country with us to save postage and have Dee Goodman mail them to resupply points as we need them. But we'll still have our neighbor pack our flat-rate mail from home and send it to every town stop so we can pay our bills and not miss important letters. We'll preaddress and date large padded envelopes to tell him where and when to send them.

Before we leave, I'll have to answer mail I've neglected for months, use up food in the freezer that's getting old, cut and dry herbs from the garden, make arrangements with the Fretzes to dig our onions and potatoes if the weather turns wet, brush up on our basic first aid and CPR, attend a wilderness medicine workshop, learn how to care for a lightning strike victim, learn all we can about llamas, find homes for our chickens and cat, mulch the garden and harvest the spinach, alert the FedEx and UPS drivers what to do with packages, and try to get in shape. And we should arrange at least a trial day hike with Katy and Wally to see if Sierra will consent to ride a llama for even half a mile. That's a big "if." Five hundred miles is an even bigger if.

Besides the prospect of a huge amount of planning work to hold us back, we also have our fears. We are concerned for the safety of our two small children. What if Bryce cracks his head on a rock and needs immediate medical care? As well as injuries, there are the horrendous electrical storms to contend with—the Colorado Rockies have one of the world's highest frequencies of lightning strikes. Then there are mountain lions. They wouldn't normally concern me, for it's rare even to spot one; *but* mountain lions are the llama's only natural predator, *and* we just learned that a child was eaten by a lion on a school track in Colorado. The town where this occurred happens to be one of our resupply points! I decide to take up these matters on the phone with Dee Goodman.

Whenever Dee telephones it's wise to put the kettle on for tea, since conversations with him are neither short nor lacking in savor. We feel like close friends before our first call ends. I share my fears of the lions, and he puts me in touch with the Colorado Division of Wildlife to discuss mountain lion habits and the precautions we can take. I share my fears of the lightning, and together we decide to ask our tent manufacturer about the advantages and disadvantages of various tent pole materials and what tactics are best in a storm. I share my fears about a medical emergency, and Dee promises to check on cellular sites—far fewer at that time—along the trail and to try to get us a cell phone for our trip.

As far as anyone knows, there has been only one other long walking journey using llamas. Peter Illiad hiked a thousand miles of the Pacific Crest Trail through Oregon and Washington. He learns about our proposed Colorado Trail adventure through RMLA and calls to offer his help. His experience gives us solid facts to gauge what we could expect from our llamas. He also relays nerve-racking stories of llamas sliding down glaciers, llamas getting loose and lost, llamas eating poisonous plants, and building bridges out of five-gallon buckets and planks to get the llamas over blown-down trees blocking the trail. I add a few more items of concern to our growing list.

I DON'T FEEL any better after this afternoon's sledding party. Although it's the spring equinox, we have sixteen inches of snow, so we decide to go tobogganing on our neighbor's hill. As we speed downward, the cold snow that sprays the kids' faces is quickly melted by their warm tears. Trudging up the hill isn't much fun either. Bryce insists on walking but can't; Sierra straight out refuses to walk. Todd ends up carrying them both uphill after every run. Sierra is hysterical over "important" things like her thumb and her pointer finger being together in her glove. They are both exhausted, of course.

I think about Colorado and slogging through the rain and cold. It's inevitable that we'll sometimes *have* to travel under those conditions. "What are we going to do if this happens on the trail?" I ask Todd.

"Deal with it," is his reply.

There is only so far you can push a child. They cannot deal with being cold and wet and hungry and tired the way adults can. They fall apart. I'm concerned that they will find *lots* of reasons to fall apart out there. I don't want them to be unhappy on the trail. If we do this, I want them to find joy—to love the wilderness.

Taking our children on the trail is like taking them home to meet our parents. The trail turned Todd and me into adults. It's the force that made us fall in love. Sharing the trail is sharing a fundamental part of our lives. We hope our kids would like it. We certainly want them to be safe.

ALTHOUGH OUR FAMILIES truly love us, we wouldn't say they perfectly understand us or the motivation behind our adventures. We should have known better than to ask them to help us decide whether to hike the Colorado Trail with our children. We talk about what could make life difficult on the trail, and my sister comments: "This isn't any different than all your other trips, is it?" "It's a lot different!" I say. "We'd have a one-year-old and a three-year-old along."

One relative thinks we'd be bringing a canoe. Another exclaims how overwhelmed she is just by packing for a trip to Disney World. We think of the elaborate plans needed to make a three-month journey happen. One is surprised that we had long discussions with our tent company's designer over pole materials and lightning. "Wow!" he comments. "You've really done your homework." (That's because this is serious stuff.)

After the discussion on mountain lions, lightning, and snow travel, my younger brother asks, "So, *is* this dangerous?" "A setup!" my mind yells. If I say yes, his next comment will be, "So *why* would you consider taking your babies out there?" But I answer, "It depends on how stupid you are."

People have wondered why we don't just take our kids to Disneyland like everyone else. After all, they're at the ideal ages for the ultimate Disney experience. Why are we bypassing the guidebooks on how to do the Magic Kingdom for guidebooks about the Colorado Trail?

We're on the opposite end of the spectrum from most people in terms of family "vacations." Our hike isn't a getaway. It's an extension of our life, our values—not a departure from life but an arrival. To us a Disney vacation is superficial, as thin as air. It blows by in an instant, a summer breeze. Our trek, however, is lasting—rock solid, like the mountains we walk on.

There are middle grounds—soft-adventure trips with outfitters and guides offering built-in safety and security—but even those leave us feeling shortchanged. A trip like that would seem to us like going back to grade school or having a baby-sitter. The child who *can* dress herself wants to, and wants to pick out her own clothes too. That spirit of independence drives us. Our hunger for independence, solitude, adventure, and risk is far greater and deeper than Disneyland could ever satisfy. This is who we are. Long-distance hiking in the wilderness is what makes us feel fulfilled.

My grandmother says to me, "If you go, you should try to leave the kids with someone." But the prospect of having the kids with us accounts for at least half our excitement. To see a waterfall, sunlight, a dancing bird through their eyes is to see it as never before. So many firsts are to come for them, and we want to share in them all.

Someone else says it's too bad the kids aren't older so they could remember it better. But the other half of the reason Todd and I want to go is for our own enjoyment. We love it out there. The kids would be along for the ride. We're talking selfish motives here. And this would be only the beginning of a long list of adventures we would like to share with them before they go their own ways in life. Sierra is three now; when she's fifteen, will she want to go long-distance hiking with her parents? Doubtful. We have maybe twelve years to experience the wilderness as a family, and twelve years can go by in a heartbeat. Why wait?

BACK AND FORTH, back and forth the rocking chair gently moves. I hold my sleeping boy in my arms and look at his beautiful face in the glow of his nightlight. I place my lips on that special spot where his nose and his forehead connect and hold them there while my tears wet his skin. I've been thinking about losing him on the trail. I've been thinking about what I would do if he were injured or attacked by a lion or struck by lightning. I think about what I would do if he died out there.

I watch as he walks and stumbles so many times in a day. At one year old, he's not very coordinated, and his verbal communication is minimal. Sometimes he seems so vulnerable to be out in the wilderness. So what *would* I do if he died? What would it be like to carry a dead baby down from the high country into town? At the funeral, our friends and family would tell us we never should have taken our children out there, and we would have to struggle with guilt for the rest of our lives.

My New Age friends would say I create my own reality, and the more I dwell on this fear, the more likely it is to occur, so I try to banish it from my mind. But am I having these fears because they are premonitions, or am I dealing with them so I can cleanse myself and leave them behind? In some native cultures special rituals attend the birth of a child—tribal members enact its funeral, simply because not all children survive. They practice death so they can better deal with its occurrence. I do the same, as I allow my tears to wash away the fear.

I lay Bryce down and walk out of his bedroom, squinting from the bright light, and brush my cheeks dry. Todd wonders what's wrong. He is usually the one with the fears, the doubts, the insecurities. When I express concern, however rarely, he doesn't play devil's advocate and bolster me up. He sinks even lower than I do. If ever-optimistic Cindy is concerned, there really is a reason to worry.

But this is something we have to work through whenever we go on a journey: fear of the unknown. I think back to my experiences on the Pacific Crest Trail, of falling down a near-vertical icy traverse and flipping two times in midair, and of crossing snow-buried trails over 12,000-foot passes for a month. If we had known what was in store, perhaps we wouldn't have ventured that first step. It's usually better if we don't know what is ahead.

If we close our eyes and listen to our hearts, they tell us to hike the Colorado Trail. All fears and concerns aside, we think it's doable with the children. We wouldn't be doing this mostly *for* them, although I'm sure the experience would help to create the human beings they are to become. Todd and I want to go out there because *we* love to hike. We seem to need a certain amount of risk and adventure in our lives, and this would satisfy that need. When we think of the high adventure to come, our thoughts are joyous. We've been "thinking like mountains" lately. Listening to our friend Walkin' Jim's music of traveling in the mountains stirs our souls. We've been there. We know wonderful things await us. The Rocky Mountains of Colorado will become part of me, just like the Appalachians, the Sierras, and the Cascades. And they will become part of our children too.

Once you have educated yourself on how to be the most knowledgeable, responsible parent you can be, it comes down to a judgment call, and this feels right and good for us. Let's do it! Whatever happens out there is supposed to happen, and we must have faith that it will be a beneficial experience in the long run. We must believe that.

THE REPORTS are coming in. The Colorado Division of Wildlife tells us the most likely place to see mountain lions (cougars) is in the foothills, where deer are plentiful. This kind of terrain occurs for a few days at the beginning of the trail, until we climb to higher elevations, and then again in the Cochetopa Hills. The wildlife specialist says mountain lions are so elusive that we would be lucky to get even a brief glimpse of one, even though Colorado has an estimated 1,500 to 3,000 cougars. We've begun hearing stories from our friends in the West, including the story about their not knowing there was a lion in the area until the pictures they took revealed one lounging on a branch above their heads!

In more than a hundred years, fewer than a dozen people have been killed by mountain lions in North America. Most of the attacks were by young lions, perhaps forced out to hunt on their own and not yet living in established territories. Young lions may home in on easy prey like pets and small children. Since Sierra and Bryce fit that description, we want to know exactly how to conduct ourselves should we encounter one.

Now on to lightning. We call the tent designer for Sierra Designs about graphite versus aluminum poles. Our tent came with aluminum poles, but we wonder if graphite is a poorer conductor of electricity. He tells us he has been debating this with a meteorologist and feels we're better off with aluminum, although he'd gladly special order a set of graphite poles. The best remedy is to avoid exposed ridges in an electrical storm. If we find ourselves in a bad situation, he feels we would be safer *outside* the tent. Bundling the children into rain gear to go outside in cold, soaking rain seems ridiculous. If we stay inside the tent, we should get into the center and insulate ourselves from the ground with as many foam pads as possible. Although we're educating ourselves, all these worries are starting to compound.

In a few days Dee calls back. He's having problems finding cellular phone sites over the last third of the trail, where the Colorado Trail stays very high in the remote and wild La Garita and San Juan Mountains. In the end, we decide to go without one.

Dee also has some concerns about the snow pack. It has just snowed two feet (in early June), and closed all the roads. "You might have to leave the buried trail and climb high onto the Divide to get to open country. If the trail is really impassable, you might need to find another route around it." This is the last thing I want to hear. I've been frightened in the past crossing snowy traverses, and I don't want to try it with my babies and a string of llamas.

THERE IS A huge chasm between the words "we'd like" or "we hope" to hike the Colorado Trail and "we're going to" hike the

Colorado Trail. Our brain chemistry changes once we make that affirmative statement and commit ourselves. This is the very first step in making any dream come true. A dream doesn't have a chance until we make that shift. Every time we write it or, even more, speak it, our dream draws closer to reality. It builds our belief and confidence that it can and will happen. As Richard Bach said in *Illusions*, "You are never given a dream without the ability to make it come true. You may have to work for it, however."

2

On the Road
June 22, 1993

"There's no use trying," [Alice] said. "One can't believe impossible things."

"I daresay you haven't had much practice," said the Queen. "When I was your age, I always did it for half-an-hour a day. Why, sometimes I've believed as many as six impossible things before breakfast."

—Lewis Carroll

SIX A.M. We're packing last-minute objects—bed pillows, cooler full of fridge food. Dewy grass soaks our sandaled feet. The morning air is still cool. I turn and head toward the waiting truck. The kids are buckled in, the back is jam-packed with food and supplies for the next few months.

The pioneers were perhaps our nation's first long-distance walkers, and folks like us may be the last pioneers. We too have had to pick and choose from our belongings what is most necessary and suitable for the arduous journey. Some last-minute luxuries we've brought along may not be worth their weight once we're into the trip. The pioneers left furniture and family heirlooms alongside the Oregon Trail. We have the option of mailing them home.

That same restlessness is propelling us westward toward the great American dream. There's that same gamble and striving and risk, and we hope, a payoff when we finally reach our goal. We too are walking away from our homes, our jobs, our loved ones; but unlike the pioneers, we hope to return. Still, Thoreau said, "We should go forth on the shortest walk . . . in the spirit of undying adventure, never to return."

We're driving all the way to Michigan tonight, across three states. Our first day and our biggest day. Todd turns the key in the ignition, his thigh muscles contract depressing the clutch, but he doesn't shift into first. We turn and glance back at our home, our security and comfort. It will look different when we return. We will see it with different eyes, for we will be different people. We are leaving behind all that symbolizes safety and security. Like the pioneers in their Conestoga wagons, we are trading our home and our property for this moving vehicle, this capsule, stuffed with supplies and loved ones. Our eyes lock, and time stands still. Here we go! Who knows what is waiting for us?

When I was a child, my family always recited Catholic prayers on the first mile of any road trip. We say them now, too quickly to be thinking of the actual words. It's more of a good luck charm—calling in the angels.

It took a little thought to decide which objects would be regularly needed on the trip and should be stored in the cab. Kids' books, crayons and drawing boards, cooler, water bottle, bags of munchies like popcorn and hard beer pretzels to keep the driver alert and the family alive are placed on the seat between us and at our feet. The back of the truck holds hiking and camping gear and boxes of trail food. All day long we take turns with the audiotapes—one adults', one children's, one adults', one children's. When we refuel, we look for a park or a playground to stretch our legs. When Bryce needs to sleep, I must contort to stretch my arm back so he can hold my hand.

Toward the end of each day, the kids need a companion in the backseat to get them through the last difficult hours. Two little sweet-smelling heads rest on my shoulders, my hands on their knees.

All the way across the country we stay with friends or camp. Late nights and unfamiliar surroundings chase sleep away. As time zones change and our internal clocks are thrown off, our fatigue increases. If we can get through this week on the road, living out of the truck, and still be healthy and still like being together, we may have the hardest part licked.

No matter how many times I drive across the country, I will never grow tired of seeing that great wall of mountains—the Rocky Mountain Front Range—rise from the plains and come into view. For days we battle heat and boredom as we drive across the Midwest. We stare at the horizon, trying to make out the snow-covered blue peaks melting imperceptibly into blue sky. Then the land begins to rise, and somewhere in eastern Colorado Todd or I will yell, "There they are! There are the mountains!" They appear like a ghost of a backdrop. The mountains represent a different world to us. They contain undreamed-of things that we have been yearning for. If we wondered for five seconds why we were doing this, when we see that range it comes rushing back. We feel like homing pigeons.

It takes five days to travel from Pennsylvania to Colorado, and it will take five more days to meet our sponsors, collect llamas and gear, and acclimate to the altitude. First stop is Dee Goodman's place. He's the mover and shaker behind this whole endeavor. Worn-out cowboy boots are nailed upside down on the fence posts around Dee's Akron ranch. Half a dozen vehicles, mostly trucks, are scattered around the drive. A dog grins at us, and millions of grasshoppers jump at our legs, eating his crops in the hot summer sun. The land is so flat and unshaded that it doesn't seem to deserve the name Colorado, which to an easterner is synonymous with mountains.

Dee bangs through the screen door and greets us like long-lost friends. He's so tall he slouches to compensate. He invites us in to meet his wife, Carla, and the kids. For dinner there are buffalo burgers and cold baked beans straight from the can. It's killing Dee not to go with us to kick off this hike. He feels it's his dream too. We drive around his farm in the sinking sun as he mends a fence and checks his wheat. He chews a kernel to test for maturity and promises us, "This is going to be a blitz harvest. Record time. So I can meet you folks on the trail and share in this adventure." Foremost among everyone who is helping, we wish this man would be there to take the first steps with us.

From the Goodmans' spread, we travel to Carbondale, Colorado, on the far side of the range. Here Charlie Hackbarth makes Mount Sopris saddles, the best llama pack systems on the market. He is an artist who taught sculpture for many years before designing and making saddles. They're flexible wooden saddles with an attached wool pad, and besides being aesthetically pleasing, they're the most comfortable for a llama to wear and a child to ride on.

At Charlie's ranch we saddle and resaddle his docile llama Thumper, which his daughter raised from a *cria* (baby). We roll up our foam sleeping pads and Crazy Creek chairs and strap them to the tops of the two side panniers. A third rolled pad stretches across these in the back, creating a brace to help hold Sierra on her wool felt seat. If she gets drowsy or the llama spooks, she won't fall off easily. As she practices riding Thumper, Charlie tells her to relax and let her upper body bob. "It's a long time since I've seen anything as pretty as you up on a llama," he tells her. "Except for the llama Stan will choose for Sierra, his 'boys' won't be as gentle as Thumper," Charlie warns. "He'll give you high-spirited llamas— llamas that are most likely head, leg, and rear-end shy. But they will work for you."

"That's OK," I tell Charlie. "We're not looking for pets. We want them to do an important job for us."

Back in the 1980s, when people were turning to llamas to harvest fiber for weaving, or as show animals, or for a "lifestyle investment," or for breeding, Stan Ebel had a vision. He left behind his cattle ranch and his pharmacy in Nebraska and moved his family to Masonville, Colorado, to become an unusual kind of pioneer. With the coming crunch on wild areas dictating that people venture farther and farther into the backcountry to find solitude and at the same time that they reduce their impact, he saw huge potential in using llamas as pack animals, for they have unique qualities and talents.

He began to breed aggressively for strong frame, sound conformation, and high performance, with wool and color as low priorities. He is perhaps the most knowledgeable and respected of all pack llama breeders and commercial packers in the country: we couldn't have found a more qualified sponsor.

Stan's five-hundred-acre ranch is home to 350 to 400 llamas that he leases to the Forest Service, among other clients, for trail work, search and rescue, and so on. He has about 50 gelded males to choose from (studs and females are too valuable to use for packing). He has a riding llama for Sierra. He matches our personalities with his llamas'. Amazingly, with hundreds of llamas, he knows them all. He's a no-nonsense man, teaching us not to depend on llama pack rain covers but to make sure everything is waterproofed to begin with. He warns us not to depend on breeching straps (around their butts) or neck straps to hold the load on but to make sure the saddle itself is snug and well-fitted. He doesn't believe in desensitizing the animals and subduing them too completely. He gets them used to the halter and saddle but keeps their spirit and independence intact. We like this guy.

From his "big-boy" selection—the ones that can carry heavy loads—we choose Jupiter, Jack, and Hansel (who looks as though one parent was a horse). Berrick will carry Sierra; he's a favorite when the llamas visit the shut-ins at local nursing homes. (Llamas are very popular for pet therapy in the West, since they prefer to move their bowels outdoors in community piles and can easily be trained to enter buildings and vans.) Unlike most of Stan's llamas, besides being sturdy and strong Berrick tolerates being stroked and handled and is considered "pet quality." The live weight of a child is much more difficult to carry than "dead" weight, for a child sits high and moves around a lot, making the llama work harder to balance itself. A llama that can carry eighty-five to ninety pounds of dead weight can comfortably carry a sixty-pound child. At age eleven, Berrick seems to have enough experience and the right kind of temperament to carry my child across the Colorado Rockies.

Before we left home, I asked Dee if he could persuade one of the RMLA members to hike with us the first few days as we learn the ropes. Bob Riley of Lyons, Colorado, evidently drew the short straw. It wasn't his idea; his wife, Jo, heard we were looking for a starting companion and thought it would suit Bob, since he loves to hike but hadn't done it for many years. Bob isn't so sure it's a great idea. He's read my books about our adventures on the Pacific Crest Trail and thinks we are hiking animals—speedy megamilers. I assure him that we now have two paces—slow and slower. He will fit in fine. (Little do we know, especially given Bob's reluctance, what a vital role he will play in a journey that will ultimately take five years to complete.)

On our way from Stan's home to meet the Rileys, we stop at Rocky Mountain National Park, and the doubts come flooding back. Looking over a sea of snow-drowned peaks, the Never Summer Range, makes my stomach churn. We'll never be able to hike through such snow.

Steep snow traverses are dangerous to cross, especially with a string of llamas and a couple of babies. There isn't always a safe way around, and turning back is never an attractive alternative. You come face to face with the ugly specter of risk and must base your decision on how much risk you're willing to take. The threshold lowers considerably when your children are at stake. Decisions could be critical.

While in the park, we try a short day hike, taking the minimum of gear. But an afternoon thunderstorm builds, pouring rain and hail down on us. The kids are wearing cotton clothing under water-repellent suits, and it's not enough. Bryce sticks his head and hands out from under his pack awning and his skin turns red and icy. He cries hard. Sierra looks as if she'd like to do the same. We run back down the trail and are overjoyed at the sight of our Ford pickup in the parking lot.

Once inside, we're wrapped in security and comfort, like scared children who have run back to grab their mother's skirt. The wind and rain can't get at us. Heat floods out almost instantly when the engine starts. The quarters are cramped, but we're thrilled to be scrunched together on that seat. We strip the kids and discover they're soaked to the skin. That decides it: not even cotton T-shirts will work in these mountains—only synthetics. Serious rainsuits. Rubbers. Umbrellas when there is no lightning. The kids *must* be kept dry, for hypothermia is a great danger. It's nearly time for take-off, and we're *still* learning. Small mistakes are all we can afford. Tomorrow this truck, which has replaced our log house as our last link to home and security, will be left behind too. We wonder at this moment, Do we have enough knowledge to pull this off?

In the Rileys' plush home, we haul in all our gear and attempt to pack the llamas' panniers. The panniers must be loaded evenly, within two pounds, or the saddle will shift toward the heavier side. We carry a handheld brass scale to weigh them. Todd must lift them into the air to read the numbers—no small feat, since they weigh up to fifty pounds.

After the kids are put to sleep, we sit quietly eating cheesecake and listening to music, each thinking about what happens tomorrow. The first steps of a dream. I want so badly to do this hike. It's been only seven months since Wally planted that seed, but so much preparation has gone into arriving at this point. A lot of people are rallying behind us. Dee calls to wish us well. He says, "What started out as a business endeavor has turned into people doing something for their friends." We don't want to let anyone down, including ourselves.

3

The First Week

JULY 6, 1993

There is little point in setting out for a place one is certain to reach.
—H. W. TILLMAN

WATERTON CANYON. For the first six miles, until we climb into the mountains, our trail is a dirt road—wide enough to allow full sun to warm us. Dry, rocky slopes support little vegetation—yucca, sage, gambel oak, and juniper. Down in the canyon, cottonwoods line the Platte River, which our road parallels. We're at 5,520 feet—the lowest point anywhere on the Colorado Trail.

The kids are cranky. Not enough sleep, no way to escape the sun, no way to cool their bodies. We give Sierra a bandanna moistened with precious drinking water to swab her neck and face. We push the water bottle on them at every hourly break, determined to avoid dehydration. We slather them with sunscreen, being careful not to get it in their eyes. At least the llamas are doing well.

A band of bighorn sheep cling to the craggy canyon side. They are gray like the rocks, but the already sharp eyes of our three-year-old pick them out. The only other entertainment is the mountain bikers, for this canyon, so close to Denver, is a popular recreational area. Solo "power riders" train as hard and fast as they can. Parents push jogging strollers. Young children practice on bikes with training wheels. Most have something to say. To Todd, who's carrying Bryce in a top-of-the-line Tough Traveler child carrier, they say, "Hey, can I ride in there?"

To Sierra, who's riding on Berrick, they say, "Now that's the way to go."

To me they say, "Either you're going in style or you're out for a long time." My least favorite question is "How far are you going?" "Durango, five hundred miles away" sounds far-fetched. We look so green—pale, actually. And I, with a few extra pounds left over from pregnancy, am hardly the picture of physical prowess.

As soon as we hit the narrow trail, Todd breaks ahead and sets his own pace, a practice rarely tolerated in our relationship, especially now, with children and llamas along. Trouble can crop up at any moment. He and his string of three llamas disappear around the bend. Docile, laid-back Berrick begins acting aggressively, butting me with his head as though he wants me to hurry. He tries to move first around my right side and then my left; I can barely hold him back with my outstretched arms. I yell to the men to stop.

"Berrick's got a very strong herd instinct," Bob concludes when I catch up. "He doesn't like being separated from the rest of the llamas. Not even out of sight." Todd's Jupiter was acting strange too, pulling back and turning around as though he wanted to wait for Berrick.

We're finding out that to make this trip work the string needs to stay together, just as Todd and I do. Before we had kids and llamas, we hiked together much of the time, with me in the lead to prevent Todd from getting too far ahead, since his pace is much faster. But I would often let him take off up a mountain, stretching his legs and going at his own natural stride, always waiting for me at the summit. That's not going to happen anymore. With llamas and kids along, he's forced to crank down his pace even slower. He's stuck with us on the trail, just as in marriage. This is a new way to hike, and I'm afraid he's going to resent it.

A little later, with the others still in clear view, Berrick begins rubbing his face on my child carrier and shoves me a step or two. It takes me by surprise. Bob says he's only trying to shoo away flies.

"They don't have a mean bone in their bodies," Bob says. "If they act ornery, they've usually got some sort of problem. Or they could be testing you."

In the last miles of the day Jupiter, who's bringing up the rear, lies down. Huge Hansel, the llama that looks as though he's part horse, pulls Jupiter along for a good fifteen feet, rubbing off his leg hair. Day one and Jupiter learns his lesson. It didn't take us long either, on this first day, to appreciate the value of Bob's knowledge.

AFTER TWO AND A HALF DAYS, we deposit Bob and his llamas at the Top of the World campground. He'll meet us in another week in the town of Breckenridge to help us resupply. In this short time, we've all grown extremely fond of one another. Bob especially took to Sierra; as the father of three grown sons, he sees her as the daughter he never had. He and Todd had a thing going on steep switchback trails. The one below would yell, "How'd you get up there?" A reply like "On the wings of a raven," would be in order. Then the one above would yell, "How'd you get down there?" and so forth.

Among the sobering things we've learned in these first few days is how much energy it takes to look after the kids, beyond our long list of camp chores. Bryce is only one and a half and must be watched. This evening he wanted to see how the broken glass in the fire pit tasted. Sierra was traipsing through poison ivy up to her neck. There is little time for luxuries like baths. Bryce looks like the character Pig Pen in the Peanuts comic strip: he loves playing in the dry dirt, turning over rocks and filling his fists with soil to put into things—like the aluminum cook pot or his dump truck or his belly button. A bandanna dunked in cold creek water is their bath, bringing screams and tears from Bryce.

We've also learned that out here Sierra needs an afternoon nap, though she gave it up long ago at home. Shortly after lunch, she'll throw a fit over something minuscule like having to eat a different flavor of energy bar because her favorite is all gone. We put her in Todd's pack, and she's out like a light.

Normally Todd carries Bryce and Sierra rides Berrick, but when Todd carries Sierra, I get Big Boy Bryce, who makes me crazy with his rockin' and rollin' in the child carrier—pulling my hair, standing up to throw his arms around my neck, jumping up and down, leaning way over, turning around to watch the llamas. I'd rather carry seventy pounds of dead weight than this kid. We should just strap him down. He has free rein, though, for the thought of sitting on your rump for two and a half months without being able to shift from one hiney cheek to the other sounds like torture. This way he's happy but we're crazy.

I tell Bob, "By the time you meet us in Breckenridge, the gray at my temples will have spread over my whole head." "By the time Todd gets there," he says, "he'll look crazed—long beard, eyes rolling back in his head, frantically trying to balance the panniers, saying, 'Two more pounds in this pannier. I need two more pounds and I can't find them anywhere.'"

Learning the individual llamas' idiosyncrasies and personalities is one of this first week's chores, as well as figuring out what order to put them in. Some like to follow, others must lead. Some pull back on the rope when they're tired. If we're leading a dragger, he gets switched back so another llama can yank him along instead of our using precious energy. I only lead Berrick, the kid carrier—it's safer that way. Some of the llamas like to snatch food along the trail while we're hiking. They should be snacking only when we stop and let them, since they need to devote their full attention to walking safely. Occasionally one gets his long neck wrapped around a tree while the rest of the string moves on down the trail. If Berrick gets into trouble, on a stream ford or stepping over a fallen tree or crossing mud, I can easily shorten his lead rope and pull down on his head to control him, or even grab Sierra off.

In this first week, Sierra and Berrick have really bonded. She hikes one to three miles a day, leading her llama, and rides the remaining six to eight miles. She scolds him when he tries to take advantage of her by stopping to eat. She compliments his performance throughout the day and points out all sorts of interesting things—airplanes overhead, flowers by their side, rock formations, rays of sunlight. In camp this evening, it begins to hail. She cries because "her Berrick" is out in the weather. She wants to make room for him in the tent, but we tell her the llamas are happy outdoors, since their wool is so thick and warm.

Bryce doesn't get much chance to hike on the trail during the day, and he must find it frustrating. He's very observant though, and he calls out, "Hill! Steep! Ditch!" (for a water bar), and "Apen!" for aspen trees. In camp, the first thing he does when he's awarded his freedom is cruise trail. He trots quickly in one direction, saying, "This-a-way. This-a-way." His tiny hiking boots are a perfect replica of an adult's, scaled down to the size of a Cabbage Patch doll's. He then makes a U-turn and says "That-a-way. That-a-way," his chubby cheeks vibrating like Jell-O.

It takes three hours to set up camp in the evening and three hours to get moving in the morning. We need to stake out the llamas, feed and water them, pitch the tent, filter water, wash out dirty diapers and clothes, roll out the pads and sleeping bags, cook dinner, do the dishes, brush teeth, wash up, change diapers, help Sierra use the "bathroom," take out contacts. There will be no opportunity to read for pleasure out here. It's all I can do to muster the energy to write in my journal after putting the kids to sleep. "It's a job," Todd says, feeling overwhelmed. "It's all work." Part of his poor attitude is related to washing Bryce's dirty diapers. He took on that job himself after brainstorming a creative way to do it. He cut the top off a five-gallon collapsible water container and duct-taped handles to it. He collects water and moves far away from the source. He first cleans the vinyl pants and then dips and rinses out the diapers, straining the feces and depositing them in a six-inch cat hole he's dug in the ground. After a final rinse they're hung to dry in the tree branches, so as to keep the llamas' pack weight to a minimum. Disposables are not the way to go on a long hike, for the weight of the wet diapers would be incredible after a week or so. Since Todd likes things done his way, I gratefully relinquish this job and stick to changing Bryce.

While Todd and I do our camp chores, the kids play with the contents of their toy bag—picture books, farm animals, a Matchbox tractor set, Barbie dolls, a teddy bear. These compete with toys found in nature: sticks, rocks, occasional dried cow pies, and piles of elk droppings. They never get the toy bag out during the day; they find enough to entertain themselves with at breaks. Mostly they eat: jerky, dried apples, crackers, and cheese. They eat every hour or every two miles, whichever comes first. Sometimes they even eat while they ride. Except for the first day, it hasn't been warm enough for them to wear shorts. Long underwear, sometimes a few layers, is the norm. They're burning up calories just staying warm, in addition to exercising. When it rains and hails, they need a huge amount of fuel just to avoid hypothermia.

The children used to get worked up when they heard "funder." Out here thunder is a daily occurrence, sometimes several times, and doesn't necessarily turn into anything more. But still we must prepare. We bark orders to the kids. "Come here! Put your foot in!" (their rain pants leg). "Point your toe!" "Pay attention!" There isn't always a lot of time. The llamas get jumpy as our anxiety increases. Popping open our large, colorful golf umbrellas doesn't help matters. We watch hail the size of peas bounce off the ground and burrow into the creases of the llamas' thick coats. As the thunder grows closer and we see lightning, we collapse our umbrellas with their long metal spikes and walk exposed to the weather. All the hatches on the kids' rain gear are battened down—cuffs pulled over their hands, pants legs pulled over their boots. When the umbrellas are down, we put pack covers over the child carriers to keep the kids dry, making them ride in the dark. In one storm Todd pulls his pack string along like a locomotive, rope taut, for the animals feel threatened. I look back at him for a reaction. He has a small smile as if to say, "This is interesting." Up ahead is the crossing of Rock Creek. A timber spans the creek rather far above the water. I lead Berrick boldly across the sixteen-inch-wide bridge, and he follows with no hesitation. Members of Todd's pack string, however, exhibit their unique personalities as he attempts to lead them across.

First comes Jupiter. You can almost hear his mind working as he assesses the situation. "Gee, Berrick, you're so brave and confident. You just went across that bridge like it was nothing. I'll try to follow you, but I don't know." About halfway across, he feels peer pressure from behind: "You're not a human. Get off the skinny bridge and cross like an animal." So he chickens out and jumps off, plunging toward shore as fast as he can.

Then comes half-horse Hansel, who despises getting his feet wet. He says to himself, "No way, man. I am *not* going in. I am *not* tippy-toeing across that narrow bridge either. I am airborne!" He flies through the air like a gazelle, aiming for the shore and making it.

Last is Jack. Nervous Jack. He takes a few seconds to think. "Holy cow, guys. I'm not as courageous as you, Berrick. And I'd rather not change my mind midway like you, fickle boy Jupiter. There's no way I'm flying over it like you, Hansel. Even if I wanted to, I couldn't reach." But indecisive Jack takes too long to make up his mind and is pulled right through the water, which is clogged with alder thickets, scraping his panniers to hell.

All this happens in seconds. I'm on the far bank, tying up Berrick and getting the kids to the safety of a tree, while Todd is staging his own personal rodeo with tangled ropes and stuck llamas, yelling at me to help as the thunder grows louder and closer. In this situation we need to unhook the llamas and lead each one out of the mess.

LATER, up on a ridge in the Kenosha Mountains before dropping down to Kenosha Pass, we see a figure coming toward us. Not until he's on top of us do we realize it's Bob Riley. Our hearts warm. He missed us. We stake the llamas out in a campsite and follow him to the road, where his motor home is waiting, making this our biggest day yet (twelve miles).

"Will you come back out and hike with us, Bob?" Sierra asks.

"No, munchkin. I'm just here for a quick visit."

After taking showers in the motor home, we roll down Kenosha Pass, which long served as an Indian trail into the fertile hunting grounds of South Park. It was crossed by white parties as early as 1830, when miners streamed over this very path. Expansive South Park lies below—a beautiful wide, spacious valley. Dark cloud shadows race across the nearly level green land. It's one of the major "parks" or high open plains in Colorado, and it's here that the South Platte River rises. After a delicious dinner at the Fairplay

Hotel—supposedly so named because the miners here dealt squarely with one another, contrary to the greed and claim jumping that characterized many camps—we fight for the check and lose. Bob is pleased: we're the guests. Warmth floods our bodies from the hot showers, from the delicious food, but mostly from the love.

This kind of rest is vital during a long hike, especially in the break-in period. It's difficult to come out here and suddenly adopt a die-hard, hard-core wilderness hiker attitude. And I've always been one for a diversion in town, where you can indulge in all the comforts you've been doing without. It helps maintain my enthusiasm for trail life.

In a few more days we hit Breckenridge, our first resupply, with seventy miles under our belts. Our first stretch is complete, and in retrospect we find that the time really did fly. We're amazed that we're out here on the trail again, after those years of abstaining—having babies, building our log home, and all the rest. As different as it is from our trail life before, to Todd and me it feels like home.

On the dusty road into town, we begin to consider making llamas a more permanent part of our future. This first week on the trail has showed us the value of our llama friends. At eye level, their long-lashed faces never intimidate us. They follow obediently, never whining or saying "How soon till we're there?" My body is burdened only with the camera gear on my back. The rest of the load rides on theirs. We feel gratitude and fondness toward them. "Maybe we should buy some of our own," we say. They are our ticket back to the long trails and the wild high country. They make all this possible. Will we be satisfied with only the Colorado Trail?

ON OUR WAY into Breckenridge, Denver's CBS News meets us for an interview. When a reporter approaches, Sierra pulls her visor down over her eyes. To the simplest questions ("What's your llama's name?" "Are you having a good time?") she remains mute. Her defiance irritates me. Before the camera crew arrived I insisted that she cooperate, so she knows this is a prime time to test her power. Or is she exhibiting reclusive tendencies? Perhaps she's begun to cherish her time in the mountains, alone with her own thoughts. These reporters may be an intrusion into her new life.

The camera crew wants us to go into town for lunch so they can shoot the hungry hikers enjoying a pizza. But we aren't hungry right now, and Todd is being rushed to unload, unsaddle, and stake out llamas at a rough campsite by the side of the road. If we leave the llamas unattended for any length of time, they could get tangled or loose, be stolen, or be harassed by dogs. Yet the publicity is important. We couldn't pull off this adventure without the assistance of the Rocky Mountain Llama and Alpaca Association. They're hoping for maximum exposure to let the public know how great llamas are and what a family can do with them. It's part of our job to work with the media, no matter how bothersome.

At the restaurant, Bryce stretches the mozzarella cheese, getting it all over his hands and face and the table. Sierra picks her nose. I take a hasty bite that burns the roof of my mouth and reflexively spit the pizza onto my plate. When we return to our campsite we find two llamas loose. Local dogs forced them to pull so hard on their stake-out ropes that the panic snaps on their halters released them.

With the interview out of the way, Bob takes us into town in the motor home to do our chores. The motor home is a hit with the kids: they climb on the chairs and sofa, play with the TV controls, and watch videos. Sierra delights in using the toilet and the sink. No cat holes, no cold water. She also enjoys striking poses in front of the full-length mirror, making faces and fish-kissing the glass.

Bob jokes, "What started out as an inexpensive sponsored trip will end up breaking us—now we've created a need for not only llamas, llama gear, and a trailer, but a TV, a VCR, *and* a motor home!"

While we do our chores, we board the llamas at a local llama ranch. They sniff and snort to introduce themselves, then make for the hay and grain. Only Berrick stands alone at the fence, nose to nose with Sierra. She cries. I'm surprised at his lack of interest in mingling or eating. She tells us that on the trail he smiles at her and talks to her, mind to mind. They understand each other, she claims. Watching this scene, I would never doubt her.

Sierra is adapting to her journey and her new life on the trail. It's the first sign that she, like her parents, is "coming home." I like to live life feeling that wherever I am is home, whoever I am with is family. People from back home pass through our memories like a sudden breeze. We wonder how they are, smile at the memory, and return to the present moment, which always feels so big on the trail.

It is not comfort we miss. In all our years of long-distance hiking, we've learned to happily do without creature comforts in exchange for the freedom this wandering lifestyle brings. Todd even chooses not to use the indoor plumbing back home, for he enjoys observing the weather and watching the birds from the open door of his outhouse.

There's not much we miss about home, at least not at this stage in the journey, and it's heartwarming to see Sierra embrace the trail as her home too.

4

The Ten Mile Range
JULY 16, 1993

Everything is sweetened by risk.
—ALEXANDER SMITH

OUR GUIDEBOOK SAYS, "The linear Ten Mile Range connects the south end of the Gore Range with the north end of Mosquito Range. Climbing is steep and strenuous. A challenge to even the seasoned hiker. Inclined snowfields may linger well into July."

Until now, I've led Berrick around every snow patch to avoid confrontation. It's safer this way. Sooner or later, however, I'll need to know what he and Sierra can deal with. At the next patch, we head straight across. His feet break through the crust and he sinks in over his knees. Not wanting to linger, he gallops through, giving Sierra a bronco ride and bringing tears and screams of anger. "Bad Mommy!" she yells.

I skirt the next patch, on a steep ridge. But because of the pitch,

Berrick leaps. More screams and tears. Up ahead is a long snow traverse. I call for a break to discuss strategy.

Todd goes out alone, kicking steps to widen the footholds. He carries Sierra across and deposits her on dry ground to wait. But Berrick, first in line, refuses to budge. Fearless Hansel is next. He won't go either.

Option 2: Climb high up onto loose scree, through stunted evergreens, and lead the llama string around the snow. Although this entire landscape is riddled with hidden mine shafts, making it very dicey to leave the trail bed, this seems the safest way.

I hear Todd and the llamas plowing through scrub so thick I can't see them, and I feel overwhelming gratitude for this man who always manages to quash his own fears and rise to the occasion.

On the next traverse, Todd carries Bryce on his back while holding Sierra's hand. I lead the entire string. "Don't dilly-dally," he warns, so I sprint, with them running at my heels. Every traverse is different. We must assess each one to decide on the safest course.

At another traverse, Todd leads *his* string first. Half-horse Hansel begins to lunge, dragging all the other llamas across much faster than they'd like. Once on dry trail, he continues to lunge. Jupiter can't keep up with Hansel's speed, so he pulls back until Hansel's saddle and panniers slide over his butt, down his hind legs and off his body. We're above treeline and there's nothing to tie the llamas to, so Todd just leaves them loose.

Meanwhile Sierra, Berrick, and I are on the other side of the traverse, separated from the pack, which makes Berrick wild. I venture out onto the snow, lead rope in hand. Trying to go faster, Berrick shoves me down the side of the slope, where there are no footholds.

Cumulus clouds are growing larger and darker, then they expand like nuclear mushrooms. The weather is deteriorating with alarming speed. The kids are tired. We need to stop. We've barely eaten or rested all day, but we still have miles to go before we reach the safety of the trees. We pull out lollipops, hoping to calm the kids, who are infected by our anxiety.

When it comes to snow traverses, Todd and I carry a lot of emotional baggage. When I was on the Pacific Crest Trail in 1982, I fell on an icy, north-facing slope. I wasn't able to catch myself with my ice ax, my glasses got covered with snow from my skidding heels, and I went limp. Fortunately, because of my rag doll body, my feet hit two rock outcrops with little resistance, sending me somersaulting down the slope until I landed without a scratch. My hiking partner watched with horror and insisted on reliving it for me, night after night in the tent, until my fear grew huge.

Todd also had a bad fall, on a snowy traverse in the Cascades. He was wearing crampons—metal spikes strapped to his boots for traction on ice. A ball of wet snow formed underneath, causing him to slide down the slope into a tree. The spikes bit into the bark and held while his body twisted. It broke a bone in his instep, terminating his hike that year.

Now that we're faced with snow, we don't want to inflict our fears on our children, who have clean emotional slates. We want to keep as calm as possible and behave as though this is business as usual, but we feel ourselves starting to crack.

At the high point, a tremendously steep cornice buries the trail. We climb up to the ridge alongside it. Huffing with exertion and anxiety, the llamas leap, making both kids cry. These snow traverses are taking much longer than we anticipated. Without the llamas, we would move quicker. They're both an asset and a liability.

The cornice encounter puts Sierra over the edge, and she begins to wail. We can't comfort her. Todd puts her in his pack and Bryce in mine so they'll feel more secure. We boogie across the open ridge, negotiating jagged rocks, strong winds, and incredible wildflowers. The other side of the ridge is so steep I can barely look down without getting dizzy. The trail bed is narrow and eroded. I shudder to think of traversing snow here. As it is, I consciously cling to the mountainside with my Vibram soles. Rock cairns lead us down to the trees, a descent so steep we can feel our toenails turning black as we pound the trail. My neck muscles knot up from looking at my feet.

In the tent, Bryce gasps in his sleep—a vestige of his convulsive crying. Todd and I are exhausted physically and emotionally. Today was almost too much. We dealt with it because we had to, but we don't want to continue being challenged so intensely by snow. We'll be forced to seek an alternative route, to drop down and walk forest service roads, which will increase our mileage. We may even have to consider going home.

This is the first time we've experienced real fear on this hike. The trail is going to force us to push our boundaries. As much as we've experienced in the past, nothing could have prepared us for trail life with llamas and small children. This is fundamentally different from anything we've ever done. Our family is being put through a stress test.

As fortune would have it, we never encounter another snow traverse, but the Ten Mile Range has taught us a lesson. It's important to explore limits. How far *can* we push these kids, ourselves, the llamas, our family as a collective whole? More important, *how much is it worth?* Just because you *can* do something doesn't necessarily mean you *should* do it. Todd and I were cracking on that ridge, and the children picked up on it.

TODAY'S ROUTE, from Searle Pass to Kokomo Pass, is a five-mile traverse at 12,000 feet over exposed terrain. Fortunately, there's no snow and the sky is practically cloudless. We wander in and out of little side drainages with only minor elevation changes. We relax in the sunshine on breaks. This is more like it. When we arrive in camp, however, we realize our tent poles are missing. Jack's pannier was never cinched closed in the morning. They must have bounced out when he leaped over an obstacle. They could have been lost since the very beginning of the day.

Our tent poles are necessities. We have precious little security out here—little protection from the elements. Our tent is all we have to keep our beds and bodies dry. It must be supported to work properly: we can't just drape its nylon body over our heads and expect it to protect us.

At 5:00 P.M., Todd readies himself. As the male, he feels it's his responsibility to care for his family in challenges like this. He is a stronger hiker than I am, and if it were up to me I think I'd just let the poles go. I don't usually sense resentment from him at times like this. These are jobs he just feels are his.

We covered ten miles today. Just how far back should he go?

"I'll walk all night," he says.

"No!" I protest. "I can't unload, stake out and tend the llamas, set up a shelter, pump the water filter, cook supper, and take care of the kids all by myself." We look up to see a thunderhead building over the pass. "And I don't want you caught in a storm without shelter and warm clothes."

"I'll go to the pass—two miles—and turn around," he says, and is off running.

As I do my chores, I gaze up to the pass and murmur aloud, "I hope your pop is OK." Bryce whimpers, "Dada, Dada," over and over.

An hour later Todd returns, poleless. His dark eyes look humble, with a hint of disappointment at not pulling through for us. But he tried, and so *I'm* not disappointed in him. His legs hurt. A few times he had to stop on the uphill to breathe, his heart threatening to explode. He cut switchbacks on the downhills, his feet pounding and his knees locked to use as brakes. So many of the physical challenges we must overcome to pull off this hike rest on my husband's shoulders. Even he didn't know how hard it would be.

To rig up the tent, we use our golf umbrellas and sticks as makeshift poles, tying out as many corners as we can. The shape is too funky to let us put on the fly, so we hope for a clear night. As we lie in the dark, misshapen tent, we realize there is no room to get cocky or comfortable out here. You never know what's around the next bend in the trail. Literally.

We come up with a plan of attack. Now it's my turn to step in and do what I do best—human relations. We'll work at getting to a phone, then call Sierra Designs, our tent manufacturer, and have them "overnight" new poles. I'll call our RMLA contacts in the area and ask for the poles to be delivered to Tennessee Pass the day after tomorrow. Todd shies away from dealing with people. It's not the forte of an introverted man, but I thrive on human contact and see it as a challenge. This is how our marriage works: we each have our gifts and allow the other one to take over when the situation calls for specific expertise.

"Look at that big camp down there," I say, as we switchback down to a dirt road. "And all those vehicles. Someone will help us." Half a dozen people approach as llamas, small children—a little happy family—arrive in their camp. I assume we look nonthreatening. The women and children stare. The men have gone elk scouting. I explain our dilemma, tell how vulnerable we feel above treeline, with no tent and a danger of lightning. We need some help. We need to get to a phone.

One woman in her late fifties offers us information: there's a ranger's office *twenty miles down the road*. I impress on her that I don't need a public phone, I just need *any* phone. I offer to pay for gas. At least six people appear to be of driving age. At least three vehicles sit nearby. My blood pressure starts to rise. I lick my lips and begin to feel trapped. My children stare wide-eyed. This isn't a luxury item we're in need of. It's our only shelter. Todd motions for me to step away. Their apathy is clear to him. He's willing to let them off the hook. I'm not. I'm reduced to tears, and my voice cracks.

A big man emerges from a camper, plants his cowboy boot on a truck bumper, and asks in a cocky tone, "Now what seems to be the problem here?" I persuade him to take me in search of a phone. I'll go alone and leave Todd with the kids and the llamas.

Accepting rides and hitchhiking are a necessary part of this wandering lifestyle. When you have no vehicle, you sometimes have to depend on other people. You assess each situation wisely and intuitively and trust for the rest.

After a few miles of silent driving, we find a private residence. "Stay in the truck," he tells me. "I'll tell her your story. You might scare her."

I stay put, speechless. Do we look so rough and wild? Is our journey so strange? After a few moments I get out of the truck. The homeowner is a potter, an artist like me, and we get along great. My chauffeur, a concrete truck driver from Witchita, looks humble and becomes quiet.

I make my calls and line up help. When we return to the campsite, the tension in the cab is a little less pronounced. In my absence, someone has turned up a newspaper article about us, complete with pictures. Suddenly everyone is friendly. Suddenly we are legit. But I'm saddened at the level of mistrust in some folks' hearts and the apathy it breeds.

SINCE OUR LAST resupply break I've noticed some internal changes. There's a power struggle under way between our children and us. Sierra blatantly disobeys when we tell her not to pull her brother's hood over his face. She does it time after time, knowing he hates it. Some would say she's looking for attention, but how can that be? We're together twenty-four hours a day.

She had a little fit today over a question she wanted us to answer. "What's Berrick doing with his feet?" she asks. I offer close to a dozen answers. "Walking." "Placing his feet." "Taking you to camp." None qualifies. She gets hysterical over my inadequacy as a mother. She's testing me for some reason, and I'm not in the mood. I turn around and yell through clenched teeth, "I don't *care* what he's doing with his feet! Forget it!" She cries, and after five minutes she blurts out, "He's making footprints!" I swing around and glare at her. "Did you know the right answer all along? Are you trying to make your mother crazy?" I realize later she probably knew the answer when she posed the question, but she forgot and wanted me to find it again.

Lately Bryce has begun to throw temper tantrums—something we've never experienced with this child. For the past twenty minutes he's been screaming and crying and flopping around like a fish on dry land. I search the ground for rocks that could hurt him. I stare in amazement at this new behavior. I hope this isn't some sort of physical problem, like the beginnings of epilepsy. But no, it's over his water shoes! He wants to wear them to bed. They're synthetic and make his feet stink. I try to remember what the books say. Hold him close or ignore him? I don't want this kind of behavior to repeat itself in public or at a host family's home.

How *do* we discipline out here? How can we do a time-out? I can't consult Dr. Spock for advice, or call a pediatrician or a more experienced mother. We have to decide for ourselves. Discipline is having the backbone to make our own decisions, based on what's best for us right now. What holds true at home may not be the case out here. The trail makes us reevaluate and redefine everything. I remember how on the drive from Pennsylvania, Bryce threw a hissy fit, so we had to pull off the highway. Todd, Sierra, and I got out and sat in the gravel and weeds to give Bryce some space.

Our time-outs on the trail take place on a pannier on the ground, a few feet away from each other, and only for a few minutes. Still, the restraint and their rejection feels unbearable to them, and they cry as though they're being tortured.

Bryce doesn't let go of his shoe problem. Night falls. Todd and Sierra are asleep, and I'm fading. Bryce sits up by the closed tent door in the dark, whimpering "Shoe. Shoe."

This behavior isn't unusual for children his age, but what we're doing on the Colorado Trail isn't the usual family setup. Todd and I don't get up in the morning, have a quick breakfast, down a cup of coffee, grunt good-byes to the kids as they're whisked off to school and day care, then come home, have a few words over dinner, passively watch TV, and go to our separate rooms. We're in each other's presence *all day long*. We even sleep together. There's no one else to take up the slack. No teacher to supply answers for six hours. It's a paradox, but here we are in the big outdoors, unable to get away from each other. There's no door to shut, no confined space to retreat to. No place to hide. No respite. Despite the wide-open spaces, we have never been so confined as a family. So much feels like virgin territory.

The stressful situations on the trail are making their way into our children's sense of themselves. When problems erupt, they're in a front row seat. In their limited way, they're trying to understand and make sense of this new life. They know, even in their young minds, that they're powerless. Clearly it's scary for them. If they feel powerless in one area of their lives, they're going to try to get power somewhere else, hence the temper tantrums and disobedience. The underlying currents that travel through our days on the trail spread out into our personalities and color how we behave. Our children are beginning to feel some cracks too.

NOW IT'S TODD'S TURN to have a fit. This morning as we're packing up, Todd asks if I'm done with the toiletry bag. I say yes. Just as we're ready to leave, however, I remember that I just began menstruating and will need to get tampons. But he's already packed the bag, which is now hard to get to. Once he gets it out again, I realize they're in a different bag.

Whoops. He holds his tongue, as is his nature, but his normally soft eyes send out daggers. He unloads the pannier with force, throwing sacks in the dirt. I tell him I'm sorry and say, with tears in my eyes, "You used to have a fit once a year. Now, you have one or two a day. You're not the guy you used to be. Treat me like you love me, like I'm Bob or a friend."

"I'm *fuckin'* sick of it all and I'm quitting," he responds. "You ought to be able to find yourself another guy to do what I do." I cringe at his choice of words, for he rarely uses such foul language. He must *really* be upset.

As we're hiking along, I tell him, "I want to hear you tell Stan and Bob and Dee and everyone else who helped make this trip happen that you're quitting because your wife needed a tampon."

"Well, you should bust your butt every morning and get up at 5:00 so everything is in order and ready to go. We still don't get out of camp until 9:30!"

"Why do you think this trip has to be so easy? Is it easy at home?"

"A lot easier than this."

"Well, you have a lot of responsibility out here. You're the boss of this trip. It's a hard job."

"Maybe this next stretch I'll just have an 'I don't care' attitude. 'Oh, we're out of water? We'll just filter llama piss!' I know we wouldn't be where we are now if I didn't care. We'd lose one day for every two."

"I really care about all that you do, and I appreciate it. It's tough being the boss. But you know, if we're successful, it will all be because of you and your efforts. You're just like some general in the army, leading your troops down to Durango. Like a Schwarzkopf or someone."

"I feel like I'm leading the Ringling Brothers Circus to Durango. Just put a rope and a harness on me. I'm just a beast of burden like all the rest. All I do is stare at a llama's asshole all day."

"You're such a poor soul," I laugh. "No one *makes* you hike so close to Berrick's butt."

Our conversation ends as we reach the parking lot and trailhead for Mount Massive–Mount Elbert. As we unload and wait for our ride to the next town to resupply, a man approaches us and says, "Wow, what a great thing to be doing. Are you having a good time?"

I make eye contact with Todd and can't help but laugh as I answer, "Really good." When he walks away, I say to Todd, "You know what your problem is? You aren't getting enough sex." He corrects me, "I'm not getting *any* sex." "Well, you're not the only one who is being deprived."

Intimacy on the trail can be an incredible challenge. First of all, Todd almost always falls asleep as soon as we put the kids to bed. I *make* myself stay awake because once they're asleep it's my time to write. It's very important that I record the day's events and impressions in my journal every night or I'll lose the moment. This *is* my job. By the time I'm finished, sometimes two hours later, I'm sleepy. Even if I wanted to have some fun, I wouldn't have the heart to wake him up, since he gets up earlier than the rest of us to saddle the llamas. And we're often on the grubby side. After a full day of hiking and taking care of the beasts and babes, not a lot of energy remains—or interest! Plus, we have small children on each side of us. They fall asleep quickly and sleep soundly, but they will occasionally throw an arm into the very small arena we have to make love in, or they'll wake up to pee. So on the rare occasions we do have sex, there aren't a lot of gymnastics going on and we stay basically mute. What fun. How much effort could anyone put forth?

There's more going on here, however. I may naively think I can plaster over the crack with sex, but a power struggle remains. It goes back to what life used to be like for us on the trail before llamas and children. There was much more sharing of all the jobs. We both could work on logistics and both devote energy to being poets in our journals. Now there's a distinct division of labor. Todd's head is buried in his guidebook, and all his energy is used in saddling and packing the llamas. Before, he just had to load his own pack. My head is buried in emotional dealings with the children and saturated with jobs like fashioning pillows out of spare clothing for everyone each night—jobs that didn't exist before. We didn't even *need* to set up a tent when it was just the two of us—we could easily do it during the night if the weather turned bad. In addition to dealing with the kids, I also must try to mentally formulate my sensory impressions during the day, so I can record the magic of what is really happening to us out here. I have to *feel* all day long, and I have to analyze my feelings and everyone else's too. It doesn't look like work, but it's an exhausting task. And my job won't conclude when we reach the end of the trail. I'll have to write articles and books and conjure up these experiences all the rest of my writing career. Neither Todd nor I could do what we're doing—long-distance hiking with our children—without a committed partner. Together, we make a whole. Apart, it would never happen. Todd and I are just now seeing the reality of this and are learning how to work together. We're babes in the woods when it comes to doing it well.

WHEN ROB FERRIS picks us up at the trailhead, he pulls out cold juice for the kids and beers for us, sent by his wife, Ginger. He's in his late forties, is in excellent shape, and moves as though he leads a busy life. We're always self-conscious about our hiking odor when we're in enclosed places. In the open air it's not an issue, but in a vehicle we're quick to roll down the windows to spare our companions. Even though our own noses are adjusted to the odor and can't detect it, we apologize profusely.

"You can take us to a motel," we offer, "and just board the llamas at your place."

"Nothing doing. You're staying with us." Rob knows little about who we are or what we're doing, just enough to be interested in helping. Dee Goodman said Rob was the first to volunteer when Dee announced to the RMLA that we needed host families.

My body is so dirty that when my wet arm touches the shower curtain, black drips run down it. The dark water swirling toward the drain is shocking. There goes my "tan." The kids scream bloody murder when I wash their hair, for they're used to their "shampoo hats" in the tub back home—scalloped pieces of blue foam with holes in the middle that stretch over their faces to keep water out of their eyes. They make them look like daisies. I try to hush their big mouths so Ginger doesn't think she invited hoodlums into her home.

Ginger happily adds entrée after entrée to her dinner to accommodate us all. "Take the Land Cruiser into Leadville in the morning to do your shopping," Rob says over dinner. "I'll give you the keys. It's yours for the duration of your visit. Whenever you need it, take it."

We are struck by the Ferrises' generosity and their eagerness to trust, considering we just met a few days ago. It's in stark contrast to the camping party we encountered when we lost our tent poles. What makes one human being fearful and closed and another open and giving? I wonder if it depends on people's history—what they were taught, how many positive experiences they've had in helping people and how many negative ones, how many times people have reached out to them or shunned them. All experiences build on one another. Having recently seen the opposite, we are even more grateful to the Ferrises.

They are the first folks to take us home: the first in a long line of supporters. They provide us with a much-needed break from the stress of the trail. As uncomfortable as our TV interview was in Breckenridge, the kindness we're receiving more than compensates for the need to promote llamas.

We feel so comfortable during our visit that we ask the Ferrises if we may return in three days for another break. Thirty miles from where we left it, the trail hits another good road crossing that conveniently leads down into the town of Buena Vista. We're ahead of schedule and need to kill a little time. Plus, the infamous Fairplay Llama Race will take place on July 28 in South Park City, and our RMLA friends have persuaded Todd to enter.

FROM TENNESSEE PASS SOUTH, we've been hiking the skyscraping Sawatch Range, which has some of the highest elevations in Colorado, including 14,433-foot Mount Elbert, the state's highest peak. Much of the Colorado Trail follows the Old Main Ridge Trail, which began as a Civilian Conservation Corps project in the 1930s. It avoids all these lofty summits but comes reasonably close to nine 14,000-footers, and many climbers and hikers are drawn here to try to bag their summits.

We pass many of these hopefuls as they ascend from the Mount

Massive–Mount Elbert parking lot where Rob Ferris drops us off. Their aftershave, shampoo, soap, and deodorant fill our nostrils. "Hello! Hello! Hello!" We need sunglasses to shield our retinas from their brilliant white T-shirts. We're a real contrast. Even when we're clean now, we look a little rough. The trail clothes that we wear every single day are worn and sun-faded, stained by sweat and dirt. Our clothes, like our bodies and faces, are taking on the rugged wildness of the trail. We are changing outside as well as inside. It takes only a few weeks of living outdoors.

At Twin Lakes Reservoir we face a four-mile trudge along its north shore. The way is treeless, hot and dry, punctuated by sagebrush. Our faces stiff with sweat and dirt, we come upon a public restroom in the power plant's visitors center. "Come on," I say to Sierra. "Let's go get cool." To the bathroom sinks we go, heads under the faucets. The sinks are small, and my head gets stuck. I have to turn it a few ways to free it. We emerge dripping and giggling. Todd just watches.

We plan to camp on the lower lake's south side, a remarkable contrast with cool forest, shade, and inviting campsites. At the first available site, Sierra and I quickly tie Berrick and rip off our clothes. You have to make your move quickly when you're going to skinny dip at the end of a mountain day, lest the breeze cool you off or the even cooler water make you lose your nerve. We plunge in and scream with pleasure.

"Come on in, honey," I call to Todd. "It feels fabulous."

"There's a lot of work that needs to be done," he says.

"It can wait five minutes. I'll help you then."

But nothing doing. He unsaddles the llamas and stakes them out. I wish he'd loosen up and have some fun. I look at my daughter, laughing and running through the water, and I find it hard to believe that a three-year-old can be such a friend, such a companion to an adult. But she is. I feel bad for my husband. It's clear he's not having a good time.

HOPE PASS feels hopeless. It is perhaps the steepest ascent on the entire Colorado Trail. On the elevation profile map, it looks like a sharp-pointed dagger. That the Leadville 100, a torturous hundred-mile ULTRA mountain marathon conducted above 9,000 feet, coaxes runners up this very trail does not make my struggle any easier. It's painful because jumping-jack Bryce is on my back. I crawl, making poor time, and I'm panting. Here I am at 10,000 feet, wondering how I ever carried a seventy-pound pack in the High Sierra. I'd almost rather have that than this squirming child.

Sierra is on Todd's back this morning and Bryce is on mine because after only a mile and a half she moaned for a break. She must not have slept well, so we put her in Todd's pack for a nap. I resent carrying Bryce if Sierra isn't really going to sleep. It seems like a waste of my precious energy. I watch her, for she's learned to fake it. If she stays alert and lively for any length of time, out of the pack she goes.

This time she does nap, and afterward she goes back on Berrick while Bryce goes back on Todd. Then she complains of a stomachache and needs to go to the bathroom, but nothing will move. Todd stands and waits, not able to put down his load, for now Bryce is asleep. "It's taking all day to cover three miles," he says, frustrated.

When we get to the steepest part of the climb, I tell Todd to go by. He's been on my butt in a futile attempt to get me to move quicker. Splitting up isn't our normal practice, because the llamas hate to be separated.

We're supposed to camp at a mountain lake at the base of the pass, so I'm shocked and angry when he zooms right by it. "Stop!" I yell. I'm exhausted, and the pond is beautiful. We've already covered our eight miles. When he returns, he says, "Why can't I pick the site? Why can't we go farther?"

"Why can't my opinion be considered? What's wrong with you?" I ask as we unload at the pond. "All you do is complain that we never get anywhere, yet we're ahead of schedule."

"I'm tired of going your pace," he says.

"Ten years you've been going my pace and now suddenly you're tired of it."

"I don't understand why you can't go a little faster uphill. Don't you like to breathe hard?"

"I breathe plenty hard at my pace. You're just a better athlete.

Look at your legs. They're much longer than mine. And your stride is bigger. Look around you, honey. Look at this place. It's beautiful. Why are you wasting it feeling like this?"

"You don't carry that kid all day, bouncing and jumping and leaning out of the pack, pulling your hair. Tell the truth, what would you rather do—carry him for two fast hours or eight slow ones?"

"Two, of course. And I don't even like that. We're all very grateful to you for carrying him."

"It just gets frustrating, going so slow with him on my back, yanking the llamas along because they're trying to eat because you're going so slow they think you've stopped."

I'm realizing how difficult this trip is for him. Besides dealing with Bryce, he feels he's constantly coaxing us down the trail in order to get somewhere. It's his resentment over the division of labor rearing is its ugly head again. He feels he does more than I do, and it's probably so, at least in terms of physical jobs. My jobs *appear* easier.

He cares for the llamas, finds our way, pumps water, rinses out diapers, carries Bryce, and helps me with the kids when he can. I set up camp, cook, write, photograph, care for most of the children's physical needs and all of their emotional needs. I'm the one Sierra converses with all day long. By about 4:00 P.M. I'm maxed out and say, "Ask Daddy. Talk to Daddy a little."

She'll ask him the same question three times, and I'll have to say, "Honey, Sierra's talking to you." He never hears her. He tunes her right out. (Something he can't do with Bryce.) That's impossible for me. I think it's a sin to squelch a child's inquisitive mind. But for Todd it's a survival tactic. He needs his private space. So much of his life is spent inside his head. If he can't physically find the solitude, he creates it, going within. And sometimes it drives me crazy.

This life on the trail invokes much greater expectations of each other. It's demanding us to be close in ways we never imagined. We have to acquire new skills in getting along and caring for ourselves and one another.

Because Todd can't go at his natural pace out here, his tendency is to stay close to the hiker or llama in front of him. Not everyone looks down while hiking, as he does. I like to scan large areas and get a greater sense of place. But Todd's knee can pop out of joint, so he must be mindful of how and where he places his feet. When he leads Berrick with Sierra and I take the string, the last one in the line ahead of him happens to be Jupiter. And the part of Jupiter's anatomy that Todd happens to be the most familiar with is what's in his limited field of vision—Jupiter's asshole, which is only about two feet from Todd's face.

As the days go by, Todd can't help noticing that "it" is getting drier and drier in this arid air. Cracks radiate from the anus like the spokes of a wheel. Todd knows this because Jupiter needs to walk with his tail raised. Its swishing evidently creates friction and pain. Finally Todd can't stand it any longer, so when Jupiter least expects it (and what llama would expect this), Todd runs a bead of Bryce's thick white diaper rash ointment down his index finger and smears it all over the sore area. Jupiter goes ballistic. The kids scream with excitement. He whisks his tail to get it off, which helps spread it all around the sore area and work it into his skin. Todd does this for a few days until his "view" is improved.

THE ELEVENTH annual Fairplay Llama Race starts off with a real bang—an authentic cannon on the streets of South Park City, a thriving, brawling mining camp during the 1860s. But with all the laughter and shouting, the forty-plus contestants never hear the starting cannon and don't take off, so the audience has to step out into the street and motion that it's time for them to start moving. What a way to begin.

The first challenge for the runners and their llamas is to sprint two blocks, past thirty-two restored authentic buildings, then stop to saddle their llamas and load them with thirty pounds. Todd is running with Jack, our most high-strung beast. All our RMLA friends are here, either competing, supplying race llamas, or organizing events.

The past few weeks of packing in the Rockies pay off.

Todd and Jack are leading in the front line. The whole of the three-mile race can be viewed from town, on a high bluff overlooking the bed of the South Platte River. The kids and I position ourselves and watch for Dad's brilliant red T-shirt. The contestants run across the cold, deep river ten times and up and down rock tailings from the hydraulic gold mining days. Then they climb hills, cross a dam and a footbridge, traverse a man-made tunnel, hurdle three jumps, and plunge through the "Willow Jungle" and up "Killer Hill." We see some runners coaxing their llamas through the obstacles. Other ropes are taut as the runners pull their llamas along, but twice we see Jack literally run up on Todd and mow him down. What high-altitude lungs and fit bodies our two boys have!

This race is run not for money but for fun and to show how great llamas are. There are ribbons for the various age-class divisions. Many of the contestants are athletes running with high-performance llamas. The profits of the race are donated to llama research at the Colorado State University.

Here comes Todd, seventh in line. He looks as though he can't possibly suck any more air into his lungs. His chest expands as he heaves. In gasping breaths he says, "A few times I thought my heart would explode. I was so grateful for the rough spots where I had to walk and was able to keep my heart rate down. Jack had no limits. He never even breathed deeply. He was trying to go even faster. He was into it."

When the winners are announced, Todd wins first in his division. He stands on a pedestal to accept his ribbon, Bryce on his back in the child carrier and Sierra in his arms, so proud of their pop they won't let him go.

It's good to see all our friends again—Bob and Jo Riley; Charlie Hackbarth, who lent us our llama gear; Stan Ebel, who lent us the llamas; Rob Ferris, our current host; Wally and Katy White, who started this whole business at that party back in Pennsylvania, and dear Dee Goodman. We roll over to the Fairplay Hotel for lunch, where we see a mountain man–gold miner dressed in authentic garb, sitting on a bench in the lobby. A sign beside him says "Get your picture taken with Poncha—$3," but rumor has it he's from New Jersey.

From the Ferrises' house in Buena Vista (Spanish for "good view") in the Arkansas Valley, you can see mountains on all three sides. The magnificent Collegiate Peaks in the Sawatch Range captivate us. This is the area we'll be traveling through next. As we drive along the highway, we see a great wall of mountains, one mile high, rising from the valley floor. Like the Ivy League schools they are named after, this collection of 14,000-footers is in a league all its own. This is the highest mountain region in the continental United States.

In 1869 Professor Dwight Whitney, head of the Harvard School of Mining and Geology, led a group of science students into Colorado Territory to compare the heights of the Colorado Rockies with those of the Sierra Nevada. They named the high peaks after their institution (Harvard), Whitney's alma mater (Yale), and the other Ivy League schools.

In addition to the dramatic mountain backdrop, this valley enjoys more sunshine than Miami (an average of 345 days) and has fewer than 40 days with snow on the ground. It has an average snowfall of 40 inches, yet within thirty minutes north, west, or south you'll find 250 inches or more.

On night two with the Ferrises, we lounge in their hot tub and look up at the stars. Life is very good. Todd finally gets his much-needed sex. (I could live without it for a long time out here. I'm more interested in some time to myself.) Not on our very first night off, as you would imagine, for Bryce has other plans. He awoke with a "hot dog thirst," an in-town ailment which strikes in the middle of the night, resulting from too much salt in hot dogs, corn chips, and soda. He then proceeded to outdo Todd in staying awake.

After the long-awaited yet fleeting event, Todd quips, "Maybe I'll have a better second half of the trip now that I've had my 'first half of the trip' sex." "You're so full of shit," I tell him. "We've been out here three weeks and we've made love three times. That's better than you sometimes get at home." But he *is* under much more stress out here. He, of course, can't recall the three incidents.

PEOPLE HAVE considered our traveling llama circus an oddity right from the start. When we're on a road walk, nearly every group that drives by slows down, sticks their heads out the window, and either fires off a few shots from their camera or scans us with their video. Sierra very skillfully bends her visor over her face when she sees a vehicle approaching. She wants very little to do with the public. She gets tired of people taking her picture (to her it's as if they were actually *taking* something from her). She sees it as a violation of her privacy, of which she had so much before reaching the public roads. These folks never *ask* if they can take our pictures, and they never offer us a cold drink, even when we're walking on a hot, dusty road—even when we see coolers in the backs of their vehicles. Todd seems to think they're too flustered by the sight of us and can't think of anything else but recording it. I don't know. So I begin saying as they whip out their cameras, "That's gonna cost you." But no one takes our threats seriously until Rainbow Lake.

Around Rainbow Lake Resort, many people are out for the weekend. We see the resort store by the road long before we descend to it. Bryce already begins repeating, "Hot dog! Hot dog!" We tell him he'll be lucky to get a cold soda or an ice cream at this tiny, remote store. So he switches to "Grapes! Grapes!" "Surely don't look for grapes," we tell him. "There won't be anything fresh." And there isn't.

But he must have known something we didn't, for after we finish our soda and head on down the road, two ladies in a car pull up to us, and one says, "I bet you would like some grapes. My grandkids all love grapes. See those two men over there fishing? They have a big bag of grapes. You go over to them and tell them that their wives said to give you the whole bag."

"We don't need to take their grapes," we protest. "And certainly not all of them."

"We can drive into town and get more at the grocery store," they say. "Just you go do it."

Reluctantly, we go over to the lakeside and deliver the message. As the men hold out the white plastic bag, we say, "We don't need *all* these. We'll just take a bunch."

"Take them," they insist. "We're obedient." I plead with Sierra to say "thank you," but she only hides under her hat. Bryce is thrilled.

As we happily stuff the cool grapes into our mouths, sweet juice running down the kids' faces, we look at Big Boy Bryce and wonder how he knew.

Hikers call this kind of serendipity "trail magic": unexplainable "coincidental" happenings on the trail, right when you need them most. They bolster your strength, your courage, your belief in humanity, and your sense that there may be something or someone in this universe looking out for you after all.

SOMETIMES THE CHILDREN puke in the evenings—in our tent. Not an all-out vomit, just a mouthful of two. Not because of anything they ate, and not because they're sick. It's from horseplay—from wrestling and dive-bombing so soon after they've eaten their large supper. It's become a ritual to spend the last hour of waning daylight immersed in this fun. They seem to need one last shot of physical contact. Although we're together twenty-four hours a day, we're in our separate spaces as we hike—on llamas, riding in packs, leading. The kids must not get enough touching in this life, for whenever we take a break during the day, they're literally on us—on our legs, our thighs. If our laps are full, they sit on our shins, climb onto our backs. If we stretch out in the grass, they're on top. It's sometimes annoying and uncomfortable and it doesn't feel much like a rest to Todd and me, but we put up with it, figuring they must need it.

When they play rough in the tent, we constantly separate them to their individual sleeping bags on opposite sides of us. (Todd and I huddle together in the middle, attempting to be a couple and to look at the next day's maps and write.) We secretly hope one will puke or get hurt slightly, so that just a few tears flow. Then they've completed their "mission"—to use up all their remaining energy—and they finally lie down and sleep. Bryce cuddles with his thumb in his mouth while the other hand holds the fabric of my shirt and rubs his index finger and thumb comfortingly together.

Some of their excess energy is expended in camp. Besides the back-and-forth jaunts on the trail that Bryce performs immediately on being released from his backpack prison, he and Sierra go off on walks together—holding hands, playing "family." (She's the mom, he's the child; the father is dead.) She leads him around and shows him things. They go to the "grocery store." They crouch under low-hanging branches, the roof of their home.

If there's a creek nearby, that's all they need till bedtime. They gather bowls and spoons and whatever pots and pans aren't being used for supper and go off to dig in the wet gravel, filling, sifting, building dams. Sometimes Bryce forgets and helps himself to a drink when he's thirsty, not understanding that the water out here needs to be purified. We can't get them to resist sitting in the water either, whether they have shorts on or not. They do it without thinking. So I let them slop bare-butted with only a shirt on. Where else could they be freer and less inhibited than in the Rocky Mountain wilderness? This mountain stream is such a contrast to the manicured herb garden where this whole adventure took root. How far we've come, how happy these children are out here. It's times like this that bolster my confidence as a mother, assuring me that I'm exposing them to things that will feed their souls.

As the evening progresses, they dump out the contents of the toy bag on a foam pad. Sierra takes her stuffed pink teddy and puts it to bed with a bandanna as a cover (never minding the dried snot all over it). She'll put her shades on her teddy if it goes to the "beach." When she's tired of playing with it, she'll perch it on a tree branch so it can watch the goings-on.

Bryce is obsessed with lining up Matchbox cars into traffic jams—along dead trees, up their branches, balancing bumper to bumper.

Only once on the trip has Bryce come running toward me with an urgent complaint while I'm cooking; he got dangerously close to our gas backpacker's stove and knocked over the cook pot containing *five* expensive freeze-dried suppers. We can't afford that. We carry only one extra day's worth of food. Now I maintain a wide imaginary No Trespassing circle around "the kitchen." During these times their father is on discipline duty. Food preparation is all-important. Likewise, when Todd is on diaper-cleaning duty, the children aren't allowed anywhere near him.

Bryce is among our greatest challenges out here. At one and a half, he's at the "testing" stage of his development as a toddler. Whatever you tell him not to do, he will attempt. He stuck his hand into a pot of near-boiling water the other day after I told him not to. He's always trying to play with the stove and the windscreen when they're not in use but are still covered with soot. We've caught him picking up rocks and dropping them onto the llamas' feet to get a reaction, or poking the extended tent poles into the llamas' sides. They just kindly move away from him. Llamas usually spit only at other llamas, over food or other power struggles, but I wish he *would* get spit at, to teach him a lesson. The limits we've imposed are real, and we set them for real reasons like safety.

MOUNT PRINCETON'S lower eastern flank is made up of huge white crumbling pillars called the Chalk Cliffs. At the base of this magnificently symmetrical mountain, flowing out from the cliffs, is a wonderful area of hot springs. It's been commercialized, but it remains very popular and inviting. On the long walk into the valley, we ask every day hiker we meet, "Are the hot springs worth it?" The answer is unanimously "Yes!" It's six dollars for adults, one dollar for children. Todd, our finance manager, is reluctant. Because we've spent more days "in town" than originally planned, we've dropped hundreds more dollars than anticipated. We have a certain amount of money allotted for each resupply, and we've exceeded it. But today we've reached our official halfway point, and that alone calls for *some* kind of celebration. When we learn that outside the commercial concrete pools there are hand-dug pools in the river itself, we get even more excited. The piped hot water empties into these pools and mixes with the cooler river water, making just the right temperature. The comfortable depressions are lined with river silt and bordered with white river rock. They're just the right size for an intimate few or a small family like ours. This natural experience of the hot springs sounds more appealing than sitting in a man-made concrete pool with a lot of strangers. The kids and I are sold. Three against one. We win.

The children are entertained for hours. They move large rocks around, drop pebbles, and pour silt between them to block the cracks, changing the temperature of the pool to suit them. I lean back in the water and think about all we've been through. Our relatively smooth first week on the trail perhaps gave us a false impression of what trail life would be like. Then we encountered mishaps and stresses on our route and in our group dynamics. Cracks appeared. But here in this hot spring, at the halfway point of the Colorado Trail (which, it will turn out, represents only a tenth of the journey we will eventually complete), perhaps the cracks are healing over in the warm water. Todd and I rest our heads on a flat rock, close our eyes in the sun, and listen to the music of the river. Our heavy concerns sink to the bottom like silt and roll away down the river.

5

The Cochetopa Hills
AUGUST 1, 1993

If you're not living on the edge, you're taking up too much space.
—LOU WHITTAKER

THE HALFWAY point in any journey is a huge psychological milepost. Todd thinks that if we've managed to come through this totally new experience and achieve half our goal, we can certainly do the rest. We are starting to develop a rhythm and a way of living on the trail that's working for us, that we're beginning to feel comfortable with. We hope that our anxieties will ease and we'll be able to focus on more than logistics and mere coping.

One of the things we'd like to do is to turn this whole outdoor world into a classroom for our children. We plan on home schooling them as opposed to a public school education. With the free and independent life we lead, we don't want the school system putting a crimp in our travel plans—telling us we can go away *only* in the summer. Once they make a decision like this, parents begin to put more energy into teaching *before* their children are of school age.

Our "schoolroom" today is a large burn that our trail crosses in the beautiful Sawatch Range. We can easily see the southernmost peaks above us, named in honor of the great chiefs and medicine men of the once mighty Ute Nation: 14,229-foot Mount Shavarno, 14,269-foot Mount Antero, and the others. The broad Arkansas Valley is clearly visible through the dead snags below us. The sky is overcast and there's a cool breeze blowing this morning, so what normally would be a hardship is a pleasure. We take the opportunity to teach Sierra about forest fires—how they start, what happens to the animals. We point out ditches that the firefighters have dug to try to stop a fire's spread. We look at the rock-hard serotinous cones of the lodgepole pine, whose seeds are so tightly encased that they need the intense heat of fire to open the cones. In the evening we build a campfire, a rarity for us, and explain fire further.

I don't believe it's a parent's job to entertain children all the time—not even out here, where they're away from toys. We play word games with them as we hike, to get them to think and learn to describe things and express themselves. They learn to use their imaginations as they ride. They look around. They learn to see, listen, smell. Since there are few people on the trail and we see very few wild animals (too much talk), they crave stimulation. Major road crossings excite them. We time our breaks to fit our road crossings. Today's highlight is Highway 50, a busy one. Bryce spends the morning fighting off sleep to rehearse all the vehicles he hopes to see on the road. "Truck! Van! Car! Motor home!" he yells. And there it is. Excitement mounts as we descend, for we hike on an open power line road with a clear view of the highway. Already there are squeals of delight when something large goes by.

Once we stop, they situate themselves on a comfortable rock with paper bags of dried banana chips and venison jerky. There are tractor trailers, dump trucks, motorcycles. Sierra cannot contain her excitement when in quick succession she sees a motor home pulling a car and, directly behind it, *a car pulling a motor home!* These are patterns to her, like our breaks interspersed with periods of hiking. They've become our daily routines on the trail, different from those back home (like school bus schedules), but familiar and comfortable in their regularity all the same.

Across the road, a backhoe is at work. When we pack up and move on, we stop to watch. Todd explains to the children that the man is digging holes. When there's a loud scraping noise, he tells them the metal bucket just hit a rock. After a while the operator shuts off his machine; he's afraid the noise will spook the llamas and thinks we're waiting to go by. "Oh, no," we say, "our son just loves heavy machinery." Bryce finally falls asleep muttering "backhoe, backhoe, backhoe." He wakes up saying "backhoe, backhoe, back-hoe." It's easy to see what's important to him. Sierra thinks he's weird. We know he's just a boy. We laugh when our friends call us "the wilderness family and their children who love earth-destroying vehicles." Not really. They do love vehicles, but I sense they love the earth more.

As we cruise into the second half of the Colorado Trail, my husband is becoming more relaxed, but now our daughter is having bouts of homesickness. Part of the problem is a game we began playing. We pick a room in our house, hold an object from it in our minds, and describe it for her to guess. She's *seeing* these images. She's back there. But it's making her remember what she doesn't have out here. Like her kitty, Olive. Time to switch games.

I could use some company myself. Since we've started to relax out here, I've begun to think about what I could do to enrich my trail experience. I'd like to take on other people. We've been travel-ing for a month with just our little family, and though the children have gotten extremely close to one another and Todd and I to them, I could use a little more adult conversation. My quiet husband doesn't earn high scores in this area, especially in the evening when he's tired and sleepy. I felt bad the other day when I realized I haven't had any lofty thoughts since I've been out here. No great insights, no revelations, no "becoming one with the spirit of the wilderness" feelings. I used to have them before I became a parent. Now I'm concerned that I've been missing out on something. There's always a nose to blow, a drink or a snack to get, a layer to peel off, a butt to wipe, a question to answer—lots of knee-jerk reactions to ever-present needs.

The simple presence of our children and llamas takes up nearly all our time and energy. On some level we *are* absorbing the beauty we walk through. We *are* being changed by the experiences and challenges we are encountering. But the real accomplishment is that we are traveling the length of the Colorado Rockies as a family. There aren't any other children out here. We don't see anyone, period. I suppose our forward movement ought to be enough.

BEFORE DROPPING into Marshall Pass, our trail crosses the Continental Divide. Clouds race up from the west, hit the crest, and shoot straight into the sky. The east side is clear and blue. We feel so high up it's as if we're scraping heaven.

A beautiful silk-screened trail marker reads "Continental Divide National Scenic Trail," pointing left and right down the ridgeline while our Colorado Trail merely crosses the saddle. I look left and right up the open green slopes and see no visible trail, no obvious treadway like the Colorado Trail.

The Continental Divide Trail involves map-and-compass route finding; exposure; serious stuff. It sends a thrill through my body to think of hiking that trail, the granddad of trails. Someday we will, but probably not for many, many years. Not until our kids are adolescents and we feel confident in our skill at finding our way and keeping our children safe. But *some*day, we will venture here and make our way from Canada to Mexico.

The rhythm we've fallen into is interrupted when I have to fly to North Carolina for four days to speak about my lifestyle as a long-distance hiker. The Brights, who offered to host us during this resupply break, suggest that my family hang out at their home in Buena Vista, Colorado, while I'm gone. When I return there's a new wrinkle: my son rejects me. All along, he's been getting closer to Todd, who usually carries him and takes care of most of his needs during the day. Todd hikes with a bright yellow sippee cup dangling across his chest, the handles hooked onto his sternum strap buckles. He can get a drink for Bryce quickly, using a handy water bottle. Bryce can handle a full water bottle on a break if we help him, but he isn't yet coordinated enough to grasp it, drink, and hand it back without spilling. With the sippee cup, Todd doesn't have to unload

Bryce to give him a drink. Todd looks comical, this big dark, hairy mountain man with a sippee cup around his neck. What a good dad won't do!

The area we're about to go into, the Cochetopa Hills—is cougar country. The land is hilly, fairly open, and remote, with few trees. The author of our guidebook encountered a cougar here. If we see one anywhere on the trail, it should happen within the next few days.

It was here that a young boy was killed while running around his school track—on the outskirts of a town where we'll soon resupply. Even so, cougar attacks are rare. When we hike through lion country, we need to stick together and make plenty of noise to reduce our chances of surprising a lion. (That's not difficult.) Children need to stay within sight. If we happen to surprise a lion, we should talk calmly and firmly and move slowly. Face the lion and stand upright. Do everything to make ourselves appear larger: open our jackets, hold up our arms, put the kids on our shoulders to keep them safe and gain height. If a lion attacks, fight back.

The llamas not only will alert us with their warning call before we are aware a cougar is in the vicinity but will serve as a deterrent because adult llamas and cougars tend to respect one another's space.

We're camped tonight at Tank Seven Creek in the Cochetopa Hills, named for the Denver and Rio Grande Railroad water stop downstream. It feels spooky, as if there's electricity in the air. All day we scan trees with thick, horizontal lower limbs—perfect places for lounging if you're a large cat. The llamas are staked out in a circle around our camp, and we're all facing different directions this evening—instinctive guarding.

After supper, Sierra announces she needs to go to the bathroom. We take her about twenty yards from camp and leave her alone on a smooth log to do her business. Suddenly Hansel emits a high-pitched call from deep in his throat.

All the llamas are on their feet, staring in the same direction, searching for movement. A second llama detects something and joins in the calling. I realize they're looking in the direction of Sierra, but beyond and above her. In the trees on the hill! Oh, my God!

Lions take their prey by snapping their necks and then dragging them away. This image of Sierra fills my mind, and in a rush of panic I sprint over and pick her up in my arms, her pants still down around her ankles, and bring her back to the safety of our camp.

For half an hour the llamas are agitated. They usually eat for hours once they're staked out, then sit down to chew their cuds. But now they all stand at attention, staring up the hill, not breaking their gaze, not moving a muscle. They pace. It makes us feel protected. We are near the only water source for eleven miles, and there could be thirsty game around. We keep our children close and go to sleep feeling like trespassers in this wild area, as if the landowners are out there watching us. We wonder if it *was* a lion they saw and if it will be back in the night.

As we hike through these remote hills, our eyesight is sharper, our hearing is keener. We pay attention to where the llamas are looking, because they'll see something before we do. Sierra is occupied all day just looking for horizontal tree limbs.

Being in mountain lion country has changed our focus on the landscape. Their presence is helping us absorb the details of the land in a way we never took the time or had the energy for before. As we watch for the shadow of this elusive creature, we're now *seeing* things. This trepidation does indeed enliven the landscape.

Other types of trepidation dampen our perspective. As we continue through the Cochetopa Hills, the skies continually rip open and dump on us. When you hear the word "hills" you think "low," but in these northern Cochetopa Hills we're at 10,000 to 12,000 feet. Even in August it's cold when the weather turns bad. Raw cold. The rain and dampness seep into your marrow and chill you until you're not sure you'll *ever* get warm again.

Even impending bad weather makes Todd and me paranoid. First one awake (Todd) unzips the tent, throws back the fly, and peers up at the sky.

"How's it look?" I ask anxiously, before he can stand upright and raise his head. It rained last night, but there are patches of blue this morning. It could go either way. By the time we break camp, the sky is threatening.

We plan to hike four miles without stopping to rest. We need to get miles in before it rains. Our body temperatures drop amazingly fast as soon as we stop moving. If we can just do our morning's climb without being burdened by rain gear and without carrying both children (Sierra gets too wet on her llama), we should be able to cover our allotted mileage.

Atop Sargeant's Mesa at 11,600 feet, we pull over in a clump of evergreens to get out of the rain and try to shove down some nourishment. The free-ranging cattle that are summering over on the mesa like the protection of the pines too. Despite our efforts to chase them away, they creep even closer. Our llamas don't like them, especially Berrick. They do their warning calls and grow increasingly anxious. We have to move again before we feel fully relaxed.

One of the worst things about hiking in inclement weather is we never really get rested. Rest allows our body temperatures to drop and invites hypothermia. Yet if we *don't* rest, hypothermia will creep even closer. We can't afford to ignore our bodies' need for rest and nourishment. It's a precarious balancing act. We have to keep tabs not only on our own condition, but on our children's too.

Hypothermia or exposure is the major cause of death in the outdoors. And a wet temperature of forty-five degrees like we have today constitutes "ideal" conditions for it. Sierra has on every article of clothing she can fit under her rain gear and still be able to move her limbs, yet she's still cold. Bryce's hands are like ice. He won't keep his gloves on because he needs to suck his thumb for comfort. Todd and I are very anxious.

We get through this day without a major downpour, just annoying showers. But at night the sky rips apart, flooding our tent. Todd takes Bryce's sippee cup and dips the puddles out. The wind is fierce outside, and we're hoping it's the tail end of a front, moving out the "bad air." But no. Todd gives me a wet report again in the morning, and we spend another day trying to out-hike clouds and deal with cold rain.

Most gaps through the Rocky Mountains are isolated notches. But Cochetopa Gap is wide, extending for miles, providing several relatively easy passages from the Gunnison Basin to the San Luis Valley. The Utes followed buffalo herds through this gap. In 1848–

49 Colonel John Fremont led a party into this region to explore potential railroad routes. Their guide, Bill Williams, headed in the wrong direction, forcing the expedition to overwinter high on the ridges of the nearby La Garita Mountains. Eleven of the thirty-five men died in a blizzard. A few more were killed by an infamous cannibal, Alfred Packer, who survived by murdering his fellow travelers and eating them.

On a saddle above Lost Creek drainage, we see Cochetopa Park for the first time. Mesas and domes are scattered throughout the pale green land. There is a fencerow, a dirt road or two, but no other signs of civilization. The gap was bypassed by the transcontinental railroad. This land is visited only by an old pickup lumbering through, kicking up a trail of dust, and a few isolated travelers like us.

In the low evening light, the ground burns with a carpet of yellow straw flowers and scarlet Indian paintbrush. The wind is strong on our faces, and the large clouds it pushes across the heavens send matching shadows racing across the floor of the park. It soothes our eyes to soak in so much open space—open land, open sky. This is "the West" to me. Sparse islands of evergreens dot the land, and we head for one to make a protected camp. It's a dry camp, for water is scarce in this land. We carry tonight's and tomorrow's supply with us.

THERE MUST BE a lot of sediment in the water in these hills. Our water filter is nearly impossible to operate. It takes about fifteen minutes instead of the usual two to pump one quart. I use a terry cloth bib to cushion the handle and prevent my hand from aching. Todd backwashes the ceramic filter to clean it, but within minutes it works hard again. Then it begins to leak. Then the hose pops off. In one last attempt, Todd wires the hose to its connector, but it's clear that the filter is dead. Boiling is the only way.

I position the stove directly behind the tent to block the wind. We prime our stove by dumping a small amount of white gas into the well and lighting it. The flame heats the fuel inside the tank, expands the molecules, builds up pressure, and sends fuel shooting up the hole. Once I light it, however, the flame doesn't burn out as usual but grows and grows. After a while Todd looks up and yells, "There's too much pressure in it! It will explode!"

We quickly push the kids away. Grass and dry pine needles around the stove begin to burn. The wind is wild. The whole forest could go up—or at the very least our tent.

"Dirt! Dirt! Throw dirt on it!" We scrape the ground and throw handfuls of soil, trying to suffocate the flame. The flames snuff out, but seconds later they burn through the debris and flare again.

"We've got to move it!" Todd yells. We each take a stick, and in my haste, I knock over the eight quarts of water in the pot. Our drinking water for tonight and tomorrow. There's only one quart in a bottle remaining. "A seam must have burst." Todd says. "It's wrecked."

When we finally smother the flames, we sit there stunned. No water filter. No stove to purify water or cook. How could two crucial items break within twenty minutes?

After the stove cools off, Todd examines it. Instead of a split seam, he finds a stray pine needle caught in the fill cap. The stove will be OK. We'll still have to boil water to drink, but at least not over an open fire.

The children and I walk out into the open, shoot photos, and watch the sun creep toward the horizon. It pauses behind a solitary tree across the park and sends out rays in all directions. When it drops behind Cochetopa Dome, the sky glows orange.

"Don't you wish you could be there?" Sierra asks, gazing into the light, her whole being glowing too from the reflected light.

"In the sky? Where it's orange?"

"Yeah."

Coyotes yip and call as we put the kids to bed.

"Do I need to be afraid?" Sierra asks.

"Only if you're a rabbit."

Todd and I crawl out for one last pee and to watch the sky. There's a meteor shower tonight, one hundred per minute. I lean back on my husband's strong chest as we tilt our faces to the heavens. A long streak races down the sky and we each say, "Wow!" We continue to be amazed at the gamut of emotions you can experience in one trail day—from terror to bliss in an hour or two. Life on the trail is so rich.

It's Friday the thirteenth. When I ask Todd the daily morning question, today's answer is, "Nearly all blue." By the time we shove off at 7:50, however, there's no sunlight left. The entire sky is engulfed in clouds. We're heading west, where the weather is coming from; it looks ominous.

We walk toward lightning and thunder, then into it, stopping to cover the llamas' panniers and dress the kids in rainsuits and fleece clothing. We're aiming to get across this open meadow to an aspen grove, to duck in as the heavens rip. The kids sit alone under a dense evergreen while Todd and I work in haste, setting up the tent.

The tent gets soaked as we put it up. When we all pile inside with our wet rain suits on, the floor gets wet. In comes the toy bag. I read the kids books, sitting cross-legged in our wet rainsuits. Todd studies maps. We snack on jerky and crackers and take tiny sips of the remaining water. Todd refuses to drink. He would rather get a little dehydrated than deprive his wife and children. Thank goodness it isn't hot. The storm rages outside. The sky cracks open. Rain beats against the coated nylon. Wind shakes the tent. The kids are excited, and Sierra giggles, "Oh, Mother! Are we all right? Is this OK?"

Once the thunder rolls away, the sky grows brighter and the only water hitting the tent is falling off the trees. Todd peeks out. "Blue skies! Let's go!" As the sun comes out, the temperature rises inside our polyurethane-coated rainsuits. We unzip. Push up sleeves. Stop to disrobe.

But before long, more storm clouds gather. Up goes the tent again. On a summer day in the mountains, there's usually a buildup of cumuli later in the afternoon. They unload and move out, and it clears up by evening. *This* weather is screwy.

Rainstorm number three is without lightning, so we decide to sit it out under the golf umbrellas amid some dense conifers. We each take a kid. They quickly become bored and stick their arms out, getting the water dripping off the umbrellas to run down their hands and up their arms, soaking their clothes. "Pull your arms in!"

They run out from under the umbrellas, switching parents. Back and forth. Getting wetter. "Stay here!"

They shuffle their feet, in their lightweight half-leather, half-fabric hiking boots, back and forth beyond the umbrella, where the ground is wet, so they can *make* mud. "Keep your feet under!"

Sniff. Sniff. "Bryce has a dump." Too bad. It could be quite a while before the storm stops so we can change him.

The kids try to hold and balance the heavy umbrellas themselves. Tip forward and our backs get soaked. Tip backward, our fronts. Sideways—dangerously close to poking our eyes. When the storm finally passes, we quickly change Bryce and try to get in another mile or two before the next deluge.

Rainstorm number four hits us when we get to Cochetopa Creek, in a wide-open meadow. This is our first water source since yesterday afternoon. We quickly set up the tent for the third time today. I'm about to boil some water for drinking, but Todd says to hold off. He'd like to cover another two miles.

When the sky looks brighter, we pack up *again* and set out. This is getting incredibly fatiguing. Todd is losing his sense of humor. Sierra needs a nap, but we don't want to stop and take Bryce off Todd's back. He just fell asleep. I want to give her some hard candy to keep her going, but Todd has absolutely no interest in stopping for even one minute. I yell at Todd, and Sierra says, "You guys quit this fighting or I'm going home!" Her comment squelches me.

We set up the tent in camp for the fourth and last time today, crawl into our bags, and collapse. It rains three *more* times while we're in camp. In two days we'll be in the San Juan Mountains. Open. High. Exposed. If we have weather like this up there, we're dead.

In the middle of the night, I crawl out of the tent and find the sky bursting with stars. I murmur a prayer of thanks. But the clear weather is short-lived. The next morning we awaken to clouds, dampness, and rain.

The kids often deal with the rain better than their parents do. They're usually smiling when they look at us from underneath their rain hoods. Todd and I work hard to ensure that all their basic needs are taken care of—warmth, nourishment, and rest. I try to maintain a positive outlook. Comfort is not something we can regulate in the wilderness. That becomes a question of mind-set. Perhaps even young minds are learning this.

One of the things Todd and I were most concerned about before coming on this trip was if the children could survive bad weather. After these days in the Cochetopa Hills, the answer is yes; we just have to be there for their needs. Can children also cope with the emotional and psychological rigors of living in the outdoors like this? The answer again is yes. Our kids seem to do best when things turn bad.

ALL ALONG Cochetopa Creek we climb. A great wall of mountains rises behind it. At the headwaters of the creek, over the San Juan Pass, we'll enter another world—the San Juan Mountains, which we'll follow to trail's end in Durango.

Cochetopa Creek is loaded with beavers—miles and miles of dams in all stages of construction and deterioration. Behind dry, deserted dams, the silt is built up to dam level, making it clear that it was time for the beavers to move on. If we crouch down to eye level with an active dam, even Bryce can see how it raises the water level a few feet. Entrance holes are clearly visible in their homes. We run our fingertips over the toothmarks on pointed stubs of trees that the beavers have gnawed down and hauled away, some so recently that wood chips are still scattered around.

The beavers have diverted the creek and built a dam right where the Colorado Trail crosses, making our ford thigh deep instead of a hop across. The beavers are in charge, and they can change a man-made trail in a matter of days.

What we have here is experiential learning. It reminds me of how my friend back home was so eager to show me the new CD-ROM nature program she bought for her kids. They took the mouse and clicked on "pond." A beaver appeared, and a voice said, "Beavers build dams on creeks." Period. It was hard for me to be excited when I know how big and rich the world really is. Some people think the classroom teaches children enough about wild areas. I believe children need to explore the wild world, be immersed in it, watch clouds expand, beavers build dams, stars twinkle. They need to feel mud, hear elk bugle. Only then can the magnificence possess us and put into clear perspective our place in the natural world. I know in my heart that what we're doing on the trail is best for my children right now. There isn't any finer way I could teach them about life and themselves than by leading them through the Rockies of Colorado.

All day as we followed the creek, the sky has looked threatening. When it finally opens up, we opt to sit under some dense evergreens. Before leaving for this trip I filled a tiny spiral-bound notebook with the lyrics of favorite songs. The children and I huddle under a red-and-white golf umbrella and sing all through the storm. They're happy. We peer out through the branches to our llamas, hunkered down in the rain. Their long eyelashes blink back the drops. Their thick coats compact as they grow wet, making them look much smaller and leaner. The rain looks like solid gray vertical lines of water.

TONIGHT WE'RE camped right below San Luis Pass. Todd fetches water way down in the steep creek drainage and returns, arms loaded, totally out of breath and upset with himself. He spilled a quart of water from the diaper bucket down one boot and soaked the other foot by slipping on a rock and going into the creek. What a workhorse.

The storm clears out, and our dining room decor is the peaks of the San Juans, with Organ Peak directly across the drainage. Its sides are long, fluted volcanic dikes that look like organ pipes. They're painted fiery red and orange from the setting sun. Maybe we'll get a break from this horrendous weather now. I've gone inside the tent for a moment to change Bryce's diaper when suddenly Todd calls, "Come out right now with your camera!" Long rays of the setting sun are shooting through the pass and lighting up just the tops of the peaks with a golden light. Bryce yells from within, "So me! So me!" He can't bear to miss anything. The wet grass is freezing cold on his bare feet, but he doesn't seem to mind. He just stares at the light on the mountains, little rosebud mouth agape. The temperature has dropped considerably since the storm cleared. We can see snow on the highest peaks. Tomorrow we top the saddle and enter the high, magnificent world of the San Juans. We finally believe that tomorrow the sun will shine on us. Just in time.

AT THREE YEARS OLD, Sierra isn't a huge help with camp chores, but her enthusiasm and willingness to learn make up for it. If we don't let children help when they're young, they may not be interested when they're older and are truly able to contribute.

Sierra helps extend our shock-corded tent poles, helps snap the tent onto the poles, unrolls the pads and lays out the sleeping bags. She also feeds the llamas a handful of rabbit pellets in the evening if the grass is scarce in camp. It's mostly to get them used to coming to us and eating out of our hands should they get loose and need to be caught. She puts a cupful in a battered aluminum bowl, a relic that dates back to my Camp Fire Girls days and has traveled 7,000 trail miles with me. She talks to them the whole time, squealing with delight: "Oh, Hansel-Man. You have such a big black nose." The llamas seem fond of her—even big macho Hansel, who's a touch-me-not. When she's finished with one, she announces, "I'm on to Jupiter!" Of course her Berrick always gets served first.

The llamas add a lot to our children's lives out here. To *all* our lives. They're a great source of entertainment and friendship. They teach responsibility and the valuable gift of mutual care. If we take care of the llamas' needs, the llamas will take care of ours. It's obvious even to a three-year-old. Sierra's learning "gratitude." I see it in her eyes when her Berrick takes her across a hairy pass and remains surefooted and calm for her. And I see it in her eyes when she feeds them. It's a simple lesson but incredibly valuable.

It gets cold after the front finally moves through. I normally sleep in my thin long underwear top and bottom, but tonight I can't seem to get warm. I have to get up and add an expedition-weight top, hat, and socks. Bryce seems cold too. He keeps inching down into his bag. I pull him up by his armpits, afraid he won't have enough air down there. I think about that sometimes. Could they suffocate while they sleep, never waking up, never gasping for air? Sometimes I wake up in the night and feel as if I can't breathe. As if someone is standing on my chest or my nostrils are only half open and can't suck in enough air. Our sinuses seem to get a bit clogged out here when we recline, but it's mostly the altitude of 12,000 to 13,000 feet. The suffocating feeling sneaks in during the night

when we're quiet and relaxed and our heartbeats slow. Once it startles us awake, we take deep breaths. Breathe through your mouth.
Keep calm. It's a scary sensation, but knowing what it is helps.

The cord of Bryce's sleeping bag hood is around his arm. I have a
hard time untwisting it, for he sucks his thumb with added enthusiasm when his sleep is disturbed. He gets more and more upset the
longer I fiddle. Somehow, in my efforts I get the cord wrapped
around his neck—tightly. He screams and wants his father. I feel so
bad. Does he think I was trying to strangle him? He's associating pain
with his mother. I can't calm him and have to hand him over to Todd.

It's been a week since I traveled to North Carolina, and still he
rejects me. I lie there in the dark on my back, eyes wide open. Tears
trickle down the sides of my cheeks. I want my son to love me, to
want me. Fathers must go through this all the time—being second-
best—but it's tearing my heart apart.

IF THERE'S one thing about this wandering lifestyle that thrills me
more than anything else, it's topping a pass in high, open mountains. As I climb the last steps up to it, I look back on the country
we've just traveled through. Soon it will no longer be visible. Only a
memory. A whole new world will break open before us as soon as
we top a pass. It makes me feel thirsty with the need to drink in this
new land. I'll stand there, raking my eyes over the scenery—the
mountains and valleys, the creek drainages, the lakes, and I won't be
able to move for a while. I won't *want* to move. It feels *so* good on
my eyes. I feel nourished.

The view from San Luis saddle stuns us. We see the trail thread
around the green-meadowed slopes—through a saddle, around
another peak. It's so exciting to view the trail ahead. Such a difference from hiking in the great green tunnel of the Appalachians.

From the saddle, it's only 1.3 miles and 1,400 feet to the summit
of 14,014-foot San Luis Peak, the closest the Colorado Trail comes
to a 14,000-footer. We see tiny dark figures making their way up the
exposed ridge. Todd and I feel drawn to the summit, but circum-
stances don't allow a detour. If we were alone and backpacking, we
could just boogie on up, but with the kids and llamas, we need to
keep moving according to plan.

For the next four miles, we will be following the old and appropriately named Skyline Trail and will stay at 12,000 feet or more the entire time. Only once will we graze the upper limits of a spruce forest at the head of Spring Creek, where we can find shelter if the thunderheads build. The wind is swift as we head down the saddle, adding an air of excitement to this glorious country.

Tonight we're camped on the saddle between Middle and West Mineral Creeks. It may be our last night alone on the trail. Wally and Katy White, the friends who first put this crazy idea into our heads, are planning to meet us tomorrow, somewhere on the trail.

It's a month and a half that we've been traveling *alone* as a family. These last 350 miles have taught us how to live together and enjoy each other. We also feel very comfortable in the wilderness. Bryce brings it all home to me tonight.

Shortly after supper, he disappears. I call and call, but no answer. So I begin to check the area around our campsite. I find him a short distance away, certainly within earshot, but totally oblivious to my calls. He's sitting in an open meadow in the lowering sunshine. A gentle breeze is feathering the strands of his sun-bleached hair, lovingly petting him. He's lost in thought, staring at a purple aster in his hand as the wind fingers the petals, bending them down, then lifting them up. He's mesmerized by the incredible beauty of the moment. My throat tightens and my nostrils prickle as my eyes fill with tears. My God, my children *must* be happy out here. A sunlit meadow, a simple flower, an evening breeze are entertainment enough for my little boy.

6
Company Arrives
AUGUST 18, 1993

The bond that links your true family is not one of blood, but of respect and joy in each other's lives.

—RICHARD BACH

WHEN THIS easterner first imagined the Rocky Mountains, I envisioned craggy, *rocky* mountains. On Snow Mesa, in the La Garita Wilderness, I feel as if I am on the rolling farmlands of Pennsylvania, only higher. But underfoot are green tundra grasses and a mesa. Mesa—even the word sounds foreign and exotic. It's hard to imagine that we are 12,360 feet high. A mesa is a great uplifted tableland with steep sides. When we cross four-mile-wide Snow Mesa, we forget we're so close to the sky.

The land feels ancient. In Spanish *la garita* means "the lookout." The Indians used the mountaintops as signal stations. Old rock towers or cairns positioned on grassy knolls and across expanses of land guided the historic Stock Driveway, the path for driving cows from the lowlands to the high country. When we see the remains of life lived long ago, the place feels spiritual. The energy endures long after the bodies pass on.

Sheep are still grazed on Snow Mesa. We hear their bleating before we see them. A murmur. A hum in the air. Our ears pick up the sound, straining, knowing we're hearing something different. About the time our minds think "sheep," we see cream-colored spots on the slopes. We might be able to pick out the herder, often a Basque shepherd brought over from the western Pyrenees of Spain. We may spot his tent home and his dogs, moving more swiftly throughout the herd since they've spotted us.

We're been advised not to approach herding dogs, not even to look at them or make eye contact, for they take their job seriously and want no confrontation. We take Sierra off Berrick and shorten the lead ropes to maintain control when they come close, barking.

Everywhere we look the land is striated; across all the slopes are shallow ridges about a yard apart, made by the sheep traversing. From a distance it looks as if the land is gently terraced. John Muir called sheep "hooved locusts," but although we can understand his animosity, we harbor no ill feelings toward them. So ancient an occupation. They seem like such gentle creatures, compared with big, lumbering free-range cattle.

We walk differently when we cross this landscape. Our heads are always up. The expanse *pulls* them up. The muscles in our eyes *feel* stretched from so much long-reach looking, compared with our other lives in front of screens and printed material. The trail here is often without noticeable tread, so we always are looking for our route—following Driveway cairns or brown carsonite posts stuck into the earth. They're thin slats of a material resembling fiberglass that nod back and forth in the wind, which seems to blow constantly in this country. We often need map and compass readings to stay on course.

As we look ahead across the mesa, something catches our eye. Bright-colored figures with animals. Could it be Wally and Katy and their llamas, coming up from Spring Creek Pass to meet us? The specks move closer and begin wildly waving their arms. Our hearts warm. They are out here for us. In such wild, desolate country, after not encountering people for so long, we feel the way the mountain men of old must have felt when they came down from the hills and met a fellow nomad.

The road to Lost Creek Ranch is an eighteen-mile jostle. Washboard ruts. It makes us feel worn out from just sitting. Wally concentrates on the road and tries to aim his truck tires toward the smoothest areas. Back and forth across the little-used road, trying to make our ride more comfortable. We don't care. We're thrilled to be taking a break with our friends. Gonna take a shower, eat a good meal, sleep in a bed, have a little adult conversation. Yeah!

Our cabin is hunting camp style. Old fifties furniture. Linoleum floors and countertops. Cardboard shoeboxes duct taped and nailed to the walls as shelves. But best of all is the "hot tub"—a World War II metal missile transporter that's been torched in half. Water is gravity fed by a black hose shoved into a creek up meadow. The tub sits in the middle of a pasture. The ranch owner's dad hauled it here originally to use as a watering trough. His son, Bob, put a fifty-five-gallon barrel woodstove into it and now uses it for a good soak. He starts the fire for us at about 2:00 in the afternoon. At midnight we put on our headlamps, leave the sleeping babes with Katy, and head down through the fields. I am not enthusiastic about this adventure.

When we climb up the ladder, I dip my hand in the water. It feels like bathtub water after the kids have been playing in it for hours—just a few degrees above cool. The mountain air is chilly, and the thought of taking off my clothes is almost enough to send me back up the hill to the cabin and my bed.

Bob opens the stovepipe draft in hopes of moving things along. Orange tongues shoot out from the top of the stovepipe—brilliant against the black sky. I slowly lower myself in and realize there are no seats. No floor either. A missile carrier is round, so you must push your back against one side and brace your feet against the other to keep your bottom from sinking. The woodstove is submerged in the water at one end, welded to the side, and fed from an opening in the tub wall. You can touch it and not get burned. Wally and I position ourselves by the stove, across from each other, and spend the next hour circulating—pulling water up with one arm and pushing it down with the other. The exercise helps warm us and distributes the heat. Before long the water is a luxurious temperature, and we ease back, rest our hands on the deck around the tub, sip wine coolers, and stare at billions of stars.

Come morning, we take a stroll down to the hot tub to show the kids and see it in daylight. It's a good thing this is after the fact, for the water is murky brown. It doesn't get changed much. I'm glad I didn't see it earlier, or it could have been just the excuse I needed to miss out on a good time and a great memory.

For the next five days we will hike into the Weminuche Wilderness, through the Needle Mountains and the Grenadier Range, all within the San Juan mountain system. With an average elevation gain of more than 12,000 feet, this is the loftiest stretch of the entire Colorado Trail, topping out at Coney Summit at 13,334 feet.

Our friends from Wisconsin, Steve Peck (who was Todd's hiking companion for the Pacific Crest Trail) and Mary Remer, will be joining us, but Todd and I feel strongly that Wally ought to come along too. The Weminuche is one of his favorite places. He has nothing pressing that he must immediately get home to. We have an extra box of dried food, and the cabin fridge, Katy says, is stuffed with fresh leftovers. Since he played a big part in our being here, it seems only fitting that he should share in some trail miles. He's easily convinced.

We're no longer alone on the trail, and we won't be for the rest of our trip. I enjoy the company, but already I feel the difference in our family dynamics. Our children are on the periphery. Our conversations revolve around adult topics, and we seem to pay attention to the kids only when they need something important ("I need to poo"). They come to us to be held when we're in our folded foam camp chairs. Until now our children have been the exclusive center of our attention. Now they must learn to share us. Sierra is afraid of Wally and Steve. They tease her. They try to hug her. They're trying to win her affection. She won't walk near them. I asked Sierra to give Wally a plate of cake the other day and she refused. Katy chimed in, "If you don't, you won't get any yourself." I agreed until I saw how frightened she was. I can't force her to feel comfortable. She is sociable to people who gently seek her out and allow her to take her time. She sees women as less threatening. I need to make sure my children know they are more important to me than friends who join us. Ultimately, this is our family trip.

People seem to understand that right from the get-go. When Bob hiked with us those first days, *we* set the pace, *we* decided when we needed to break and for how long. *We* chose the campsite and when to quit for the day. This could be hard for seasoned packers who are used to running their own backpacking trips. But our kids run this trip. We have to cover miles while allowing time for playing in creeks and climbing boulders. If they aren't happy, then Mom and Dad won't be happy, and this whole experience won't be worth it.

When friends join us, we have a responsibility to them too. Although our plate is full with caring for llamas and children, no man is an island out here. At the very least, their performance influences ours.

On our second day from Spring Creek Pass, we have an eight-mile stretch of exposed high trail and our highest point, Coney Summit, to climb over. As we head out of camp, the clouds are gathering, the weather deteriorates, and we grow concerned for our friends, especially Mary. We know that when the weather is bad we have to push more and breaks are few and short.

Steve is an animal. He rigorously trains every day as though he were entering the Olympics. He regularly rides his bike two hundred miles in a single day and pushes his body until he pukes. We're not worried about his performance. We know he would continue in a crawl if he had to. Mary we're watching warily.

After crossing Jarosa Mesa, velvety looking with its thick cover of willows and loaded with elk, we begin our climb up to Coney Summit. There's no trail, just a general direction. The land drops off steeply to our right, in jagged, eroded volcanic cliffs. But our route is smooth and grassy and gently sloping. We hike right along the edge of the cliffs and need to turn around periodically and scope out the land we came from.

The higher we climb, the more country comes into view. Mountain range after mountain range appears in the distance. The sky is turning cobalt, and storms are filling the heavens over all the distant peaks, but still we walk in sunshine. We watch the neighboring skies, watch the direction the storms are moving and the way the clouds are building and spreading. Each mountain range has its own weather system, and we try to decide *if* we'll get nailed and how long until it might happen.

By the guys' calculations, Coney Summit should be only another mile and a half climb. An hour at the most. Let's push over it.

Once we hit a peak summit, we take a break and eat some food. Wally's altimeter seems to be off, for his calculations don't jibe with where we are on the map, which shows each peak's altitude. We don't pay it any mind; altimeters are often off. We're pleased with everyone's performance, especially Mary's. She says she's feeling fine. Looks as if we'll get into camp early. Always a treat.

Before we head across the open tundra, rain begins to fall, so we suit up in full rain gear. We spot another point up ahead. Todd mentions that the guidebook says we skirt a knoll just before dropping down off the ridge, so we figure that's the knoll ahead. When we see five women backpackers coming toward us, I ask, "How soon till we drop down?"

"Oh, you have to go over Coney Summit yet. That's another couple of miles. You'll be exposed for a few hours yet."

Oh, my God! Now we really feel the need to push to get off this ridge. Todd and I crank it into high gear and leave the others behind. About the time we approach what appears to be the true Coney Summit, we hear cries from behind. Steve is yelling for us to stop. In the saddle, we hold a powwow.

Mary is doing poorly now, nauseated and light-headed. Steve wants to head down, cross-country, drop off the ridge, and cross the high point tomorrow. Todd and I want to keep going. Wally is indifferent. We haven't heard any thunder, so lightning isn't a concern yet. The wind hasn't picked up, and the rain is still gentle and manageable. We want to get it over with. The weather could be even worse tomorrow. If we can do it now, we think we should. It looks as if it's pouring in all the surrounding valleys. Whole ranges have disappeared in the rain clouds. We take Mary's entire pack and load it on one of Wally's llamas that's training with light panniers. Mary thinks she'll be fine now. And she is.

We know we've reached the true summit when we see four-wheel drive vehicles parked on the crest. The guidebook says this is a popular spot for motorists. Kind of bursts our bubble after all our physical struggle.

Our descending route past the ghost mining town of Carson is extremely steep. We stumble past the remains of a few miners' cabins, trying not to fight gravity. Our bodies feel limp from fatigue. I've carried Bryce all day. When I'm pumped with adrenalin and barreling over a ridge, trying to out-hike a storm, I can disregard the fatigue. I'm numb to it. I don't have time to acknowledge it. But as soon as we slow the pace and relax a bit, it rushes over me like a flash flood. I'm starving. My body aches. All of a sudden my neck feels painfully stiff.

The men are ahead of Mary and me, scoping out a campsite. When our trail crosses a creek, the water source for the night, they begin to climb again. I get bitchy. "Where are you going?" I yell. "To find a flat spot." A good answer. When you're extremely tired, *any* incline feels monumental.

We set up camp in the stunning Lost Creek Valley, in a field of periwinkle and white columbine. A golden eagle circles above. Coyotes yip. We watch an elk go in and out of laurel thickets across the canyon. Ptarmigan call. Low white clouds drift over the peaks. Who knows what tomorrow brings? Today wasn't *so* bad.

WAKING UP to rain on the trail is unlike anything we experience in that other world of protective structures and vehicles. Your ears first pick up the sound of raindrops pinging on the stretched nylon fly of your tent. I may have heard the rain in the middle of the night, so I listen now. Is it merely dripping off the trees or is it the real thing? If so, is it intermittent or steady? If it *doesn't* quit, a feeling of dread hits.

Todd and I roll toward the center and look into each other's eyes. Twist up our faces and stick out tongues in disgust. We lie there and listen to the rhythm. Smile when it ceases. Frown when it begins again in earnest.

We discuss a game plan. Next break in the rain, Todd will suit up and bring in the llamas from their picket lines. He'll saddle them up, come back to the tent to retrieve gear from me, and begin packing panniers. I'll stay in the tent with the kids—dress them, stuff bags, roll pads, feed them a cold breakfast. Todd will fire up the stove and deliver cups of hot chocolate and coffee. Invariably, at least one will spill.

On this particular morning, none of our friends are eager to leave, so we remain extra long in the tent. We read books, but we begin to get on each other's nerves. Todd arrives with extra layers of fleece clothing and rain gear. It's a feat of strength to stretch the kids' rubbers over their hiking boots, and trying frustrates me.

Sierra announces she wants a chocolate Power Bar for breakfast. I rip open the metallic wrapper with my teeth, fold it back, and hand it over. She refuses it. She didn't want it opened. She wants to eat it while she's riding, which is only *minutes* away. I give in and exchange it for an unopened one, but then I lose it and flip out. She begins to cry. Bryce begins to cry. Todd ignores them, and I grow more irate over his ability to shut them out *and* his depending on me to deal with them. (The way I depend on him to deal with the llamas when they act like meatheads.)

I push the kids out of the tent to stand under umbrellas and wait. By this time I don't care if it's pouring, I want to move. I help Todd shake water off the rain fly and stuff the tent.

Once on her llama, Sierra asks to have her Power Bar opened, and I quietly open this second one. Our friends think I have amazing patience. Funny. I often feel like the mother from hell. Poor kid was probably seeking some fragment of control in her uncertain wilderness life. The weather is beyond her control, and so are her headstrong parents. The wrapper on her Power Bar is something she can at least *attempt* to control.

I try extra hard out here on the trail to be patient. These kids didn't ask to come along. This is Todd's and my gig. I remind myself of that a lot, especially when the weather challenges us. As a result, even through the rain, Sierra and Bryce are usually smiling.

It rains steadily for two hours as we climb up broad and green Lost Creek Valley. As we switchback past some hoodoos (eroded volcanic pinnacles), we're reminded of flames and gnomes. The kids say they look like a line of soda bottles with chunky lids or people wearing hats.

Sierra consented to ride her llama this morning, even though it's raining, to cut me a break. For me, carrying Bryce uphill is the worst. So Sierra is exposed and feeling cold, even though she has on most of her clothing. We sing Walkin' Jim's song "Pika Pika" when we hear the big-eared rodents squeak in the rocks. I'm trying to keep her mind off her discomfort.

On the pass, the wind hits with a vengeance. We stop to add some insulation and hoist *both* children onto our backs. We pull their rain pants down over their boots to close the gap and keep their socks dry. When it's not blowing so hard, we gather the coated nylon pack cover and hold it in place with a wooden clothespin so the kids can see out. But now the rain is driving horizontally into our faces, so all hatches are battened down and snapped tight. They're set up for a nap in the dark, warm and gently moving. This morning, however, it's a setup only for boredom. Bryce wants to hear a silly children's song, "The Cannibal King." I repeat it dozens of times as he fires off " 'gain!" as soon as the last line is sung. My voice is breathy, for even though we're moving downhill, he's work to carry. But he's happy, and he's staying relatively still while he listens.

When the rain lets up, we stop for a break on the soggy ground. I peel an apple and section an orange, and the moisture freezes my fingers. It's cold. Bryce insists on feeding himself even though he's wearing thumbless mittens. We laugh, watching him struggle. It's hard enough out here. I switch to cheese and candy. More calories and easier.

When the rain begins again, I pull balaclavas over the kids' hats and dig out plastic bread bags from my rain jacket pockets—waterproof mittens. Wide enough to grasp an umbrella handle and a lead rope but enough protection to create a vapor barrier and keep my hands warm. Sierra asks where we're heading. I say, "To camp." She says, "I want to go home." "I don't blame you, honey."

Down in Pole Creek Valley, the sun abruptly breaks through, making the landscape bright and glistening. The sun's warming rays are soothing on our faces, but our rain gear suddenly makes us feel as if we're wearing portable saunas. We peel off our coated nylon and bask in the warmth. There are smiles on everyone's faces. "We've just entered Paradise," Steve comments. Sunshine, when it's been absent for a time, can transform nearly any place into Paradise. We couldn't feel better. We come from a state of feeling downcast and victimized and wondering Why are we here? to thinking Why would I want to be anywhere else? just from the presence of the sun. It doesn't take a lot out here to fill us with joy.

We move closer to the water to get a closer view of impressive Pole Creek Falls. The surging water cut through the volcanic rock to create an arch and high rock pinnacles. But in a minutes the sky again fills with nasty clouds and thunder rumbles. We slide back into our clammy rainsuits, saddle up, and go in search of a flat spot to camp. As large raindrops fall, we set up and start to cook dinner in our tent vestibules once again. So disappointing. We haven't been able to share an evening meal with our friends *yet*, for the inclement weather drives us into our individual tents. This suits Sierra fine, for she's still having trouble relating to the men, especially Steve. She repeatedly tells him and Wally that she doesn't like them. Come evening, we have a talk and I ask her what the problem is.

"I don't like Steve's hair."

"What's wrong with it?"

"It's too straight."

"My hair *and* your hair are straight."

"His is *all* straight in the back. I don't like the way it all goes down. He looks like a duck."

Oh, my God. We talk about accepting people for who they are and not how they look. Then I say, "The real problem is they're always pestering you for hugs and kisses, isn't it?" She nods. "How about if I get *them* to promise to leave you alone, will *you* promise to not say you don't like them and to give them a chance?"

"OK, Mama."

She probably longs for those early days on the trail, when it was just our little family. But Sierra may as well learn to get along with all kinds of people. That's one thing about this lifestyle. Sierra and Bryce don't have children their own age to play with. Their comrades are often much older. It's both a drawback and a gift. We can experience long-forgotten childlike wonder, and they can experience greater depth and meaning in their world. We learn that all people, no matter their age, are entitled to respect, acceptance, and space.

THE SOUTHERN San Juans are at the tail end of the Mineral Belt, which stretches from Boulder down to Silverton. Colorado's prosperity of the late 1800s was based chiefly on silver mining. Large, rowdy mining towns sprang up in the valleys while remote little settlements like Carson and Beartown, which we're walking through, clung to the high mountainsides close to the Divide. Like Carson, there's not much left of Beartown: just a fallen-down cabin and a few long-abandoned mine dumps.

When we see an old miner's log cabin, it's hard to pass by without checking it out. They're not all that different—smallish logs, weatherbeaten, crude notches, chinking gone, roof falling in, debris inside. They all look as though they were put up in a hurry without much craftsmanship. These men had only one mission—the quest for precious metals.

We run our hands down the grooved wood of the cabin, peer in the paneless windows and try to imagine what life must have been like in this spot, high in the rugged San Juans. Did this miner ever find his fortune? Was he young or old? Happy or lonely? Did he die here, or was he driven out by hunger and disappointment?

We think about this as we climb up to the Divide, swimming through dense fields of wildflowers. The riot of color and variety— purple asters, yellow daisies, scarlet Indian paintbrushes—makes us want to lie down and roll in the sunshine, inhaling their fragrance.

Up on the Divide, we're amazed at the great green expanse, the rolling meadows at 12,680 feet. The wind is ferocious and biting. A cold front moved through last night and pushed the clouds away. We have on as many layers of clothing as will fit—five above the waist, three below, double hats, double mittens, double fleece coats, and windsuits.

The roaring wind keeps Bryce from sleeping, and even the youngest feel the excitement and beauty of being up so high. "Don't go to sleep!" the land and the wind seem to say. "Don't miss this experience!" We don't want our children to be afraid of the wild wind, even if it does take our breath away. We want them to realize that only in wild open places does it blow with such abandon and freedom. So few of these places are left.

As we say good-bye to the Continental Divide, we silently tell it we hope to be back and walk its backbone across the rooftop of America someday, children and llamas in tow.

Our Colorado Trail switchbacks thirty times through the narrow Elk Creek gorge, so precipitously that it seems to drop us. The canyon is so steep that we reach out and use the rock wall for balance in places where the trail is eroded and the footing is treacherous. Sierra is uncomfortable but learning to trust. She grasps the wooden horn of her saddle and widens her eyes, but she doesn't complain. She's maturing. You can't cross the Rocky Mountain range and not have it affect you, even if you're only three years old.

I SEE SOMETHING I'm not looking for, and I can't hold it in my mind's eye. The flashing red light ahead on the trail makes no sense to my brain, nor do the two sets of dark llama ears that appear behind it. Only when we hear a voice saying "Here comes the Llama Family now" do we recognize Bob Riley, who is filming us with his video camera.

He did it again! Surprised us! He gives out T-shirts that he's had silk-screened in honor of our imminent completion of the trail. On the front is a large symbol of the Colorado Trail enclosing a llama and "Rocky Mountain Llama and Alpaca Assoc." Underneath: "Cindy and Todd, Sierra and Bryce, Hiking with Family and Llama Friends on the Colorado Trail." On the back:

Why Llamas?
* Hiking the Colorado Trail with llamas is just a walk in the park.
* Llamas will carry over 100 pounds of camping equipment, children's toys, plus diapers for 470 miles.
* Llamas never ask how soon we will be there.
* Llamas have little impact on the environment.
* For a llama, the whole world is a salad bar.
* Berrick is a good friend of Sierra.
* Llamas only need grass, water, love and Stillwater Minerals [Bob's company].

We take a break in a meadow, and Bob breaks out chilled sodas and beer. Once again this wonderful man warms our hearts with his love.

Steve and Mary are beginning to make the mental transition from one lifestyle to the next. From a wild, free world to one of schedules, vehicles, and material things. If one is truly in love with this life, the reentry always entails culture shock. It can't be avoided. It's something you have to go through whether you're in the back-country for a week or six months. Steve becomes sullen and a bit withdrawn, for he knows where *his* heart lies. We empathize with him, for we know that before long we'll be in exactly the same place.

Tonight we're reminded of how small this world really is and how connected we are to the spirits of other long-distance hikers. Another soul wanders into our camp by the Animas River. He comes from the south. Another through-hiker. He has thinning gray hair in a long ponytail under his baseball hat, a long gray beard, and a much more youthful face than his hair would have us believe. His legs have many miles on them. He puts down his pack, and we recognize him as Joe Fennely from Connecticut. He hiked the Appalachian Trail the same year I did back in 1979. We've been running into each other over the years at hiking conferences. Bob is amazed that out of the dozen or two hikers he's seen on this trail, one is a friend.

Amid the long green river grasses, we make a common kitchen where we cook and share a meal. A huge pleasure, but a rarity on this rainy stretch. We talk with Joe of trails and adventures. Joe pulls out his penny whistle and plays sweet tunes to us and the San Juan Mountains.

Animas is a reference in Spanish to "river of the lost souls." It runs cool, green, and spirited. There's another familiar sound in this valley. The trains of the Denver and Rio Grande Railroad—a narrow-gauge line that was constructed in 1882 to haul ores, especially gold and silver, from the San Juan Mountains. An estimated $380 million in precious metals rode this route. It remained part of the line until 1980, when it was sold to a company that maintains it as one of Colorado's historical highlights. Visitors can ride forty-five miles from Durango to Silverton and penetrate the Weminuche Wilderness, accessible only by horseback, foot, or the D&RG. We plan to ride the train as a congratulations gift to ourselves when we reach trail's end in Durango.

We switchback out of the spectacular river canyon, see the beautiful Grenadier Range come into view, and wait at an overlook for the morning train to pass. A great column of black smoke is visible first, as the authentic coal-fired steam locomotive pulls the long train around the curves. The train reminds us that on the other side of this mountain is Molas Pass—the checkout point for Steve and Mary and our last resupply. One final stretch is all that remains of this long Colorado Trail.

We feel comfortable and confident now in this lifestyle, with our children and the llamas. Gone is the fear of the unknown. This trail is our home, and long-distance hiking is our love. It's wonderful to see that our children seem to be enjoying it as much as Todd and I are, perhaps even more. We are able to share with them what means the most to us in our lives, have them experience the same joy, see them really "get it." This is the real surprise, the real reward, the real reason for our trek on this trail.

7

The Last Stretch
AUGUST 25, 1993

When work, commitment, and pleasure all become one and you reach that deep well where passion lives, nothing is impossible.
—NANCY COLY

AT WALLY AND KATY'S house in Durango, we resupply for the last time. We will return here in a little over a week, the entire Colorado Trail completed, and prepare to return home.

Breaks from the trail are not necessarily easy or relaxing. The longer we are in town, the more fatigued the children get. Their schedule is thrown off: although they go to bed late, they continue to get up at the crack of dawn. Their sleep is disturbed by "hot dog thirst" and a need to use the bathroom. If they're on the floor with blankets, they seem to miss their sleeping bags, but the bags are too hot for indoor use. If they're in a bed, they tend to roll out unless we set up barricades. I'm up half a dozen times a night tending to their needs. Todd sleeps deeply. I yell, shove, and insult him to get him to wake up and help. It takes so much energy that I'm sleep deprived too. We know why our children get irritable on those rare occasions when they do. Sleep is the only fix. But neither child will nap in town during the day without being in a car seat or a child carrier.

Wally and Katy want to take us to a commercial hot springs for a picnic supper even though it's late—nearly 8:00. Bedtime. Bryce has been sucking his thumb for an hour—a sign that he's more than ready. And the kids are starving.

When we arrive, half a dozen adults are lounging around the pool looking half comatose—clearly into the comfort and relaxation. And then our children burst in. "The hot pool is too hot!" Sierra screams. The cooler pool is too cool. She sits outside and shivers loudly. Everyone stares, either entertained or annoyed. Bryce has a full diaper and complains vigorously while I try to change him. It starts to rain. We hurry to eat under a tree as the wind picks up and the night grows cooler. Why did we even come here? Because we are trying to be good guests, and Wally and Katy are trying to be good hosts.

Our kids have limits in town (society) as well as on the snow-fields of the Ten Mile Range. We could selfishly push them to extremes so we can do what we desire. But if we didn't keep our children's best interests at heart, it would backfire and become a nightmare. The key to making this long-distance hike a success *as a family* is to make absolutely sure our children's basic needs are met. Then, and only then, as individuals and as a family, we are close to limitless.

When we resupply, we need a solid day in town to do chores. Laundry is first. We pick through the panniers and pack pockets, sorting dirty laundry. Peed-up underwear, snotty hankies, and food-encrusted bibs often seem to hide and miss the boat. Fleece coats and wind gear do not get washed unless they're visibly filthy.

Todd goes through all the gear and makes a list of things to resupply or repair. Fuel bottles get topped off. Our container of Band-Aids is refilled. The water filter is backwashed or cleaned. The rims and threads of the water bottle lids are subjected to soap and hot water to remove dirt and mildew. Pots and pans are scoured. Four pairs of boots get greased. New maps and guidebook sections for the upcoming stretch are packed while those sections already completed are pulled out. I often need to replenish my supply of envelopes, writing paper, sunscreen, lip ointment. We compile a list during the last day or two of a stretch before heading into town.

And there's food. We figure out how many breakfasts, lunches, and dinners we'll need for the upcoming section. After looking at what's left over from the previous stretch, we decide what we want to buy.

On this last leg of our hike, we're suffering from menu burnout. You'd think that after our thousands of miles of trail experience we would have our act together when it comes to food. Not so. I bought cases of fat-free health food from a co-op before we set out in an attempt to lose weight. The stuff got so dry and tasteless that I chose not to eat it. Katy's scale shows that I've lost seven pounds and Todd has lost fifteen. The children have lost nothing, thank goodness. I vow that we are going to eat well on this last stretch, dammit! We're done suffering with tasteless backpacker food. We'll cart the remaining boxes of crackers and bars back home and feed them to our chickens (even they refuse to eat them). It's an all new, mouthwatering list: canned ham, cheese, bread, fresh fruit, cookies, salami, and pepperoni.

Gone is the haughty purist sense that we still need to live like backpackers, that if our llamas carry "real food" we're somehow cheating. If ice cream wouldn't melt, we'd load a couple of gallons of that on their backs.

How we've grown as hikers. It wasn't many years ago that we turned up our noses at picnic-toting llamas on the trail. Now it's whatever it takes to get out here, and with kids the only way is with llamas. And if their packing ability relieves us from eating tasteless mush and dried food, why suffer? It's rough enough out here.

We get a lot of mail in town, sometimes more than a dozen letters and care packages. I am the family correspondent, and I try to write back to everyone before heading out again. This eats up time, leaving none for entertaining the kids. Before leaving Pennsylvania, I stockpiled little presents for each town stop—new storybooks, card games, vinyl farm animals, coloring books and sticker books. I wrapped them all in gift paper, rewards for a job well done!

While we're in town, we get on the horn to Stan Ebel, owner of our llamas, to discuss prices. We want to buy them. With our new knowledge of llama packing and our experience with hiking and camping, we could create a very lucrative commercial pack business back home by drawing on clients from Philadelphia, Washington, D.C., New York City, and our home near the Lehigh Valley. The only similar businesses on the whole eastern seaboard are a packer in Maine and one in South Carolina. We've been weighing the pros and cons for weeks. We could continue long-distance hiking as a family and have "the boys" pay for themselves at the same time. We're not quite ready to hike that rugged 3,100-mile Continental Divide Trail, but we could use them to do shorter trips in the meantime. By bringing the llamas home, we would be taking the excitement and adventure of the trail with us. This new enterprise is risky and full of complexities, like the trail. I think Todd and I need that element in our lives. This way, going home will be an adventure too.

Hansel is ten years old; Berrick, eleven; and Jupiter, twelve. Stan tells us we could have the three for $3,000. We should be able to get at least five more years of commercial packing out of them—full-time hiking, carrying heavy loads—and an additional five years of "light duty"—day hikes, birthday parties, and such.

"Ten years old seems to be the deciding age," Stan explains. "If they're not falling apart by then and have good muscle tone, they'll keep going."

We're excited. We'll need to buy a trailer when we get off the trail, then fence in a pasture and build a shelter when we return home. We need to assess our savings account before we get too excited. Still, our brains are in overdrive. Todd is designing pack saddles and panniers, calculating shed dimensions and roof designs. I'm thinking of a company name and creating business cards and a logo. Who will we cater to, and where will we advertise? Our connections with hiking clubs should provide us with many hikers who no longer can (because of bad knees or backs) or want to carry heavy backpacks, but who still want to get on the trail for an extended time. And there are families like us who simply cannot physically carry gear and kids on their backs. The time feels right for us to set out in a new direction.

THE CHILDREN'S fatigue continues as Wally drives us to the trail-head at Molas Pass. Bob is along and will accompany us on this last stretch. The motion of the truck is just enough to remind our children how sleepy they are, but sitting upright with seatbelts on makes them too uncomfortable to pass out. It's raining. Setting out in the rain is one of the hardest things to do. Even if it starts raining five minutes after we're on the trail, it's better. Packing up in the rain is so depressing. We can't hide our collective sour mood. Bryce is especially cranky. Sierra is loud during most of the hour-long ride, except when Wally asks her to be quiet.

I look at the back of Bob's head and wonder if he regrets coming along. He has children of his own, as does Wally, but still . . . Here they are dealing with someone else's children. A lot to ask. But what we're asking of our children is a lot too. Todd and I hold on to this thought, but can our friends? We feel anxious.

It's difficult for me to keep the kids happy and out of trouble while Todd saddles and packs the llamas. The dirt turnaround where we're parked is muddy with standing puddles. The kids get wet and dirty, of course. As I change Bryce's diaper on the tailgate, he cries and fights. I drop two clean diapers into the muddy water. If we can just get on the trail and get them into their child carriers, there might be peace.

After just five minutes of walking across the open rolling high-lands above Molas Pass, they're both out cold. A fine rain. No wind. Umbrellas protect our now contented cargo.

A fire devastated this area in 1879. Despite efforts at reforesta-tion, it has never been able to recover. Black snags still protrude from the meadows. The air feels soft, and the land is quiet and hushed. We talk in whispers. The rain falls so gently it makes no sound on our colorful umbrellas. A feeling of relief and peace engulfs us.

The bad news is the weather forecast. A hurricane moved up from the Gulf of Mexico. Although it broke up, the low pressure is hanging around and is expected to create long-term precipitation.

Many days of it. What a way to end a trip. In this seven-day stretch will we see the sun, or will it stay hidden all the way to trail's end?

In camp tonight, Bob surprises us with a feast prepared and sent along by his wife, Jo: zippered plastic bags full of beef stroganoff, broccoli and wild rice, butterscotch pudding, blue corn chips and salsa, and espresso. As we eat, we hear what sounds like children's voices in the distance. We look up to the ridge line and see domestic sheep walking single file, silhouetted against the sky. The moon is visible through light clouds. No stars and no wind, however. We have our doubts about the sun tomorrow.

UGH. RAIN. The kind that has staying power. A thousand-foot climb kicks off the morning's hike. Both our children are on our backs. Sierra hates to be confined all day, but she gets too wet and cold on her llama. She's tired of this trail life and wants to know how many days are left. I share her anticipation of The End.

We're able to use our umbrellas until we climb up and join the historic Rico-Silverton Trail, a former mine road, and the wind picks up. It's 11:30 and we haven't yet stopped for our first break. I feel weak and light-headed from hunger. I find a hard candy stashed in my front waist pack and suck on it vigorously, hoping for strength and stamina. Todd talks to the kids about Cheez-Its and plums—snacks we'll eat on break—hoping to entice them onward. I play the "dog game" with Sierra, where I say a friend's name and she has to tell me the name of his pet. We're trying to get another mile out of them. But Bryce is screaming in my ear. Todd asks to pass; my pace has slowed to a crawl. He disappears into the fog. Then I think, "This is ridiculous." Bryce's diaper could be soaked all these hours or, worse, he could be sitting on a dump. The kids could be cold and wet and hypothermic. And I'm starving! "Todd!" I yell. "Take a break!" We set up the tent, bring in the stove and make hot chocolate. The children smile radiantly, ever resilient. Bob joins us with sticky buns: stale, but still a treat. We sit in water and mud tracked in by our boots. Our leg muscles hurt from being stationary, cold, and cramped in the crowded tent.

The afternoon brings more rain, as well as pretty waterfalls dropping over steep-sided canyons. We see wildflowers, their colors even more intense for the lack of sunlight. Our views are short: what's at our feet or right off the track. The far-reaching panoramas of the La Plata Mountains and Grenadier Range and the exciting cliffs and gorges that make this stretch famous are nowhere to be seen. We can only imagine the beauty and the exposure. We trudge along in a world of tight focus, one that pulls our thoughts inward.

We talk about home these days. We fantasize about deep baths in our sunken tub, crackling fires in our woodstove, apple pies coming out of the oven, the yeasty smell of home-baked bread. When the weather deteriorates and it's late in the journey, we need something to propel our hearts homeward, lest we pine away over wanting to remain. It's actually good to experience uncomfortable conditions in the last stretch. It helps make the transition from one life to the next more palatable, as if the trail is a parent that's trying to wean us.

MORE AND MORE and more rain. Falling steadily all night long, waking us so we roll over in disgust. It means I carry Bryce for another day. I hate it. His weight rides low in the pack. My hips ache so badly in the night that it keeps me awake. Sierra will ride on Todd's back again, which is uncomfortable for them both.

We walk around Hermosa Peak. Wisps of fog play with its pointed summit. A slope of cold, hard talus ends abruptly at a lush green meadow. The contrast is startling.

It's a comfort having Bob along. He's easy to be with and makes us feel happy in these tough conditions. The rain doesn't tarnish his good mood, though he remarks that it's getting a bit old. It's amazing how the presence of one friend can transform my mood in hard times. I don't know if we try harder with nonfamily members or if the friend's presence raises the energy level of the group, creating more support and good feeling. It probably depends on who the person is, for inserting an outsider can be stressful too. At this point Bob feels more like family. I enjoy company when the weather challenges us, especially a person as amiable as he is.

Sierra has finally warmed up to him, stopped saying "I don't like you," and switched to slightly less obnoxious behaviors like stepping on his toes, gently poking him in the arm, and sticking her

bare feet in his face. She clearly wants to connect with him physically, and I encourage her to give him a hug or sit on his lap and listen to a story instead of behaving aggressively. She finally breaks
down and admits to him, "I like you," hiding her face with embar-
rassment. In an attempt to cement the friendship, Bob takes it one
step further and replies, "I love you."

The bad weather fosters such intimacy, for he comes over and
joins us in our tent every evening. The constant rain forces us to
spend more hours lying around inside than we care to. The tent is
the symbol of security in our children's wilderness lives, one of the
few unchanging things about this uncertain, adventurous lifestyle.
It's our only shelter, and Bob's presence in it affects us all, including
Sierra.

Bob looks around and announces that he needs to get a roomier
tent. When he returned to join us on this stretch, he came outfitted
with a golf umbrella and a Crazy Creek chair like ours. When we
mop up the rainwater in our tent with a very absorbent synthetic
chamois, he adds that to his list of necessities.

Bob's been bitten by the long-distance hiking bug. Since those
first few fateful days outside Denver when he joined us for our kickoff, he's had a dream brewing in his heart of hiking the entire Colorado Trail himself. Before this it had been many years since he
traveled long distance in the mountains. But he's been reminded of
its joys. And to think: he was initially reluctant to join us and had to
be persuaded by his wife. It's a rare human being who is able to hike
in the wilderness through stressful times with young children and
not only be tolerant but end up loving them *and* hiking.

Sierra wants to walk this afternoon, although the rain hasn't let
up. Todd is reluctant. Our pace slows way down when a three-year-
old is setting it. But I convince him that she needs to walk sometimes. It's her trip too. She hasn't walked since the Cochetopa Hills.
The folded-up cuffs of her jade-colored rain pants scrape the trail
and her vinyl rubbers scuff along as she holds my hand and walks by
my side, happily pointing out flowers and moss and all the beautiful
things she might otherwise have missed.

It's a delicate balance. As conditions worsen and the end draws
closer and we see how well our children roll with the punches, Todd

and I are starting to realize the extraordinary thing our family is accomplishing.

Tonight in bed, we're resorting to prayer to blow away the clouds. They parted for just a bit this afternoon, revealing fresh snow on the peaks. A degree or two colder, and all this precipitation would be snow even at our elevation. Yuck!

THIN, GAUZY CLOUDS this morning with some blue showing. Just the right amount that the sun *could* burn through. We're hopeful, trying not to be disappointed about all the beautiful scenery we've missed recently.

The terrain is mellow and forested until we get to Indian Ridge, which the guidebook warns against crossing if the weather is bad. It's very exposed and narrow, with steep rocky drop-offs on both sides, and it makes me nauseated to think about it.

We walk the Divide for miles, with sweet-smelling fir forest to one side, open meadows to the other. The hellebores or corn lilies are golden and dry. The wild strawberry plants have turned crimson at our feet. The season is changing. Sierra holds my hand and talks about her favorite subject, "What are *you* going to do when you get home, Mom?" I have a hard time believing our wilderness life will be coming to an end in just four days and three nights. More than two months away from home is a long time. I'm ready, but I'll miss what we have out here: cuddling and reading books, all sleeping together, telling stories, petting heads and rubbing backs, Bryce sucking his thumb and looking up at me with his big blue eyes, waking up and seeing my children's faces. Here our whole family comes together daily inside the tent. Like a cocoon, like a womb, it holds and protects us. As we go through our individual and collective metamorphoses, our bodies are tanner, leaner, and stronger, but who knows what deeper, longer-lasting changes have occurred in our souls from these hundreds of miles?

Sierra wakes in the night complaining of the cold. I find she's mostly out of her sleeping bag. She's had an accident. All the clothes she wears are soaked—three long underwear tops and two bottoms, wet to the cuffs. Even her socks peel off wet. This is why I make sure they're covered and zipped in the night: they don't have as much control over their bladders when they're cold, and digging dry clothes out of the clothing bag outside the tent is more of an inconvenience than the preventive steps. Her sleeping bag feels pretty dry, thank goodness. We'll stop at a Laundromat when we get off the trail.

Tonight the rain has returned.

RAIN ALL AFTERNOON. We're never surprised anymore. We expect it. But today we see something different—hail! Sierra talks to Berrick about it as she rides, picking it out of his fleece, holding the cold, melting balls in her red hands to show him. Dark-wooled Hansel turns white as the balls nestle among his fibers. Some mornings he is white with frost. Yet if you slide your hand down under the llamas' layers and get close to their bodies, they're remarkably warm. We always feel sorry for them when they stand out in the rain, looking as if they're soaked to the skin and appearing to be fifty pounds thinner, but they really are warm and well insulated.

Todd figures we've averaged about nine and a half miles a day out here, with ten days off, for a total of sixty days. Soon to be over. Sierra says she likes it out here but likes it better at home. Her latest topic of conversation is her birthday party, in late January, half a year away! She has the guest list figured out, the menu, the kind of cake she wants. She even knows that she wants bunnies on only *her* party hat and that all the guests will take a bath together after they eat cake, since they'll be messy. (Our kids love bath time at home.)

As a parent, you just do it. You talk with them and try to get excited even if it goes on for half an hour and is repeated verbatim day after day. At least Sierra is behind me and I don't have to conjure up facial expressions too. She doesn't let much go through her head without sharing it with Mom. But we all get obsessed with our thoughts from time to time out here, and we sometimes get stuck. When the weather is bad, the topic of choice is usually home.

This evening, as we sit back and cook dinner, Todd announces, "I don't know if we should get llamas."

"What!"

"I'm afraid we're going to spend $7,000 [including trailer, shed, fencing] for pets in our yard. How do we know anyone will want to hire us?"

I'm so upset. "You can't just kill *my* dream too. I want to do something different with my life. I'll save my own money and buy llamas back east and start my *own* business."

Todd says to Bob, "I don't want to run a nursing home for llamas. These guys seem a little old for us to be just starting out. Seems as if we ought to be buying younger boys, even if they have little or no experience, or we may find ourselves looking for replacements before long." We've got only a few days to come to a conclusion.

I feel frantic when Todd voices his doubts over the llama packing business. Deep in my mind I know it's not the business, really, but my need to lead a life that is as robust and uncertain as this one. Anything less doesn't feel like truly living. At an early age, I indulged myself in hiking the entire Appalachian Trail. It gave me a standard in life that is very difficult to keep up with. There always has to be the next dream, the next adventure, or I feel I'm just coasting.

I flick nearly done macaronis over to my children on their eating mats. They're whining from hunger, and I notice Bob is watching me, smiling. "Throwing food across the kitchen," he laughs. "You're going to have to clean up your act if you bring clients out." "Nonsense. I'll just advertise my company as being laid back, informal, and relaxed." I know some of my wilderness habits have deteriorated to the point of being crude—blowing my nose with my fingertips if a handkerchief isn't handy; spitting. Six thousand miles can do that to you. At least it has to me.

The sky clears enough come evening that we can go out to look at the view and scope the upcoming terrain. We try to decide which is Indian Ridge and which is Kennebec Pass, the last high point before we drop down into the Durango Valley. Many distant peaks have new snow. I'm glad we're getting out while it's still "summer."

WE WAKE in the middle of the night to rain. Oh, Lordy! We were hoping for a good day to cross Indian Ridge. The views are supposed to be spectacular, and it's our last day above treeline. I roll over and bury my head in my pillow. I am *so* tired of this.

It hails at least three times today. The air is so thick with fog that it drips even when it isn't raining. The hair of our heads and Todd's beard are soaked with droplets. But the wind is calm as we cross the ridge, and for that we're grateful.

The drop-offs are straight down. Because we can't see how far the rock slides go, our imaginations run wild. The trail is muddy and slippery and slanted at times. Bob can't believe what I trust Berrick with, allowing him to carry Sierra across the most treacherous trail. But he's incredibly cautious. Bob watches his performance and concludes that he's truly a remarkable llama. Buy him.

Sierra stays calm through it all until Berrick takes a large step and is forced to leap. Her upper body is thrown back so far that the her head nearly touches Berrick's back. Thank goodness for the rolled-up pad acting as a brace.

On a break, we pull out only the candy bag. It's the snack of choice late in the day. Our healthy diet has really gone to hell. You can tell it's late in the trip. Candy is mess-free, quick, and delivers the energy when you're cold. At this point in the game we're just trying to get through. Saltwater taffy, licorice, Gummi worms, and caramels for the kids. High-quality chocolate for the adults.

Bob laughs as we struggle to make progress. Sierra needs a drink. Water bottle pulled out. Water bottle put away. Bryce needs a drink. Water bottle pulled out. Water bottle put away. Sierra needs to pee. Lift her off her llama, find the toilet paper, help her with her many layers of clothing. Sierra needs to put her gloves back on. Push in her fingers. Then I think I smell a poo from Bryce. It's hard to tell if it's the real thing or just "bad air." The many layers of fabric and coated nylon rain suit hold in the stink. I've pulled off his six layers before (some with shoulder buttons, some with leg zippers, some with elastic waists), *and* taken off his shoes and socks in inclement weather, under windy, wet conditions, up high on the Divide, struggling with umbrellas—only to find it's a *false alarm*! It's gross, but now I use the "inserted finger test." It's the only sure way to tell. The inconvenience of a soiled finger is a lesser evil than totally undressing him. This time we're lucky. We sometimes wonder how we've gotten anywhere this summer.

We drop off Indian Ridge and switchback down to Taylor Lake, and then the fog clears. A man walks toward us. It seems so strange to see any humans up here. We have felt so far removed from the rest of the world, swimming through that deluge of rain and sea of fog all these days. It's our friend Terry Price, here to photograph and interview us for his llama magazine.

"I can't believe you're right where you said you'd be. On schedule to the minute, even after all that horrendous weather for all those days."

Todd beams. He prides himself on keeping to our schedule. Before we left each town stop, we needed to arrange our pickup for the next stop. Sometimes it was ten days away. A lot can happen in that time in the wilderness. A lot to slow you down. A lot of storms to stall you. But if we ever *did* get behind, it wasn't by much, and we always made it up. That's why we push. When you are depending on people to be at the road at a given time, people you don't even know, who are giving up their time to help you, you'd better not let them sit and wait and wonder and worry. We've *never* been off schedule more than ten minutes.

"Do you know how much rain we've had?" *(Do we know!)* "One storm dumped three inches. It's been the wettest summer in history. Durango is flooded!" We feel shriveled. Saturated.

In the parking lot at Kennebec Pass we meet more visitors. "How long have you been out for?" they ask. "Two months!" I hoot. "And we're done in one and a half days!" It feels fabulous to say it. To realize that success is within reach. We've met so few people on this trail to talk to about what we're doing. We get very little feedback. These men can't believe we've been out here all this time, crossing this kind of rugged terrain with such small children.

"What a tremendous accomplishment," they keep repeating. We begin to entertain the idea that perhaps what we're doing, what we've almost done, is *big*. After all this time, after all these miles, it had begun to just feel like our life.

IT'S OVER, really. All the hard stuff. All the hairy stuff. All the dangerous stuff. In fact, it's nearly all downhill into Durango. The valley below, where Durango sits, is covered with a blanket of puffy clouds. It looks as though angels with harps could surface from them at any given time, singing of our joy. *We* walk in sunshine.

"That's a sign," Bob says. "You should move to Colorado." "I don't know, Bob," I laugh. It *is* flattering to know he's become so fond of us that he'd like to keep us.

We undulate in and out of drainages all day in the timber. Uneventful. One last time, the sky darkens and we scramble for cover.

As the day draws to a close, our last full day on the trail, we are a little disappointed, for it doesn't look as if any of our friends will be coming to meet us and share our last night on the trail. Just as I add boiling water to our freeze-dried packets, Todd exclaims, "Oh, my God, it's Dee Goodman!" I drop what I'm doing and run to hug him. "I hope you didn't eat yet," he says, "because I've got supper!"

He left his Akron, Colorado, home at 3:00 A.M. to make the long drive down the state. He arrived at 3:00 P.M. and hiked seven miles uphill nonstop, with David, his five-year-old son, keeping up beautifully. I'm so touched.

His wife, Carla, prepared buffalo burgers, sliced potatoes, carrots, and seasonings in eleven aluminum-foil packets. No one will go hungry. As we build a fire, my kids can't keep their eyes open. They eat the freeze-dried food and fall asleep.

In the fire's glow, I grab the hot foil with my fingertips and carefully unfold it, letting the steam and delicious aroma waft up to my face. Real food!

"How does it feel to be finishing?" Dee asks.

"It seems like any other night out here."

"A lot of people I lined up to help you this summer were very skeptical about this whole thing. Nearly everyone exclaimed, 'With two young children?' *I* never had any doubt, though, that you'd be successful. I knew after our first telephone conversation that you not only know your stuff, you have common sense as well. I called every one of your hosts after you left town to check how it went. They all said that they originally wanted to help to more or less promote llamas, but that it developed into helping their new friends from Pennsylvania instead." It feels good to know that.

IT'S SEPTEMBER 2. We all put on Bob's "Llama Family on the Colorado Trail" T-shirts for the big day. Sierra refuses to wear hers until I threaten her. A power struggle. Bob even made sure to get her a pink one, her favorite color. I have a talk with her and ask her to *please* smile for the cameramen that I know will be waiting for us at the trailhead. She was so reluctant to get her picture taken when Terry Price joined us that I *know* there'll be trouble today. I take off the baseball hat that she so notoriously hides behind. As I lift her into her saddle for the last time, I think about what Terry said: "She reminds me of a nomad child. She hates to have her picture taken, but when she relents for an instant to look at the camera, her smile radiates a joyfulness and sweetness seen only on the faces of aboriginal people. After nearly five hundred miles and two months in the mountains, passing only a few people every other day, Sierra has come as close to living a nomadic existence as any child in America—and she's just as shy of unwanted intrusions into her splendid solitude." What could I expect from her?

On the way down, we all practice sticking our thumbs up in the air and yelling, "We did it!"

Around a corner appears another llama and a bearded man smiling. Wally! Of course he should be here too. Bob, Dee, Wally—the three biggest movers behind this adventure.

On the last mile I ask Todd, "What higher thoughts do *you* have on all this?" "Nothing." "Me neither."

It isn't the most exciting place to end, either—by a road and a parking lot with a sign showing a large-scale map of the trail. When we gather up our aboriginal children for a picture by the sign, Sierra presents only her profile, with no hat brim to shield her face.

The newspaper man interviews us, and I can think of nothing profound to say. In fact everything that comes out of my mouth sounds shallow and lacking, even stupid. We don't realize what's happening. We know that much from past endings. It doesn't feel at all like an ending. It just feels like going back to Wally's to resupply again. Sierra is playing in the creek as though it's just another day on the Colorado Trail. Bryce is rolling llama turds around on the ground. We load the panniers into Wally's truck and the boys in the trailer and climb aboard ourselves. Our lives are about to change drastically. Dragging our feet won't help. All we can do is sit back in our seats and watch the future come rushing toward us.

8
At Home
September 4, 1993

The person who risks nothing, does nothing, has nothing, is nothing, and becomes nothing.

—Source Unknown

We keep the words above in mind as we shell out thousands of dollars for llamas, llama equipment, and a stock trailer to haul them home in—our ticket to freedom and the start of a new occupation as llama packers. It isn't what we had in mind when we came out to begin this big adventure. A trip of this magnitude is expensive enough, with neither of us bringing in income while we're traveling. But if we're going to do it, let's not do it halfway.

Dee Goodman plans on sticking around after this season's grand finale and the success party the llama folks have organized on our behalf. At Wally and Katy's, he helps us pore over the classified ads in newspapers from Colorado and neighboring New Mexico, looking for a suitable trailer at a price we can handle. They find a five-by-twelve-foot W&W for $1,200 in New Mexico. It even matches our cream-colored truck, as if that matters to us. Todd is concerned about the tires. They're on the small side, with tons of hairline cracks that look like dry rot. The salesman says not to worry, they could go to Hong Kong and back. How about just to Pennsylvania? Todd figures on replacing them en route until he learns that our image of our savings account balance is a little off from reality. We'll drain nearly everything in this endeavor. There will be fence and shed materials to buy, too, once we get home. And with our occupations—freelance writing and furniture making—it may be months until there's some cash flow again.

We're living on the edge financially. We haven't had full-time jobs for five years, but neither do we have any debt. We've managed to adopt a lifestyle of "voluntary simplicity" that lets us have the freedom and mobility we crave. Still, there are periods every year when we get a little nervous about money. One is right now, as I write check after check and drain our account.

Dee's generosity is unceasing as he takes time away from his harvest to help us get this trailer on the road. A new jack needs to be bought and welded, as well as a trailer hitch ball, an electronic brake controller, wires, and more. Dee doubles as an electrician, so his aid is invaluable. Poor Todd is having enough trouble just learning to back the rig up.

After we say our good-byes, we head up to Stan Ebel's Buckhorn Llamas to return Hansel and Jupiter and Jack (we've decided to get some younger llamas) and buy Sierra's beloved Berrick. What he tells us right there in his parking lot floors us.

"In all honesty, I never expected you to make it. I told Bob Riley after you left, 'I hope you're going to be around in a few days when they quit, because *I'm* going to be busy.' "

"You're kidding! Why?" For outside of injury, we never dreamed we wouldn't be successful.

"I looked at your résumé just the other day, not months ago when you sent it. I consented to lend you llamas on Dee's recommendation alone, knowing very little about you. Between the kids and the mediocre llamas I gave you, I didn't think you stood much of a chance."

"Really?"

"All my best llamas were already leased out. Jupiter is a slug. He always wants to sit down."

"He only tried that once; Hansel pulled him for yards and he never tried it again."

"Hansel can be wild. He had his jaw broken when his previous owner tried to cut out his fighting teeth" (a necessary procedure or the adolescent llamas will hurt each other fighting). "He threw his head up and got it caught in the chute. Now he's extremely head shy."

"We never needed to touch his head; we left his halter on all summer. He mellowed out some too, from all Sierra's interaction as she hand fed him every night."

"I believe llamas can sense vulnerability, whether it's children or handicapped people. I've seen radical changes in their behavior when they encounter someone like that. And Berrick, I figured he'd be a good kid carrier with his laid-back disposition and being the hit that he is in the nursing homes, but he never carried a child before."

Oh, my God! I shudder to think of the narrow plank bridges and steep traverses I led him across with my precious daughter on his back. Trust goes a long way, even with an animal. If we weren't convinced before, there's no doubt in our minds now that Berrick is a very special llama.

We buy two sets of panniers from Stan and head on up to Charlie Hackbarth's Mount Sopris llama saddlery to return the gear he so generously lent us for the summer. We'll also buy complete outfits for Berrick and the other new members of the family we plan on buying from Dee Goodman and Bob Riley.

It's at the Rileys that Todd and I get our first glimpse of what *really* occurred this summer. From our past trail experiences, we know you can't really get it until it's over and you're separated from the experience. The video footage Bob shows us is from Indian Ridge, on the last few days of the trail. The children sit on the wet ground in their colorful rainsuits, stuffed with layers of clothing to keep warm. They peer out from under their hoods munching on snacks and smiling their beautiful smiles, while little balls of hail ping around them. He shows me leading Sierra over the rocky knife-edge trail. I hear the tinkling of the llama bells and see Sierra's body swaying as she and Berrick move as one over the trail. I can smell the wet llama fur and the dampness of the day, and I'm struck by how comfortable and at home our children look. The scenery, the cliffs to our side, the exposure shake me. Babies being brought across the Rockies of Colorado, for months, one still in diapers. I feel so good as a parent and so glad we found enough patience to deal with their needs and help them be happy so it would be an enjoyable experience for them. When you're immersed in the trail, it feels like normal, everyday life. You're too close. But as I leave and look back, I'm beginning to see it as a truly extraordinary thing that ordinary people have done.

Sierra has been crying this morning as we roll across totally flat, arid eastern Colorado. With no air-conditioning in the truck, the heat is oppressive. We can't make out what she's saying at first: "I miss. I miss." I suppose she doesn't know how to put it into words, so we help her. It's Colorado she misses. When we fell out of the mountains into Denver, she was convinced she had just then left the state. To her, Colorado meant high mountains. And it's boring to look out the window here and not be entertained, especially for a three-year-old. Todd says, "Don't you want to go home and see your room, your kitty, and jump on the trampoline and play with your toys?"

"I want the mountains!" she cries.

"We have mountains back home," Todd replies. "We have the Appalachians in our backyard."

"Where?"

Yes, exactly. Her idea of mountains and what they are has changed. Mountains are very high and grand with passes and views and elk and meadows of wildflowers and *wind*! She doesn't remember any of these things about the mountains back home. It's interesting to see that a three-year-old can feel the same way we do on leaving the high mountains. They're "soul vitamins" for her now too.

We are already beginning to see how the trail has affected our children, even at their ages. It's hard for even Sierra to return home and leave this most beloved life of her parents.

I feel so wealthy, driving down the highway with our llama trailer and our llamas behind us. We're probably the poorest we've ever been monetarily, but when I look out the side window of our truck, I see our new life ahead. What we are pulling behind us, because of this hike, changed our lives. We're wealthy in memories, in dreams, and in future goals. We're wealthy in opportunities for new jobs and new trails these boys can lead us down. When driving through Denver, we hear the blast of a car horn. Right away we're afraid that the trailer door is open and one of the llamas is ready to make a break for it. We slow down and the driver comes up alongside, still leaning on the horn. But he gives us a thumbs-up sign instead, and we smile. Someone else thinks this whole thing is pretty cool.

When we camped last night, Sierra accidentally wet her bag, one of the few times ever on the entire trip. But somehow we'd gotten her and her brother's sleeping bags switched and she wet his instead. First thing this morning, we plan to take it to a Laundromat. But either I never shut the back of the cab or it wasn't secure and flew open, for the loosely laid bag has disappeared. We drive up and down the highway searching the sides of the road, asking the highway workers if they've seen it. Todd is upset with me, for we'll need to replace it. But our wise three-year-old says to him, "So what, Dad. It's only a sleeping bag. It's not like we wrecked the truck or something." That's right, honey. Keep it in perspective. Listen to your little daughter. Of course it's her brother's sleeping bag that's gone, not hers.

A few days into our exodus east, I have simply had it with kids and living in a vehicle. And with Wee Sing tapes, and handing back snacks, and filling water cups, and retrieving Matchbox cars, and fixing barrettes, and tying dolly ribbons, and covering cold bodies at night, and wiping mouths and hands and hineys, and keeping my husband awake when he drives, and sitting on my ass and feeling my hips and thighs spreading and all my hard muscles loosening up. I'm ready to be home and have these kids entertain themselves and get a baby-sitter and go away to talk with adults or be in my studio *alone!* Three solid months in the full-time company of my children and my husband. I'm maxed out. If we were primitive people, Todd would at least have gotten away on a hunting trip, and I would have gone gathering herbs and roots!

Our house, which we haven't seen for three months, is only yards away. Still, we sit in the driveway in the truck, buckled in, after driving across the country for five days. Poor Todd is backing the trailer up and backing the trailer up and backing the trailer up. He has a definite vision of where this trailer ought to be parked. Up the incline, right by the woods, near the garden, exactly so many feet away. I get out and try to direct him, but what do I know about which way to turn the wheel? So I say nothing for a change and just observe. But he's exasperated because I'm *not* saying anything. Smoke is pouring out from under the hood and a foul odor fills the air. "I burned out the clutch," he says. "Now I'll have to replace that."

He stops the truck and sits there motionless. "I don't know what to do." Oh, Lordy, I think. Here we go.

After that problem is solved, we have to figure out what to do with the llamas. We need to build a fence, but not today. Todd will have to calculate what we need, telephone for prices, buy the materials, and put it up. Two of our young boys are not rope smart, so we're afraid to put them out in the field where they could get dangerously tangled and we wouldn't know. It would be good for them to be close and get used to the children's voices and squealing and rapid movements, so we stake them out on our front lawn. We have to make sure their lines don't extend to any of our shrubs, or they'll kill the plants and possibly poison themselves by eating the rhododendron. But they'll quickly run out of grass, and their urine will burn the scant grass we have.

After we unload the truck, there's the mountain of wash and mail to deal with, and equipment to clean, repair, and put away. There's leftover food to find homes for, and a filthy house with three months of spiderwebs, and no clothes in the kids' drawers that fit them or the season.

The kids start to fight, something they rarely did on the trail. Sierra is bossing Bryce around, taking his toys, pushing him off chairs. I believe she's using him as a source of entertainment. Her "What can I do?" upsets me. There were practically no toys on the trail, yet they were always content and got along.

Todd and I can't deal with it. It's overwhelming. Reentry is the often the hardest part of the entire journey. Everything looks as if it ought to get done right now. And our heads and hearts are still back there in the high Rockies. We feel paralyzed and displaced. If we had a television, we'd resort to turning it on this first night back and just zoning out. Instead we all sit down as a family, on the sofa and easy chairs, and page mindlessly through mail-order catalogs for hours.

PART TWO

THE CONTINENTAL DIVIDE TRAIL

CANADA TO CHIEF JOSEPH PASS

MONTANA, 1995

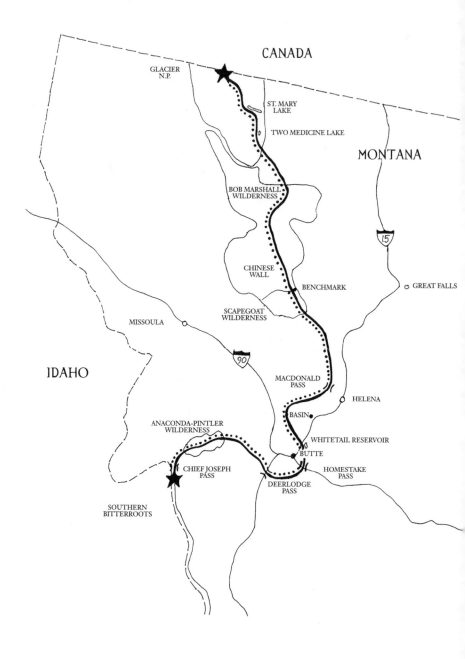

CANADA

GLACIER
N.P.

ST. MARY
LAKE

TWO MEDICINE LAKE

MONTANA

BOB MARSHALL
WILDERNESS

CHINESE
WALL

BENCHMARK

GREAT FALLS

SCAPEGOAT
WILDERNESS

MISSOULA

IDAHO

MACDONALD
PASS

HELENA

BASIN

ANACONDA-PINTLER
WILDERNESS

WHITETAIL RESERVOIR

BUTTE

CHIEF JOSEPH
PASS

HOMESTAKE
PASS

DEERLODGE
PASS

SOUTHERN
BITTERROOTS

9

A New Dream
SPRING 1994

Eastward I go only by force, but westward I go free.
—HENRY DAVID THOREAU

IT ISN'T LONG before Todd and I abort our dream of starting a commercial pack business. It was the hefty liability insurance that convinced us. To make it worthwhile, we'd have to run frequent pack trips. But our mid-Atlantic summers are hot, humid, and buggy. Clients would expect us to control those discomforts. That left only late spring and early fall.

Then we discovered how poisonous to llamas are the rhododendrons that cover much of the high-elevation forest in Pennsylvania. On a short pack trip, Berrick nearly killed himself by eating the leaves bordering the trail. Once he got sick, he projectile vomited every fifteen minutes until we got him to a vet. It was touch and go

117

for days. To hike through this kind of country requires constant attention to each individual llama, or they will indulge every chance they get. It's too much to expect from ourselves and clients.

All the commercial packers we talked to said they got into the business because they enjoyed hiking. Invariably, they got so busy that they usually had to farm out their trips to hired guides while they stayed home doing paperwork. We love hiking so much that it seems foolish to go to all this work and get out on the trail even less. So we decide to keep the llamas solely for our own enjoyment. We're adjustable. But this leaves a void in our lives. We have to think up a new dream.

Then one day a lightbulb goes on. It's the spring after we returned from the Colorado Trail—1994. Todd and I are stringing high-tensile wire around the llama pasture, threading the wire through plastic sleeves at the posts, hammering in staples. I say, "How do you feel about starting the Continental Divide Trail next summer if I find out we'll be safe with our llamas and children in grizzly country, and if we can get the money together?"

Todd just smiles. We both keep stringing. He doesn't say a word. He's thinking. The big think. I've opened a door for him. He's looking in, looking around, not ready to cross the threshold. I'm the one who gets the big dreams. He makes the dreams happen with thorough planning. I'm the fuel, he's the engine. I give the dreams power and life. He's the machine that makes them happen by carefully going over them, looking for weaknesses and flaws, and turning them into workable material. This is why we've been able to accomplish so much. It's rare that two people are so complementary.

The Continental Divide Trail is a long-distance National Scenic Trail, like the Appalachian Trail and Pacific Crest Trail. It runs along the crests of the Rocky Mountains from Canada to Mexico and literally divides the waters of the North American continent. All the waters flowing east empty into the Gulf of Mexico and the Atlantic Ocean; all the waters flowing west drain into the Pacific. The Continental Divide is the birthplace of the nation's waterways, and to the West's native peoples it's known as the backbone of the world. The range is the highest land in the country. To walk it is to scrape heaven.

What sets this trail apart is that so much of it is yet to be built. There is a tremendous amount of route finding involved, using map and compass. Much of the country is remote and wild and far from resupply points or help. This is more serious than the Colorado Trail, although we were green as grass on that trip. It's the big league.

When I first saw the CDT sign on the Colorado Trail, which follows the same route for a few hundred miles, it stirred my being. I wanted to hike the whole thing. I think about this obsession of mine. Do I have some sort of calling to lead my children over the most rugged mountain range in the country? Something that's never been done before. What a calling. It sounds strange even to me.

Grizzly bears dampen my desire to hike the Continental Divide Trail. One thousand or so remain in the American West, and the greatest concentration is in Glacier National Park, in northern Montana, where the CDT originates. There are maulings nearly every year and an occasional death. It's the kind of place where you need to keep your wits about you. You can't even sleep in the same clothes you cook in. We figured we'd need to wait many years until the kids were older, stronger, and able to make conscious decisions about keeping themselves safe.

In the national directory I look up some llama people who live in the Glacier National Park area and talk with them about their grizzly experiences. They assure me that there have never been any grizzly encounters with llamas in the park, or any with horses. It seems the llamas and the grizzlies keep their distance, giving each other the space they both need to live in harmony. One says grizzlies have yet to discover they can eat llamas. Once that happens, the truce may be over. But it hasn't happened with horses, and they've been in that country for a very long time.

The size of a party has a lot to do with the degree of safety, and llamas are included in this number. Grizzlies avoid confrontations with a sizable group. And then there's decibel level: my children are often boisterous and unceasing in their chatter. The human voice carries and is the best deterrent. There are some important things we need to consider. When the kids walk, they will have to be sandwiched between adults and llamas, and they won't be allowed to wander outside camp. Todd says it would be great to have Bob Riley along to help with the route finding, fords, and so on. Bob is planning on finishing the Colorado Trail this summer (1994), and I suspect he'll be ready for another adventure come summer 1995. I'm sure I can persuade him to join us. When Todd says the only way we can "go back out there" is if Bryce is potty trained, that he's not dealing with diapers again, I know I have a chance. Good incentive. The children will be two years older and should, in all respects, be easier.

It must be daunting for Todd. Here we go again, he thinks. Am I ready for this? Is this really what I want to do? We have so much history. We know what all this entails once we make the commitment to do it. The amount of work. The logistics. It's an all-encompassing project. But leading an adventurous life seems worth it to us, and Todd and I begin to go off in our individual directions to make this dream real.

One of the first things we do when preparing for a trip is write to all public land sectors—national forests, Bureau of Land Management lands, national parks—requesting information about their trails, alerting them to our presence the upcoming summer, learning if there are any new trails not in the guidebook or any hazardous areas (such as cliffs of scree) to negotiate, finding out about private land crossings, feed restrictions, and such. Most forest districts are extremely helpful, sending us lots of material. Some make detailed maps just for us, with the route highlighted on a copied topographic map. For this particular stretch, we have over a dozen districts to write to. The letter I'll send to Glacier National Park will discuss backcountry permit policy. Permits are issued first come, first served, a maximum of twenty-four hours in advance.

I don't write to Glacier right off when I write to the national forests. But one evening we get a phone call from Richard Hedd, a backcountry ranger at the park. He's gotten wind from the neighboring national forests that we're planning on hiking through the park this summer, and he takes it upon himself to call us. He tells us there's a good chance we won't be allowed to bring the llamas into the park. They're in the process of banning them, he says, because they might carry Johne's disease, a contagious intestinal disease common in cattle, which causes sometimes fatal diarrhea in hoofed mammals. We had heard the llama community was having trouble with these same restriction threats in the Canyonlands National Park of Utah. The horse concessionaires want llamas out of that park because the commercial llama packers compete for permits. There's been no evidence showing that llamas transmit the disease and lots of evidence showing that they don't, but the horse packers used it as a reason for banning llamas (the ban was later rescinded). We don't know much about this whole scare at the time of his phone call, but we do think it's unusual when Ranger Hedd launches into a long discourse about the advantages of using pack horses rather than llamas in the park. He doesn't consider that we have absolutely no experience with horses and couldn't possibly travel a hundred miles safely and successfully using them. Plus, our children are too young to ride horses. We don't own horses; we'd need to rent them from the horse concessionaire. We wonder about his motives.

After we hang up, I call a friend from Montana who's done extensive backcountry research in the park. I ask her what she knows about Ranger Hedd, and she says he'll make life extremely difficult for us—that he's famous for it. I decide to consult his superior.

Jack Potter, assistant park supervisor, is a joy to work with. He assures me he will do everything possible to make our trip happen. But he tells us there's been severe flooding in the park. Torrential rains in June caused extensive trail damage; forty-three bridges have been washed out. In the Belly River area, the place we'll begin, damage was most severe. Jack says the trail crews raft across the swollen creeks instead of fording them. He advises us to begin our hike farther south and head north, reaching the park toward the end of summer when the waters are lower and the most vital repairs have been made. He's most concerned about the fords for us. Thinking about leading llamas and small children across floodwaters makes us all shiver.

Homestake Pass, near Butte, Montana, is 375 trail miles from the Canadian border. This will be our kickoff point. Once we reach Glacier and the Canadian border, we'll shuttle back to Homestake Pass and hike south for another 150 miles through the Pintlers over to Chief Joseph Pass and the Idaho border in the Bitterroot Mountains before calling it a season.

The greatest problem with Jack's suggested schedule is that we'll be walking through Glacier later than we'd planned, and competition for campsites will be even tougher then. We can stay overnight only at certain sites designated for stock party use. Backpackers can use the stock sites, along with many other sites unavailable to us. Our situation limits us greatly, however. We can't hike megamiles between sites. Most stock parties can, because most use horses, which cover greater distances. For us a twenty-mile day is impossible. A fourteen-mile day is extremely difficult and is asking for trouble. If we have to sit and wait at the park entrance for campsites to open up, we could lose a lot of time and throw off our whole schedule. We'll be inviting quite a few friends to join us on this stretch. All pickup points and rendezvous times have to be determined long before we depart so they can make flight arrangements and ask for time off from work. When folks rearrange their lives and put out big bucks to join us on the trail, it's our responsibility to do everything we can to see that we stay on schedule. We need to be guaranteed campsites so we can get through the park on schedule. When I express these concerns to Jack, he assures me he will help.

In the meantime, an irate Ranger Hedd calls back and says that, unfortunately for me, I'll have to deal with him, and that he has a policy of following park rules to a T—no exceptions. But there are exceptions we want them to consider making, like getting our permit and campsite schedule ahead of time and putting Bob on the same permit so he can camp with us, even though four is supposed to be the maximum group size. No way do we want to travel through that grizzly-infested park without another adult to help should we have a confrontation. The more rules we must follow, the greater the challenge and the greater our limitations. Because of this situation, we are not looking forward to traveling through "the most astoundingly beautiful place south of Canada."

JULY 1995

MY GIRLFRIENDS are having a hard time saying good-bye. They make an hour-and-a-half drive four times this past week to see me "just one more time." They bring gifts of silver bracelets and silver heart pins to remind me that they're with me always.

It's the grizzlies that have everybody worked up, even cool-headed Bob. He's agreed to hike the whole summer with us and wouldn't think of letting our little family go through bear country without his assistance. But he's been seeing bears everywhere lately. They're popping up in his life at every turn, and he wonders about their significance. When his wife, Jo, visits a psychic and learns she'll come into a large sum of money in July, Bob wonders if that might be his life insurance.

On the long drive west, I realize the worry in my husband's heart over these bears. I sit on the passenger side and make knotted friendship bracelets out of colored embroidery floss to pass the time. In Guatemala, where they originated, the custom goes deeper. They're also considered wish or dream bracelets, and the person who wears one is supposed to attach a well-thought-out dream to it. If you wear it until the threads break and it falls off, your wish will come true. All that positive energy put into wanting it to happen turns the bracelet into a physical reminder, an affirmation. The power of suggestion helps create a reality that you very much desire.

About every one of our male friends I made them for, Todd commented, "He won't wear it." But they all did; every one accepted the gift in the spirit intended. I think Todd thought they were juvenile or looked like hippie bracelets. He made the comment a while ago that I shouldn't make one for him because he wouldn't wear it. I didn't press the issue. Anyway, as we're cruising across North Dakota he says, "I'll take purple and black for my colors." (Purple is the color of safety.) I don't say a word but smile to myself and fish around in my box for the colors. His dream, of course, is that our family will make it safely through our trip with no bear encounters.

10
A Challenging Start
JULY 12, 1995

Everywhere is walking distance if you have the time.
—STEVEN WRIGHT

THE CONTINENTAL DIVIDE TRAIL'S northernmost point is at the Canadian border in Waterton-Glacier International Peace Park. It feels best to hop on a long trail at one end and walk it in an unbroken line until you reach its far terminus, rather than hopping around and hiking chunks. But our main objective in hiking this 3,100-mile trail is to make it easy on ourselves and as enjoyable as possible, so flexibility is the key. When we heard that it was best to go through Glacier later in the summer when its floodwaters had receded and repairs were completed, we set our sights on Homestake Pass, near Butte, Montana, where the trail crosses I-94. We'll head north and hit Glacier in mid-August, then shuttle back to Butte to hike to Chief Joseph Pass in the Bitterroots on the Idaho-Montana border before calling it a season.

The CDT around Butte is only a route, not a "trail." The actual trail isn't built yet, so we walk a patchwork of roads and cross-country stretches. The Divide is somewhere to our west, and we won't be joining up with it for many miles. Road walking, although boring and hot, breaks us in more gently, for most roads don't have a very steep grade. Bob appreciates this, since he tends to put on a few extra pounds every winter. We're all—people *and* llamas—out of shape.

Only twenty yards from the Homestake Pass parking lot, we hit our first obstacle—a cattle guard in the road, with no gate in the surrounding fence. Bob and Todd dismantle the wires so we can get the boys through, then stretch and staple the fence back together. This kills half an hour, and we haven't even left the trailhead.

We aren't sure which dirt road the Continental Divide Trail follows. Todd has to read the guidebook data backward, because it was written for southbound travelers and we are now traveling north toward Canada. Every right turn in the book is a left for us; every descent, an ascent. He hikes with the book open in his hand.

I flag down a pickup, and the occupants, who have lived in these parts for thirty years, send us the wrong way. In the meantime Todd is having a rodeo with his string of llamas, which is running circles around him. They're worked up because of Bob's llamas, the two new boys on the block; one of them is a stud, causing great commotion.

Around Delmoe Lake we lose the trail and are forced to scramble up a rock cliff. There are limits to where we can take our llamas. Once the climbing gets so steep that we must use our hands, a llama is going to consider only his own neck. He'll try to leap if we lead him, but *only if* he trusts us and *only if* he's brave, as most pack llamas are. But they can't be asked to leap while they're tied in a line, and they certainly can't leap carrying full panniers.

Bob would have left a lot of his crap at home if he'd known he'd be hauling it up a mountain on his own hairy back: nine cans of evaporated milk for his nine morning lattes; his cappuccino maker; and a dozen cassette tapes for his Walkman, along with battery-operated speakers, among other toys. Rain has begun to fall, just in time to make us sweat bullets in our rainsuits. We grab the unwieldy forty-five-pound panniers and wrestle them over the rocks. God forbid we might start out easy.

Tonight in camp, we see horseback riders coming from the opposite direction. We ask about tomorrow's hike.

"Hey! How's the trail around Whitetail Reservoir?"

"Marshes are as deep as your hips. High as a horse's belly," they reply.

We're skeptical.

"Where you headed?" they ask.

"Canada."

They laugh. It's 375 miles away.

"Where did you start?" they query further.

"Homestake Pass from I-15." Ten miles ago.

They laugh even harder. "Keep your sense of humor in the bog," they advise, riding off.

When we first see Whitetail Reservoir, we are taken aback by its beauty—a big deep blue lake surrounded by the largest mountain meadow I've ever seen. It's miles across and the water source for much livestock and wildlife, especially white-tailed deer. We stop to let the children play on its sand beach and watch the wind pull plumes of yellow pollen off the evergreens across the water.

The wind stops as we begin to cross Whitetail Park. We feel as if we've descended into hell. The mosquitoes are so thick that we brush off dozens with a single swipe. In the short time it takes to pull head nets out of the panniers, the children's necks and ears are covered with welts. They attack the llamas' eyes, drawing blood and making them hum, which sounds more like a moan.

The riders were right. There are swamps. Three times I fall in up to my waist, trying to leap across. Todd's string is giving him lots of trouble. None of them are big on getting their feet wet. "Trail-wise llamas" are expected not to leap across water or mud but to bravely walk through, no matter how deep. But this is their first big trail adventure, and except for a three-day pack trip back home, they're green. They're adolescents, and they act like it. Jerry, our most spirited llama, bought from dear old Bob, is the butt of most of the jokes—"being turned into jerky" jokes—for he'll mow us down if we're on the other side of the stream. Chips is the one exception. He adores water, even seeking out puddles. In one swamp hole he gets submerged and refuses to budge. After much rope yanking, Todd jumps in and shoves on his butt with all his might while Bob pulls from above, only to realize that what Chips is moving is his bowels!

The route around the lake is more or less to go where you want across open meadows, then strike up a feeder meadow between two peninsulas of trees. *Which* two peninsulas is the question, for there are many, and we ask it while we swat and scratch and search and moan because we're tired and we can't stop for a decent rest because the insects attack with a vengeance every time we quit moving.

On this day fifty years ago, "Billy Bob" came into the world. Yes, today is Bob's birthday, and we conspire never to mention it the entire day, thereby adding to his misery and enhancing the later surprise. Come evening, we blow up balloons and string them from the inside roof of our tent with dental floss. Before leaving town, I baked a pound cake with so much butter that it couldn't possibly dry out for weeks. We decorate it with candles and wildflowers. Inside the tent, away from the bugs, is the only sane place to be, so we light the candles and call Bob over, belting out a boisterous "Happy Birthday to You!" We're all so pleased with ourselves—until he announces, "We're celebrating my very last day at forty-nine. *Tomorrow* is my birthday!"

FOURTH DAY OUT, and we're still wading through boggy meadows. It's such a challenge to find our way through them because if there *is* an old stock trail we're supposed to be following, it keeps disappearing in the meadows. Figuring where it reenters the timber is what eats up the time. Todd and Bob split up to check out the country ahead, then come back and together decide which way looks best. We try to go high around the bogs because the kids hate to ride across them. The llamas walk unevenly, stepping on the clumps of grass, sinking into holes, and jumping across anything they don't like the looks of. Todd ends up carrying Bryce in the child carrier. Sierra whines and squeals with fright.

Leisurely rests aren't on the itinerary yet. Route finding consumes too much of the day. On breaks, we undo our bootlaces, pull off our bog-soaked socks, and lay the smelly things flat on a rock in the sun, flipping them like fish frying in a pan until they're dry or it's time to go. When we come to a dry, bug-free meadow for a change, even if we haven't been hiking for long, the kids and I are reluctant to pack up and move. But Trail Boss Todd announces, "I can *see* where we took our last break. We've *got* to keep moving."

All day long, as we follow the topo map and compass, we continually stumble on visible sections of trail and realize we've been on the right track. This pleases Bob and Todd no end. The guidebook cautioned that this section would test us, and that is accurate.

Add to this that our family is testing Bob. He says it's going to be a lot longer trip than he anticipated. Bryce hasn't been real happy. He's not thrilled about riding. Although his llama, Monty, has the perfect disposition for a kid carrier, he waddles when he walks down hills, throwing poor Bryce from side to side—like an amusement park ride minus the fun. The conditions simply aren't conducive to fun. It's too boggy.

Bob is good to our children. He pulls out presents for them nearly every night this first week. He gives Sierra a real thirty-five millimeter camera and Bryce a flashlight with a monster on it. Sierra is so excited that she keeps asking, "Do I *really* have my own camera, Mom? Do I *really*?" He gives them audiotapes (with accompanying storybooks) that he plays on his speakers in camp. He loves them so much that he's asked that he and his wife be put in our will as guardians should something happen to me and Todd. Out here we need someone with this kind of tolerance, or he would have thrown in the towel back there on Delmoe Lake's cliff. It's challenge enough to travel this "trail," let alone with "the Llama Family."

We can see the tiny town of Basin off I-90 from our long descending road walk: a cluster of roofs, a few signs. We're looking for Rosie's Café, hoping that Rosie still exists and that her café will be open on a Monday morning. We're hoping for a meal to lift our spirits. It's been a tough first week.

Basin may well have more dogs than people. They're loose but seem well behaved. They come to the side of the street to greet our llamas as we head into town.

Next comes a short lady dressed in a too small, too hot for summer, blaze orange acrylic sweatshirt. Her snow-white bangs stick out from under her navy watch cap. The screen door of a little cinder block shop whose sign says The Helping Hand slams behind her.

"Welcome!" she says. "I run this secondhand store here. Everything is for free. Whoever needs anything just comes and gets it. Do you need anything?"

"Not that I can think of, but I'll take a look around." I find a Snow White barrette for Sierra, a Santa Claus ring for Bryce, and a few business envelopes for me and thank her kindly.

Folks from various homes and businesses come out to chat and take our pictures. When we worry about the dogs' bothering our llamas while we eat (Rosie does exist, and the café is open), a woman who looks like Willie Nelson offers her fenced-in yard as a temporary pasture.

When we enter Rosie's, it takes a second for our eyes to adjust to the cool, dark bar. A skinny old lady sits at the pool table, carefully trimming the frayed edges off bath towels with sewing scissors. (Could this be Rosie?) She directs us to the dining room. In a matter of seconds, Ms. Helping Hand returns with a plastic bag of powdered doughnuts, speckled bananas, and two large cake cookies.

After burgers and fries, we're heading out of town when a van pulls up. An older couple get out and offer us a package, "Don't suppose you could use some homemade sticky buns?" they ask.

There *is* one resident on the outskirts of Basin who isn't fond of travelers. We hear he held a hiker at gunpoint for two hours for trespassing. Gotta get twelve miles out of town before we're safely past his property.

We take a break in the grass by the side of the dirt road, ignoring the No Trespassing signs. Road walking in the sun gives me a bad headache, and I barely raise my eyes when a driver in a beat pickup pulls up and kills the engine in the middle of the road.

"Are you bringing those up to my place tonight?" asks a face with a long gray beard. I focus on this rough-yet-kind-looking man of about sixty. His sparkling light-blue eyes are shaded under a leather Australian hat two sizes too small. He drapes a burly forearm clad in plaid flannel over the door. Big planks and lodge-poles stick out from the flatbed of his International truck, flagged with a greasy red rag. His face and hands are covered with the ground-in dirt that only a day of logging in the mountains can create.

"You can't camp for miles on account of my neighbor," he goes on. "But on my property I got a nice spring and a green patch for your critters there. Only four miles up the road. Gotta go right by. Give you a loaf of homemade bread when you get there. My girl-friend just baked. I don't suppose you'd like that? Maybe your kids would. Second cabin up Jack Creek."

Gordon and his girlfriend, Georgia, a soft-spoken geologist, just happen to have an "excess" of steak, and because their primitive log cabin has no refrigeration, it needs to be eaten up. After we make camp, we light a fire to cook supper. These people are angels dropped into our path exactly where we need them.

I'd been questioning our purpose in being out here this week. Not that it was so difficult that we couldn't do it, but the element of fun seemed remarkably scarce. People like Gordon give us the strength to keep going.

THE LAND within the Pegasus Gold Mine looks unearthly: no warmth or richness to the soil, no humus, just a funky light gray color. In such a large expanse, it's strange that nothing is growing anywhere. Not a weed in a ditch or a draw. The ground looks steril-ized or poisoned.

An alternative CDT route misses the mine but incorporates a cross-country section that could be dangerous for our llamas. On our road walk out of Basin, we met the mine foreman, who told us to stop by the office for a drink of water. We're hoping he's around, or at least some friendly folks. We're not sure how excited some officials will be over a family and a group of llamas trying to walk through such a private place.

The office is open. Lights are on. The place is totally empty. We find the bathroom, and above the sink is taped a sign that blares, "Do Not Drink the Water!" A scary brown stain covers the sink and the toilet bowl. We were told that this area has been poisoned by heavy metals. For years, cyanide was used to separate gold from the rest of the rock.

Two pickups pull up—general foreman and project manager—cameras dangling around their necks. They take our pictures. Two more men with cameras pull up, and I ask, "Are cameras some sort of required gear for miners?"

"Actually, we take pictures of our reclamation progress all the time. We mined this land for ten years and got all we wanted out of it. Now it's mandatory that we spend another four or five years and $2 million to clean it up. We'll recontour the land, move the topsoil back, plant trees and shrubs."

Dave, the project foreman, escorts us through the mine, driving slowly as the llamas follow, passing machinery and settling ponds. He unlocks and relocks half a dozen gates. We take a break at the trailhead and share some of Georgia's homemade bread and jam.

"Thanks for stopping by," he says. "Too bad it's not later in the day. You could have spent the night. We had only one hiker come through last year, and he stayed. We don't get many visitors. It gets lonely."

Bob and I talk about the way we seem to encounter the right people in our lives just when we need them most. How no event or person passing through is a coincidence. As we walk side by side, I ask what he thinks is *my* significance in his life.

"To teach me something. I see you as a teaching aid."

"A teaching aid? Like a blackboard or a pen or a notebook?" I ask. "Yes," he says. Oh, isn't that flattering.

I've been working on Bob for a week now. I make him give me a hug every morning and evening. If he's not going to be around his wife for weeks, he'll shrivel up and die from no one touching him. I can share a little. He's uncomfortable with my display of affection, but I don't let that stop me.

But tonight, when I give him his evening hug and tell him "I love you," he replies, "I love you too," in a slightly sarcastic, singsong voice. When he sees the surprise on my face, he says, "You wore my front down."

We live too close to the natural world and to each other to not feel connected. It's my nature to acknowledge our affection for one another, push through the uncomfortable stage, and honor the great gift we are to each other. "All my relatives," as some Native Americans say when they greet each other. I hold that idea in my mind and realize there's little difference between me and Bob, or Gordon, or even Dave, the mine foreman.

When we walk along our route in the Helena National Forest, north of I-15, we see signs of labor. Everywhere there's digging—holes with mounds of dirt piled up. Prospects. On the topo map there are tiny Xs showing claims that somebody, somewhere still has a right to. But it looks as if the miners just picked spots at random and began scratching away with their picks and shovels. They remind me of moles doing busywork. Somebody must have found something, though, for in the nearby Marysville district a billion dollars worth of gold was recovered, mostly in the 1880s and 1890s.

The piles are littered with quartz rocks, a telltale sign that gold *could* be present. My children stoop to pick up the chunks, turning the rocks in the sunlight to see if a streak glistens. There are abandoned cabins with rusty woodstoves, pieces of track, ore cars, winches, and cables lying about, and broken wooden wagons that once hauled miners' belongings into the mountains. Such high hopes. Such rough living.

Near Mullen Pass, we pause to watch a freight train go by and spot a hobo slumped inside an open boxcar, looking tired and down on his luck. His dark eyes lock with ours for the second it takes to pass, and we're left wondering if we really saw what we saw.

Here at Mullen Pass, the first good road was built across the Continental Divide in 1863, the historic pathway to the heart of Montana—the Wild West. It's still wild. There are still miners scratching for gold, hoboes riding the rails, and cowboys riding the range.

Like "ole Slim" here. He's a range rider on the BLM lands. He's in his Ford diesel pickup today; his horse is back at the cabin. He wears his gun backward in the truck so he can draw it quickly. He's showing the country to some visiting relatives—Cornhuskers, flatlanders from Nebraska. They shovel themselves out of their seats and line up in front of us. Round bellies with sweatshirts stretched over them, spotless cream-colored straw cowboy hats, and shiny, pointed cowboy boots bought for this visit to the Wild West. One says, "My feet were killing me. I had to put my leather wingtips back on." Slim doesn't get many visitors. It's just him and the horse and the range cows, living simple and eating beanie-weenies.

The big Montana sky opens up north of Dana Spring as we make the transition from thickly wooded country and jeep tracks and mines to cross-country on the open, rolling Divide. We can look ahead and trace our route going up and down the grassy hilltops, and we get a strange sensation, like after your roller-coaster car climbs that first long hill and you see the exciting dips in the ride ahead. You *feel* yourself moving over the land before you actually do. Throw in the power of the never-ceasing wind that feels like a living creature, and it makes me hike with my arms spread wide, gesturing to all that's out there to enter into me. It does. It makes me hoot. It fills my eyes with tears. It's what I come out here for.

We pick up my friend Bruce, from Pennsylvania, at our resupply in Helena. He'll be hiking this stretch to Benchmark Ranch, where he'll be replaced by my best girlfriend, Nancy. Bruce is a handsome, gentle man who just turned thirty. Although he's strong from his occupation of building log kit homes, he's slim and looks burdened under his full backpack. He loves spelunking as much as hiking. A third-generation caver, he travels the world in search of exciting caves and is just as happy crawling around the dark innards of this earth as climbing its peaks. We've made some memories underground; now he wants to experience a part of my family's CDT adventure. He's happy to be here. We walk hand in hand on the Divide. Todd is used to my displays of affection and doesn't mind. Bob looks on with interest.

The climb over Black Mountain and Nevada Mountain challenges Bruce's right-off-the-plane condition. Even Bob still gets tired by the end of the day.

"You've got to pace yourself," Bob says to me on a climb. "You've got to leave enough energy for camp, so you don't fall flat on your face when you get in and embarrass yourself. I get stiff when I stop for too long."

"So, you loosen up in a few minutes of walking, don't you?"

"No. It takes me about an hour, and that's about when you stop again." Essentially he's saying that he's stiff all day long.

We do seem to stop for a break every hour or so. Our pace is healthy when we're moving. Bruce is having trouble with our style of hiking. He says it tires him more, and he'd rather go on for miles once he gets into a rhythm. Our family's rhythm is definitely a staccato of spurts and frequent breaks. Not everyone has the tolerance to hike with us. You have to relinquish a lot of freedom. But the route-finding challenges put you at a great risk if you decide to go it alone, as Bruce decides to do after a few days. When we see him way below us by a lake that our route does *not* go past, we smile and know he's taken a wrong turn.

THERE ARE more reasons than route finding to stay together. The day the wind knocks us over like bowling pins, blows the llamas' saddles loose, and leaves Sierra and me screaming for help above the roar of the wind, we understand the importance of being there for each other.

The cut in the mountain is acting like a wind tunnel, and when we descend into it the wind hits us from the side and knocks us flat in the dirt. Bob finally hears my cries; he crawls over to grab Berrick's lead rope and directs us to the back side of the mountain, where Todd and Bryce and Bruce, who has rejoined us, lie waiting in the scrub.

We try to decide what to do. Going on is out of the question, with miles of exposed ridge ahead. "We have to get out of the wind. Get to safety. The children are shivering, and they already have all their clothes on."

Bob and Todd take the llamas in stages and make their way around the back side of the knoll. They'll come back for me and the kids last. Bruce will stay with me in case I need help. We slide the coated nylon backpack rain covers over the kids' bodies and snap them up their backs. Bruce and I zip up our jackets and tighten our hoods around our faces to as small an opening as possible. We hold the children in our arms, shivering as much from fright as from the cold.

"Do you want to say a prayer?" I ask, and they nod yes.

We all hold hands, and I blurt out a few lines, asking God to keep us safe.

Seconds later a huge, brilliant rainbow appears right in front of us, arching over a peak across the valley. We stare in disbelief. It hasn't even been raining.

"That's God. He's letting us know we'll be OK." This sets Bryce off with a whole string of questions. "Where is God? Is he in the clouds, the rainbow, the wind, me?" In a few minutes, the rainbow fades.

When Bob and Todd come back and lead us into the next saddle, we realize the wind has picked up since we were here earlier. Once again the children are frightened, and Sierra says, "Let's say that prayer again." Within seconds the rainbow reappears, just materializes before our eyes, as though God was saying, "If you didn't believe me the first time, that I'm here and will keep you safe, here's my sign again. I'm with you." This is too much for us. We stop and stare, our mouths dropping open.

In camp I embrace my men and thank them for all their help. I tell Bob how Bryce asked if we were going to die. "Oh, no," he says. "*This* is really living." Yes, sir. We know we're alive on a day like this. No doubt in our minds.

"Hold onto your television viewing seats, ladies and gentlemen," Bob says, "We're just getting rolling." Day eleven out here. This morning everything was calm, safe, and easy.

It takes a while to relax, and even longer to get warm. My stomach flutters, and my body feels shaken up from the anxiety and the excitement. The children are exceptionally helpful with camp chores tonight; they're feeling grateful to all the adults for taking care of them, for keeping them safe.

What an unbelievable lesson to learn at ages three and five: to be so scared you think you are going to die; to ask for help and get such a radical sign; and then to have everything turn out OK. They could go through a whole childhood of Sunday school lessons and never get what they learned today on that windy Divide.

In the tent tonight, after the kids fall asleep, Todd rolls over and asks, "Should we be out here with these kids? Is it too much?"

"It was OK," I say. "We made it through. Now we know what we can't handle when it comes to wind. The kids were troupers. Did you ever notice that when things get rough, they never complain? They might whine over what we're having for supper, but the wind, the storms, the serious stuff, they seem to deal with. Could it be they're learning so young that there are some things in life you just have to deal with and get through the best way you can?"

Because of the challenges we're facing, our children are being forced to grow up. The risks are good; they just need to be managed. Despite these troubles and dangers, the CDT feels like the right place for our family to be.

Scapegoat and "the Bob"
July 25, 1995

Nothing would be done at all if a man waited until he could do it so well that no one could find fault with it.
—John Henry Cardinal Newman

From Roger's Pass north, life as we know it will change. We're no longer at the top of the food chain, for we've entered the domain of the grizzly bear. *Ursus horribilis* is king from here north through the Scapegoat Wilderness and the Bob Marshall Wilderness, Glacier National Park, and on up through Banff and Jasper National Parks in Canada. It's a rare place, "where man himself is a visitor who does not remain." This huge corridor of magnificent wild lands is critical to the existence of this once dominant, now threatened creature. As we hike north, the great bear's density will increase.

From Roger's Pass north we are entering not just the domain of the grizzly but also a statutory wilderness, changing the whole character of the trail. We'll soon become almost solely reliant on an actual trail instead of a patchwork of roads and cross-country stretches. The route here is frequently the established "official" CDT route, all backcountry travel, with no recreational vehicles allowed.

There's a sign at the road crossing announcing the grizzly's territory. It instructs us that it's now the law to hang all food, trash, and other odorous items out of reach of bears. As if the bears could read it and know they're not permitted to cross the highway and venture south. But we comply, and at our break by the road, we tie bells on the children's bootlaces, on our fanny packs, and around each llama's neck. Most bears want to avoid humans and appreciate our announcing our arrival. We get out large canisters of bear deterrent spray and hook them to the outside of each backpack with a carabiner. We just have to grasp the handle, pull out the pin, and spray. Attaching them to our hip belts sounds dangerous; we heard of a woman who suffered second-degree burns on her leg after her canister accidentally deployed. The Glacier National Park rangers have had good luck with the spray, successfully deterring grizzlies three feet away, although it will carry up to nineteen feet. We also have a boat airhorn that makes an eardrum-piercing sound when the button is pressed. And from now on the kids won't be allowed to walk.

It isn't many miles after we cross the pass that we spot a huge pile of bear dung and see large areas where a bear ravaged the soil for roots. It puts us on our toes. After seeing fresh signs, we hike with great alertness. We scan open areas. We listen for movement. We watch the llamas and notice where they are looking, for they see movement long before humans can detect it.

Hanging our food is a real challenge. First off, it isn't just food we must hoist up into a tree, but our trash and all items that have any odor—toothpaste and brushes, soap, lotion, insect repellent, shaving cream, first-aid kit, diaper rash ointment, pot scrubber, any container that ever held food, and even the clothes we've worn while cooking. The panniers are huge and very heavy, and the longer the stretch of trail, the more food we're carrying.

Everything must be suspended at least ten feet above the ground and four feet from any vertical support. The tree needs to have a limb that is growing more or less horizontal and is thick enough to support the load. Now a good campsite needs not only enough grass for the llamas, flat ground for tenting, and proximity to water, but also the right kind of tree!

We must plan to quit an hour early to find a tree and get the ropes in position. Between Bob's and our numerous panniers, we often need two limbs. The men take turns throwing a rock with a rope attached over the limb. Each tries until his arm is tired, then they switch. Bob tries for a perfectly shaped dead limb, but when he yanks on the rope, the limb comes crashing down. "Limb fishing," Todd laughingly calls it.

We encircle our camp with the llamas, spotting one by the food hanging tree, if possible, and one each as our personal tent guards. Jerry is so close he could crawl in. He does poke his curious head in for one of his famous nose-to-nose touches. We feel very safe with Jer just outside. He's a live deterrent. If you were a grizz and approached our tent, wouldn't you rather eat a tied-up llama who can't get away than an obnoxiously screaming human who's toting bear spray and an airhorn? We'll feel safe in camp through Scapegoat and "the Bob," but once we're in Glacier we'll have to keep the llamas separate from us, at their own corral, which could be a considerable distance away.

The 1988 Canyon Creek Fire burned 240,000 acres in the Scapegoat Wilderness. Ignited by lightning, the blaze burned entire drainages and threatened the town of Augusta. The Forest Service let the fire burn, in accordance with its wilderness fire management plan, but drought and high winds fueled the flames for three months across an area eight times larger than predicted. Yet all this destruction is actually beautiful.

We have many miles of exposed ridge running, right on the Divide. The whole world opens up. Besides seeing waves of mountains and valleys, you can see into the mountains, through the trees to the ground, for the burned land is covered with needleless spikes of trees. The rounded hills look like an old man's scalp when Brylcreem separates his thinning hairs. If you sit perched high with binoculars, you feel certain you could spot game moving through the skeletal trees.

Periwinkle forget-me-nots and yellow buttercups poke up through the scree, tossed like tiny ships on a sea by the unrelenting wind. The children's faces are chapped and their eyes are bloodshot. I keep my sunglasses on whether it's sunny or cloudy to prevent my contacts from drying out. We run from cover to cover, nervously remembering how bad the wind was not so long ago.

It's cold, too. Below twenty degrees counting the wind chill. We're reminded that this is the area where the coldest official temperature was ever recorded in the continental United States: seventy degrees below zero on January 20, 1954. In the winter of 1888–89, one of the most severe in Montana's history, a radical thirty-degree drop in temperature burned the needles on some of the remaining conifers, turning them brown.

When the wind is wild up here, poor Bryce can't nap. The sound and the feel of it pushing against his face keep him awake. Last night he slept badly, waking up with cold legs. I put his hat and a third layer of long underwear bottoms on him. Bryce needs a lot of sleep. Fatigue creates the worst behavior. If the children are well rested, we can ask them to go through some rough conditions. If they're exhausted, it seems they can't do anything. Bruce and Bob are looking tired themselves from Bryce's moaning and crying. "Hey!" I shout, defending my baby. "Look around. See any other three-year-olds up here on the Continental Divide Trail battling the wind, cold, and exhaustion? Let's cut him a break!"

Bryce has been acting ornery lately, bucking for more attention. He poured hot tea from his cup on Bob's leg the other evening. He ripped up grass by the fistful and threw it into neat-freak Bob's tent. He pokes everyone in the side with sticks. He peed on his sister on purpose. Then he walked past Bob, stepped directly on his foot, and continued walking by as if he never did it. The men have even less patience than I do when he cries and moans from fatigue. It all stems from not getting his needs met. If we neglect even one need of one child, things don't run smoothly for anyone.

BENCHMARK RANCH is a horse packing outfitter that offers guided trips, cabins, meals, showers, shuttles into town, and a beautiful wilderness setting—stream running through, pond stocked with trout. The ranch is seventy miles north of Roger's Pass in the southern end of the Bob Marshall Wilderness and thirty miles by gravel road from Augusta, the closest place to buy supplies and do laundry. Bruce will hop off here, but not before footing the bill for a cabin rental as a thank-you for the trip, he informs us. Nancy, my best friend from home, will take Bruce's place. We've been close friends for about ten years, ever since she took the backpacking course Todd and I teach at a community college back home. She's one of my many single friends who has bonded with the entire family.

Twenty sociable mules and horses greet us at the double wooden gates, braided tails swishing, bells ringing, soft muzzles sniffing. Here comes Nancy, auburn hair bouncing as she runs to meet us. After a layover day, with fresh supplies and clean clothes, we hit the trail again.

The Bob Marshall Wilderness is a preserve of 1.5 million acres named after the legendary young forester whose vision of preservation sparked the wilderness movement. Many of his efforts were channeled into identifying roadless areas to be classified as primitive and protected as wilderness. This area is most famous for the Chinese Wall, a massive reef of limestone cliffs thirteen miles long.

On Nancy's first two days, Todd hits her with a fifteen-and-a-half-mile day and then a thirteen-mile day (we had told her we average nine miles a day). One of those days includes a "death march" of four straight miles at the end with no stops for rest or nourishment. It isn't Todd's fault; there are no flat spots to camp, and all the creeks are dry. He asks if we think he's a slave driver, and we nod yes.

When I turn around to look at Nancy, she hangs out her tongue to silently show me she's dying. She whispers to me at the top of ascents to take a picture so she has another minute to catch her breath. She worked out like a maniac before coming west, hauling her fully loaded pack over mountains back home. No male friend who ever joined us put himself through such rigorous training—or any training, for that matter. But it's the altitude that's whipping her butt. And she has performance anxiety. She doesn't want to be a burden to Todd, whose quiet strength and skills intimidate her.

The Chinese Wall is one of those places that feels bigger than life, like the Grand Canyon, Crater Lake, Yosemite Canyon. It's that first view that you remember most. That first stunning sweep where you gather it all in—coming through your retinas, into your body, down to your soul. It feels as if your eyes never really saw before. You stand there and get choked up because the beauty just bowls you over.

We top a rise, and there it stretches—a continuous cliff rising a thousand vertical feet that looks like a massive serpent draped over the land. It's not straight at all but gracefully curves and bends over the earth. Layers on layers of limestone contain many hues. The low sun creates deep vertical shadows and brilliantly lit columns. At its base are jumbled piles of scree and talus. Dark-green pointed conifers pierce the brilliance along the base of the wall.

The trail meanders along its base for five miles, going through meadows and strips of intermittent forest. The Continental Divide itself runs along its rim. Every mile or two our trail rises to go over a low pass, and it's at these points that the wall makes a gentle curve. From this vantage point we can see ahead to another section, look behind to the last one, and appreciate its magnificence. From this height, it is also easy to understand how the forces of the earth thrust the wall up, for the west-facing slopes resemble humpbacked waves that break eastward.

After the Chinese Wall, our route takes us along valley bottoms, following streambeds and river drainages. Some of the trail sections are through thick, overgrown forests, barely used by the myriad horse outfitters that work the Bob. Vegetation is thigh-high, too much for Bryce to wade through, so he's stuck riding all the time. Since I lead the pack, my bare arms and face get covered with sticky, gauzy spiderwebs, an indication of an infrequently used trail. "No free riders!" I say, flicking off spiders.

It's hot on these valley floors, humid and close like summers back home. I take off the kids' pants and boots and socks. They enjoy riding in their underwear and giggle at the feel of the soft llama fleece on their piggies. When there are huckleberries by the trail, if the children have to watch them go by they act as if we're torturing them. So I let them get down to pick. It makes Bob and

Todd crazy—not making progress. Bob says our pace is like watching paint dry. He's considering cutting his trip short this summer. I think it's getting to him—that he's subjected to our pace, our needs, our wishes and has so little independence and private space. Todd can't get away from us either. He has to keep on being trail boss.

When the trail is closed in like this, our thoughts go inward too. But the kids get bored, for they don't have decades of experiences, relationships, and feelings to draw on. They live for the moment. Bryce reminds me of this in camp tonight, when he gravitates toward the mud after I wash him up.

"Please don't," I say. "You're tired and it's time for bed."

"I'm tired, Mama, but playing in the dirt will make me happy."

In camp tonight, I feel myself unraveling. I'm trying to measure out rapidly boiling water for the four individual freeze-dried suppers around my feet. Bryce wants help with a preschool workbook and is yelling while he pokes a stick in my back. Sierra is pushing a pen in my side to let me know she wants help writing a postcard. Thomas the Tank Engine is playing loudly through Bob's speakers. (Todd is somewhere else, tending to the llamas, alone in his quiet world of personal thoughts.) Amid all this, Nancy and Bob are having an adult conversation. Bob is disappointed that this trip isn't as spiritual as he had hoped. (Guess why, Bob, you're with us!) Nancy wonders why she's "choosing" pain as her reality, for her feet are killing her. Bob starts spouting quotes on how we have total control of everything in our lives and everything is a choice. At this point Bryce dive-bombs my head. I throw him off without trying to be gentle and yell at Nancy, "Maybe all it means is that you're supposed to buy larger boots when you get home!" They give me a "Where did that come from?" look, and I get up in a huff and go for a walk by myself.

I am feeling inadequate because I can't seem to prevent my children from destroying my peace. The group dynamics have been different since Nancy arrived, through no fault of hers. Sierra follows her around like a shadow and gets annoyed if I even speak to her, let alone ask her to help me with some chore. She hogs my friend. Nancy and I have barely talked since she arrived. Since Bryce has lost his sister as a playmate, he's always in my face, vying for attention. Nancy spends so much time entertaining them on the trail, telling stories from Greek mythology, that they no longer want to entertain themselves. It's hard on Todd too. The larger the group, the more stress and work it is for him. We're together twenty-four hours a day, with no escape.

Todd must have viewed my fit as permission to have his own. The next day, he loses it. All morning long, the children and I sing as we hike, happy to be together. Our emotions swing from one extreme to the other. It rained hard last night, so the trail is muddy and covered with puddles. The kids wear rubbers and have a great time plowing right through. The light looks like liquid gold, the wet vegetation sparkles like diamonds, light rays pierce the forest canopy, and I'm busy shooting pictures. We take our time, and Trail Boss grows more and more impatient.

At a beautiful, dry meadow, the children announce they're hungry. We probably haven't covered much distance, but I'm oblivious to this. That's not my job. Todd refuses to tie up the llamas and remains standing, a message that he doesn't approve of the break.

"Take a break, honey," I say, "it's a beautiful meadow," as I sit down to take off my boots and socks. I fell in a creek this morning and want to change.

"We just left camp an hour ago. If you have to take a break, this ought to be a short one. We have work to do."

"We deserve a break. We've worked hard the past few days."

"You're such a slave driver, Todd," Nancy chimes in.

As I rummage in the food pannier, he says, "Why do you need to eat? We just ate breakfast."

I ignore that comment and ask, "How many miles left in the day?"

"Lots! We're lucky if we covered one mile!" he yells. "I'm no longer in charge of the map and guidebook! I'm done! All I get is a hard time and complaining that we don't take enough breaks, that they're not long enough, that we get into camp too late. You make fun of me by calling me Trail Boss, and you give me too much shit!"

Nancy tries to reassure him: "We have nothing but the utmost in gratitude, awe, and admiration for you." He doesn't budge.

"OK," I say. "I'm not going to do my job anymore. You can dress the kids in the morning, entertain them, tend to their needs." Bryce begins to cry.

As we proceed down the trail, I lighten up and turn around to smile at Todd, trying to make up, but he continues to be a sourpuss.

After a while the kids need another break, but I stop only for a minute to get out some cheese crackers and put them in bags. But Bryce can't eat and at the same time hold onto his handles, as he needs to for balance, for the trail is muddy and the ride very bumpy. When he moans, I say, "Ask your father. He's in charge of when we take breaks now." Once we stop, I figure Todd will come around, but he doesn't.

"I don't care if we get lost," he says. "Then we can call the whole thing off and go home."

"Do you want to be a quitter?" I ask. "Come on, let's work this out. Bob, help us."

"I'm staying out of domestic squabbles."

I begin yelling at Todd. "You think you do all the work!"

"He does do a lot," Bob says.

"I do a lot too! He might do more physical work, but I'm doing more emotional work with these kids!" I go over to unhook the llamas and fall flat on my face. I'm crying. Bob comes over and puts his arms around me.

"You do a lot of work too," he says.

"I'm supposed to pussyfoot around him when we have a fight and try to get him out of his sour mood. I'm not going to do it this time!"

Bob hikes first; he's our leader now. It begins to rain. I yell ahead to stop so I can put on the children's raingear. I avoid Todd's eyes while I work. As we hike in the rain, Sierra gibbers joyfully on her llama as she twirls her Little Mermaid umbrella. I begin to relax and let go of my anger. When I turn to look at my husband, his dark eyes have softened. The next time I look, he's smiling. The next, he gives me the peace sign. And then he throws me a kiss.

When the rain stops and the sun comes out, we break to take off our raingear. I get down on my knees at my husband's feet and beg him to take his job back. He smiles and takes the map and guidebook from me. I get the candy bag out and say, "Let's have some candy. Candy makes everyone happy."

We sit on a log and rip red licorice with our teeth. "You're both overworked," Bob says. "Perhaps we need to reconsider why we're out here and quit and go home if we want to."

"We're not quitters, Bob. We're fine. We just needed to blow off steam."

The truth is, community living is hard. This is the first time I've had a woman friend along, and we gang up on Todd. Nancy and I break out in rounds of "We love you, Trail Boss, oh, yes we do. We don't love anyone as much as you. When you're not with us, we're blue. Oh, Trail Boss, we love you," every time he clears the trail, hangs our food, or performs any gallant feat. It's too much.

Nancy is my best woman friend. Todd and I are close, but there's something very special about the women friends I share heart-and-soul matters with. Most men don't really understand that bond. So Todd may be feeling a bit abandoned. I'm giving Nancy a lot of my energy and attention to make sure she's doing all right and is enjoying herself. This takes me away from him. Nancy shares my differences with Todd over the pace and taking breaks, so it could feel as if we're ganging up on him. This is the first time, though, that I have an ally in my frustrations, and I'm taking advantage of it.

Nance and I both know that Todd has tremendous responsibility to make sure this whole circus continues moving down the trail and stays on schedule, but sometimes he behaves like a bit of a tyrant. We work best when he nudges us onward, and I temper his pushing by making sure everyone's needs are met, especially the children's, including the need to have fun. It's a balancing act, and from time to time it needs to be checked and adjusted. Right now we're teetering.

It rains all the time now. The trail is a sea of mud, mostly because of the fifty outfitters that work the Bob, leading hunting parties and summer horse pack trips. The deep quagmires can suck your foot in, get down inside your socks, and swallow your leg. You can't tell how deep they go by looking. Hundreds of hoofprints mark the rich black ooze, but only the top few inches of the holes remain open, masking their true depth. The llamas tread with trepidation, having no idea where the bottom is.

The children hate to ride through the mud. One llama foot sinks down three inches and another three feet, throwing their balance off. The llamas tend to hurry through and get it the hell over with, giving the kids a real bronco ride. Once Todd screamed from behind because Bryce was hanging off Monty's side, inches from the mud, still gripping the saddle handles. When the llamas leap and scare the kids, I get told what a bad mommy I am.

Mud is everywhere, so we repeatedly take the kids off their llamas, carry them in our arms or swing them across, challenging our balance, then hoist them back up. By the twentieth time, our arms are worn out.

Sometimes the llamas don't like the route I select and go their own way, forcing me either to swim across a mud field or let go of the lead rope. Then they're on their own. This makes the kids scream, as if they've been abandoned and the llama will take off. The rope can get tangled around their legs or between their two toes, causing quite a ruckus.

Often the mud is only a half inch deep and glazes over the trail. It allows no traction, and when we try to push off our boots slide around as though we're skating.

The mud soaks the moisture right out of our skin. The muddy lead ropes turn our hands white and flaky and cracked.

The children are being forced to hike more, and we've finally learned that this is what Bryce needs to be happy. You'd think by this point we'd already know this about our son, but no. It's not as if he's old enough to understand what he's feeling and what he needs and can articulate it. He's simply bored riding, which leaves him with too much energy in camp. Then he gets into trouble. When they hike, the two children take turns at being leader. One time Bryce raced to get past his sister and fell flat on his face in the mud. His eyes, his nose, his mouth, and his hair—the whole front of his body was covered with brown ooze. He cried hard while we tried to swab him off.

He's a superb hiker, keeping a pace of two and a half miles an hour. His little butt sashays back and forth, and he usually carries a stick of some sort as a hiking staff, but it often has unruly branches at the top so it looks like a claw. We've relaxed about letting the children hike. So far we haven't seen a single bear throughout the Bob Marshall Wilderness and have found very few signs of their existence. The grizz seem like a myth. We'd be just as surprised to see Bigfoot.

But the long-distance hiker we meet today has had a personal encounter with a grizzly. One chased him up onto a ranger station's roof and kept him there all night. Skinny little Luc is Canadian and is on his way down from Jasper National Park to Yellowstone. It's his first long-distance hike.

"I knew nothing about hiking or trail food before I left. I bought raw oats for breakfast and dried beans for supper because they were cheap. I had no lunches. I often went to bed before having my dinner because I fell asleep while I was cooking it. I lost twenty pounds in twenty days," he says laughing.

"It rained the first twenty days, too. I went to sleep in the dark, got up when it was dark, and it was dark all day long. I thought that's just how it was when you hiked."

We're in stitches over his accent and dry sense of humor. He doesn't seem at all discouraged.

"Are you folks all teachers? " he asks. "Is that how you get time off to do this?"

"No, our family does this for a living. This is our job."

"Wait a second," he says. "Did you folks build a log home? Did you write a book about the Pacific Crest Trail? What's your name?"

"Cindy Ross."

"I read your book before coming out here. I only read two books on walking. Peter Jenkins's *The Walk West* and your *Journey on the Crest*. Hey, whatever happened to your friend Skip and all the others?"

I'm amazed. Here we are in the middle of the wilderness. We've seen no other hikers on this entire trail. The first one we run into knows all about our personal lives from reading my book. When things like this happen, it makes me feel that this world is really small and we really are connected.

THE TRAIL along the south fork of the Two Medicine River is an obscure one. We lose it over and over again, but as long as we follow the river, no matter how many times we cross it, we'll get where we want to go: Route 2. It's easy to tell when we're approaching a ford. The river undercuts the bank, making a steep slide, sometimes twenty-five feet high, forcing us to the other bank. We go back and forth like this, in the rain, stopping to take off our boots and socks, put on our water sandals, cross, dry our feet on the other side, and put our boots and socks back on. After crossing three times in ten minutes, Nancy, Bob, and I decide to leave our Tevas on. But Bryce has just fallen asleep, and Todd doesn't want to take him off his back to change his footgear, so he wades through wearing boots and socks.

All the moisture in the vegetation makes the llamas urinate with unbelievable frequency. It comes out in squirts and goes on forever. You'd think they could push it out faster. Elderly Berrick uses it as a stalling tactic. He often piddles five times on one ascent. Bob says that if we had a hundred llamas we'd never move. Llamas can void while they're walking, but they'd rather set themselves up to pee— stop, spread their rear legs apart—for they aren't fond of "splash." The first goes. The next in line takes a sniff and in a few moments he begins, and so on down the line, a chain reaction. A smart string, however, can work you by staggering their timing, some choosing to hold it for later. I think we're being taken advantage of!

By the end of the afternoon, after fifteen fords, Todd's aching feet are pale and deeply lined. He says it feels like sores are forming under his skin. Today's fording, plus having wet socks for days through all that mud, has caused the start of trench foot!

Over the past ten days, tension has been building. Todd has exerted his role with a little more inflexibility and impatience because of the level of stress. I left his side as supporter and volleyed against him. But all is resolved now. As Nancy's time runs out, we're feeling relaxed and close.

I look at her and think, you've had yourself one helluva "vacation." You battled fatigue, blisters, rain, and mud. You spent all that money on a flight, gear, and food. She thinks about this as we cross Route 2 and walk north along a great wall of mountains to East Glacier, Nancy's dropping-off point. The tips of the rugged pointed mountains go in and out of the clouds. Every now and then a patch of brilliant sunlight lights up a small section of rock. We look for a space in the wall, a view into the Shangri-la that lies on the other side, "the most astoundingly beautiful place south of Canada." It's a land of cascading waterfalls, turquoise lakes, mountain goats, bighorn sheep, and lots of grizzlies. Nancy drops back and watches our family move across the landscape. The children gently sway to the rhythm of their beasts, looking comfortable and at home. This isn't our vacation, it's our life.

Nancy tells me, "Last night in my tent, I asked myself, What have I lost by living this rugged trail lifestyle? If I were back home, I wouldn't have put on soaking wet socks in wet boots in forty-degree weather, slogged through eight hours of rain, exhausted my body, and lived with filthy hair. But if you avoid the hardships, you never experience the gift. You have to live with the discomfort to receive the gift."

The gift for her is the closeness of community and the connection to the earth. There is a bond that naturally and inevitably comes from sharing the same sun, the same sky, the same river fords, the same highs and lows. At home, working in climate-controlled cubicles, we stay protected from the wind and the rain and the sun and live a life where we share very little with our fellows. We naturally begin to feel isolated from one another and the natural world. We use money to buy what we need, or we get a machine to do the work. The luxuries separate us from one another. We have to work at finding common ground. We've lost community. Trail life requires bonding. You can't pop dinner in the microwave but must depend on each other to help get water, help hang the food away from bears, help get across a ford. Luxuries don't replace people. Like the pioneers many years ago, sharing a lifestyle, we're working together.

12

Glacier National Park

AUGUST 9, 1995

Life is lukewarm enough. Give us a little heat.
—ANN LAMONT

I HAVE MIXED FEELINGS as I climb over the eastern mountains that form the border of Glacier National Park. When we hike north, the wind and rain sting our faces like BBs. The kids duck their heads low as they ride, shove their mittened hands deeper into their raincoat pockets, and are silent. If we squint through the blast, we can look way out beyond the mountains into the vast empty plains of northeastern Montana. They look bright and warm, for out there the yellow sun shines without reservation. When we turn the switchback and head south, forever climbing, the wind and weather at least are at our backs.

Since we got flattened on the ridge a month ago, we all have a sensitive fear gauge. When the wind starts to blow beyond a certain velocity, our internal mercury rises, and we're filled with anxiety. When it's bad down below in the trees, we have good reason to be concerned about going higher. No one needs to speak, not even the children. Everyone is aware of everyone else's feelings, and it's enough just to know you aren't alone.

Up top, the wind is fierce but manageable. We give each other the thumbs-up sign and smile as we head across the open rocky ridge, following cairns toward jutting Appistoki Peak. When we're practically on top of it, we round its side and see the incredible Glacier country laid out before us. It's easy to imagine the force of the glaciers carving out this land. Two Medicine Lake and Lower Two Medicine Lake stretch out like fjords, with Mad Wolf Mountain (8,341 feet) and Rising Wolf Mountain (9,513 feet) thrusting up from behind, their uppermost peaks shrouded in fog. This was the location of two sacred Indian medicine lodges of the neighboring Blackfeet Indians, the largest tribe in Montana. Peak after peak fills the sky.

Sierra hops off her llama to walk the three miles of the 2,200-foot descent to the lake. I hold her mittened hand tightly as the wind flaps our pants legs like a lofting sail. She gets me to skip down the trail, past the gnarled limber pines and low mats of common juniper, and she yells, "Oh, it's so much fun, Mother, to be up in the wild wind once you know you're going to be OK!"

The wind and rain are our initiation rites into this fabulously wild and beautiful country. You can't have lush green meadows, wildflowers, and waterfalls without a lot of precipitation. The beauty of a long-distance hike is knowing that sooner or later the sun will come out again.

But it doesn't appear the next day either. Bryce woke up soaked last night. The rain came right through the tent floor, his foam pad, and his sleeping bag, and wet all his clothing down to his underpants. We lift the sleeping bags and pads to find puddles across the entire floor. Every half hour we sponge up about a quart of water with the chamois cloth. The tent sites in the backcountry are tiny cubicles with soil so compacted that it behaves like concrete, preventing any rain from percolating through. Since it's still raining, we set up a tarp in the cooking area, which is a good distance from our tent. We carry the kids over in their dry socks and set them down on a mat under the tarp to eat their cereal. Their hiking boots are soaked from yesterday's rain. In the morning their dry socks wick moisture out of the leather, making their feet wet and cold, so we wait until we're ready to leave to put on their boots. During the day, Todd and I hike with their wet socks plastered against the bare skin of our bellies. We tuck the tops over the elastic waistbands of our rain pants and let our body heat dry them through the day. It's horrible to put on cold, wet socks that suck the heat out of your feet. We want to spare them this hateful experience if we can.

Backcountry campgrounds in Glacier National Park have tent sites, pit toilets, food storage facilities, food preparation areas, and stock rails, all separate. Absolutely no food is allowed in the tent sites. You're supposed to plan your meals so there are no leftovers, which is never a problem with Todd's voracious appetite. He's usually capable of cleaning up everyone's leftover dinner. (When Nancy was with us back in the Bob, Todd told her it was a rule that you had to drink the dishwater in bear country, that we'd all take turns with that camp chore, and she could be first. He had her going for a while. The proper procedure is to strain out the food chunks and dispose of the gray water.) Packing foods like canned tuna or sardines is asking for trouble. Anytime you're not cooking or carrying your food, it must be strung up on the food pole provided by the park service. Because of this, we mostly ignore our daily before-bed hunger pangs.

The llamas seem to be starving all the time now. They look emaciated. We've been hiking for more than a month, and all their winter fat is gone. Being wet so their fleece loses its loft doesn't help—they look about fifty pounds lighter. Good grass is always a priority when selecting a campsite. They usually replace a lot of their calories during the evening in camp, but they're not allowed to graze in the park. There's nothing green anywhere near the stock rail, for the horses turn the ground into dirt. We're carrying rabbit pellets to feed them at night, but it isn't nearly enough. We couldn't bring a huge amount of extra food for them because the park rules state that stock parties can have no more than six animals, and with Bob's two llamas we had seven (we boarded one with a friend), so we have even less carrying capacity than normal. This rule was based on horses, which have a greater impact on the land than llamas and can carry more than twice the load. The park caters to horse travel. We're forced to do three fourteen-mile days, since stock campsites frequently are far apart. Llamas are only as speedy as the person leading them, and a family with small children is even slower than the average backpacker. We're handicapped.

Before we do our three butt-kicking days, we must climb over Pitamakin Pass to Morning Star Lake, a short five-mile day, where we'll sit for a full day and a half. That's how our permit itinerary reads. The subsequent sites are probably occupied, so we must wait until the last stock party moves on and they open up.

The view from Pitamakin Pass is extraordinary. (The name comes from a female Blackfeet warrior who dressed as a man and led raids into the Flathead country. A great horse thief, she said she'd marry only the man who could steal more horses in a night than she could. She died husbandless in 1850.) A thousand-foot cliff drops straight down to a turquoise lake. Beyond the shelf where the lake sits is a square notch in the mountains that abruptly drops off another thousand feet. Beyond are brilliant white mountains, totally covered with snow and glaciers. Farther yet are the sunny, never-ceasing plains, coaxing us on. This is the highest point (8,050 feet) reached on the CDT in Glacier National Park. Bryce stands calmly on the rock ledge with the very exposed and rugged view behind him; pink cheeks and blue eyes the color of the mountain lake peep out from his dirty hood. His rosebud little-boy lips curve up in a smile, and he looks like the prince of this exquisite domain—his kingdom, his gold. My Continental Divide son.

WHEN WE ARRIVE at Morning Star Lake, we're in a bad way. It's sleeting, and the children, even though stuffed into their rainsuits with three fleece coats, are shivering and crying hard. We sit them under an evergreen with an umbrella while Todd and I frantically set up the tent, afraid they may be in the beginning stages of hypothermia. A ranger arrives and reprimands us for still having the llamas at our site, where they are not allowed, instead of at the hitching post. We explain that it's imperative we get the tent up and our children warm in their sleeping bags and that it will be only a few minutes more. She says to make it snappy.

Morning Star Campsite is not a designated overnight stock site but is for day use only, so its hitching post is only six feet long instead of twenty. Horses stand when they're tied up, but llamas need enough rope to lie down. A single horizontal rail is not safe to tie llamas to, because they can go under it to the other side and get tangled in each other's ropes. They could strangle themselves in short order, and since the rail is so far from our tent, we might not even be aware of any trouble. So Todd and Bob satellite a few llamas off the sides of the hitching post to avoid a dangerous situation. The ranger sees this setup and says nothing, so we assume it's legitimate.

After we get the children comfortable in dry clothes, playing cards and coloring in the tent, Todd goes off to help the visiting ranger make log benches for the kitchen area. They work side by side for a good hour, hammering long spikes into logs sawed in half.

In the meantime a couple arrives toting a small baby in a pack. The child looks dazed. She has on only a thin layer of wet cotton and a skimpy nylon windbreaker. Her exposed skin is red. This child is suffering. I offer my children's extra layers, but the mother declines and says the baby is fine. We make hot chocolate for them and lend them an umbrella to keep them from getting even wetter as they set up camp.

The wind blows fiercely throughout the night, pushing out the low-pressure system. When we pack up the next morning, we discover that the umbrella we lent them blew away in the night, probably because they left it open. After much searching, Todd finds it upside down in the lake, fifteen feet from the shore, filled with water. Naked except for his raincoat, he wades out in the freezing water; a snowfield is still melting across the way. When the water reaches his waist, he bends down but still can't get it, so he returns to shore dripping. He devises a hook—a tied-open carabiner attached to a rope, and fishes for close to an hour in the frigid water before he's successful. Every piece of gear out here is necessary, and we can't easily live without any one thing.

Entering Grizzly Country
Although there are certain inherent dangers associated with
wilderness, you have come here voluntarily to enjoy the natural scene and all of its natural environment. There is no guar-
antee of your safety. Efforts have been made to reduce the
hazards, however, bears may attack without warning and for
no apparent reason. Respect the wild country and its inhabi-
tants. Follow the rules posted at the trailhead. Visitors have
been injured, and killed by bears.

This is the sign we read at every Glacier National Park trailhead. It
sent a slight shiver up our spines when we entered a few days ago,
but we put our emotions on hold—until we get to Atlantic Creek
Campground. A rope is stretched across the spur trail to the campsites, preventing anyone from entering. It's hung with Day-Glo
orange plastic ribbons and a large sign stating, "DANGER! This
Campsite Is Closed Because of Bear Danger." When a bear moves
into an area, to eat ripening berries or for some other reason, it is
given the run of the place, and we humans move out. That's as it
should be. If a bear successfully steals food from a camper, an area
can be closed. Removing the opportunity helps a bear stay alive, for
"a fed bear is a dead bear." Bears that get accustomed to humans
and attracted to our food become a danger and can be terminated.

We walk more cautiously now. I put Bob first, so I can take better care of the children. A squirrel skitters down a tree, and the llamas jump. They are wired. I can imagine their olfactory nerves, on
red alert. We feel safer because of their concern.

The side of the trail has been torn up by bears. They have
turned over large boulders looking for grubs to eat. The size of
those displaced rocks gives us a good indication of the animals'
strength. It's scary. In numerous areas the soil is dug up in a swath
ten to fifteen feet wide where bears fed on the tubers of glacier
lilies. This has to be very recent, since the overturned dirt is dry and
it stopped raining only last night. Huge piles of fresh scat lie about.

Every year, at least one person gets mauled in the park. We
heard our share of grizz stories before we came west. We heard that
two rangers were sitting by a lake when a grizzly came up from

behind, bit one of them in the back, and carried her down the trail curled up in a ball, then dropped her.

The other reported attack was in the fall, when the bears were trying to put on their last ounces of fat before the winter. A hiker was walking down the trail listening to his Walkman, so he didn't hear the bear, which supposedly bit him in the head and carried him down the trail, tape still playing. Both victims lived. I don't know how much truth there is in these stories, but you can be sure I told Bob the second one so he'd leave his tape player off in this stretch. No sense courting danger.

The long, skinny waterfall that drops thousands of feet off Mount James reminds us more of Hawaii than Montana. It races past hanging emerald-green gardens and plunges into Medicine Grizzly Lake. From our trail, dynamited out of the side of the mountain, we have a good view across the valley of the trails leading into the lake and all the areas cleared for campsites. This area has been permanently closed since 1986 because of bear danger. We scope the valley below us as we climb toward Triple Divide Pass, wondering what horror might have occurred down below and looking, looking for bears.

Two bighorn sheep surprise us near the top of the pass as they hop to a closer ledge and check us out. They cock their heads curiously as though they'd like to play with our llamas. They are ewes, with short spike horns instead of the magnificent full curls of mature rams.

Another whole world bursts upon us as we top the pass. A view can stir your soul like beautiful music. I can tell my children are moved when they feel the need to get off their llamas and walk—to make a physical connection to the land.

Triple Divide Pass is unique in all the world, for from its lofty heights meltwaters descend to three bodies of water: the Pacific Ocean, Hudson Bay, and the Gulf of Mexico. Razoredge Mountain, with its summit of jagged teeth, rises abruptly in your face. Triple Divide Peak and Split Mountain guard the flanks of the pass. The most brilliant turquoise lake lies nestled at its base; it's not translucent like some but is opaque because of the glacial silt suspended in the water. A thousand-foot waterfall plummets from Split Mountain, its spray lit with dazzling sunlight. Everywhere throughout the descent are waterfalls, cascading over olive-green and mustard-colored cliffs of shale. To see this intense, radical beauty, you have to learn to live with the grizzlies. Once you're here, the exchange seems reasonable.

Our route makes a tedious ten-and-a-half-mile traverse around St. Mary Lake, through some of the thickest, most overgrown trail we've ever walked. On the far side we see tourists, walking a short distance from Going-to-the-Sun Highway, the major auto route cutting through the park. It took more than ten years to blast the route through the mountains and cost more than $3 million to build the road. This fifty-mile road was dedicated in 1933 and is considered one of the country's greatest engineering feats. I'm sure it's impressive, but I can't help but think of the "engineering feats" that the glaciers and all the other forces of nature performed in creating this fabulous country. Man's efforts pale in comparison.

Our backcountry permit is good for only six days. After that we must come out to a ranger station and get another one issued for the rest of our trip. It's a safety precaution, in case a campsite or an area has been recently closed because of bear trouble.

We don't mind, because the Swiftcurrent Motor Inn at the Many Glacier facility has a restaurant. We have "real" food on our brains. It occupies our conversations with the children, imagining what will be on the menu, picking first, second, and third choices. It's only recently that Bryce's three-year-old brain has realized that the Oscar Meyer song he likes to sing is about one of his favorite foods. He is so taken by this discovery that he shouts to every hiker he sees on the widened, graded trail that leads to the parking lot: "Do you know that an Oscar Meyer wiener is a hot dog?"

We must forgo food for a little longer as we wander through parking lots. We're tired and hungry, but we keep pushing because we're anxious to end the day. When we get the usual questions from the tourists, we have more trouble dealing with them. One man asks, "Where did you begin your trip?"

"Butte."

"No, where did you begin this particular trip?"

"Butte." He's amazed.

Another man asks, "Just getting back?"

"Just stopping in for a quick hot dog," I reply as I whiz by at three and a half miles an hour, a woman with a mission.

One of the park rules is that stock are not allowed on the blacktop roads. Sometimes it can't be avoided, like going to the ranger station to get a new permit. The flagpole is the only place to tie the llamas, so we hook them up and go inside. Who should we see behind the desk but the ranger we met at Morning Star Lake, the one who reprimanded us for still having our llamas in the site while we set up our tent for our hypothermic children, the ranger Todd helped build log benches. She looks past us through the window and says, "You aren't allowed to have the llamas tied to the pole because they'll eat the grass."

"If I go out and hold them, they'll be on the road and that's not allowed," I reply.

"You trashed Morning Star campsite," she announces.

"It probably did look worse after we left, but there wasn't anything we could do about it. We were placed at a site that rarely sees any stock use and isn't equipped for overnight. The park made us stay there for a day and a half. In that time, sure, the llamas were going to eat the grass around the rail and make an impact."

She is not happy. We're wondering if she is buddies with the backcountry ranger who called us before we left on this summer's hike and more or less ordered us not to bring our llamas but to use horses instead. Todd is very upset. He feels bad that the park may view our hiking as unethical.

He says to me, "Sure, they were going to eat stuff down. The way we had to stake them out to keep them from strangling themselves let them go beyond the dirt area. But she was there. She saw how we had them tied, and she didn't tell us to move them. Besides, they were starving. They normally get little bites to eat while they walk, but our permit made us sit there without moving for a whole day and a half. Plus, because of their rules, we have one less llama, so how are we supposed to bring supplemental feed if we lose our carrying capacity?"

Todd is afraid the park will revoke our permit and not allow us to continue. We're wondering if the backcountry ranger is trying to get back at us for going over his head. He did get in trouble from his supervisor for prematurely calling us up and saying that llamas were going to be banned from the park because of Johne's disease. That whole issue was thrown out. Todd is looking forward to getting out of the park now, and it's a shame, because we do find it, as the brochure claimed, to be "the most astoundingly beautiful place in the United States south of Canada" and it's sad to have negative feelings attached to it. In the end, we manage to get our permit and enjoy some great fried food despite the ranger's poor attitude.

AT THE TRAILHEAD to Poia Lake, a ranger stops us and asks for our permit. "I heard you were coming through," he says. We're sure of that. Every ranger from here to the border has probably been told to watch what we do.

"Could you please get your llamas to stop eating the grass?" he says as he studies our paper. Todd and I glance at each other, wondering how he expects us to do that. He made us stop here at this grassy area. As soon as llamas stop moving, they look for something to munch on. Short of putting muzzles on them, we can't prevent it. And what's wrong with trimming the weeds along the sides? Our ten-and-a-half-mile traverse around St. Mary Lake a few days ago was like hacking through a jungle. Since basically only CDT hikers walk that stretch, it's a very low priority for trail maintenance. It's probably been years and years since it was clipped, because there are trees—saplings—growing right on the trail that we had to bushwhack through. There the llamas would be doing them a favor if they ate a branch or two. This is getting ridiculous.

When we arrive at Poia Lake we are appalled at its condition. It evidently is a popular spot for horseback day trips; a huge area around the stock rail is trashed. There are ditches under the rail where the horses have pawed the ground. Manure is everywhere. Some excursions bring up to twenty-five horses in a party. Horses are acceptable in the backcountry no matter what their impact, and the concessionaires give the park money for their permit fees.

The trail to Elizabeth Lake is equally trashed. Horse travel has widened it and turned it into a quagmire. The hoof-churned mud is so deep we can't walk through it but must cling to the bushes on the sides of the trail and jump from rock to rock to keep our feet from being swallowed. Why all this fuss about our llamas? They should be setting standards for environmental impact for the horses to comply with. We are beginning to feel discriminated against.

Tonight we experience a place that's burned into our brains. Elizabeth Lake. It's the end of the day, and we're thirsty and footsore from a long descent. Gentle waves lap at the shore, little white ridges coming across the water.

Bob says my shoes and the children's automatically fall off whenever we stop for a break, and that when we get near water, our clothes do too. Bathing suits seem like such a hindrance out here. We swim to wash off the sweat and dirt and body odor, and because we're hot. We'd need to dig a bathing suit out of a pack and find a private spot to change, maybe quite a distance away. Taking off all your clothes to put on other clothes seems silly. Skinny-dipping ought to be part of the trail experience. I want my children to know the joy of running naked along the shore, kicking up spray, with sunshine warming their bare skin.

The children and I lie naked on our bellies in the warm shallows of Elizabeth Lake, turning over the tiny pieces of smoothed shale that cover the beach. They are flat and rounded, in hues of aqua, gray, and olive. When we rub them between our fingers they feel like velvet. We roll over onto our backs and soak in the warm afternoon rays, feeling content and refreshed.

After dinner, we return to the lake with our foam pads and sleeping bags. I lie with one child cradled in each arm and watch puffs of cumulus clouds rise over the peak of a nearby mountain. In seconds, each cloud completely dissolves into the azure sky as the water vapor is absorbed. We watch cloud after cloud come over the top as though someone was firing clay pigeons for target practice. We use our zipped-open sleeping bags as blankets, holding each other, watching the craggy mountain peaks take on a rosy afterglow, and I can't think of any finer or purer peace. We don't feel the need to be anywhere else or to have anything more than this experience right here.

In the morning we get an extremely early visit from a ranger stationed out of the Belly River, our final destination in the park. He says he was told by radio to watch for us and pay attention to our practices. To "catch us in the act," he had to get up in the dark, possibly 4:30 A.M., and hike the three miles from his cabin to the campground. He's probably looking at where and how we have the llamas staked out and whether we bring them into our campsite, but he finds our practices impeccable. He doesn't understand what all this fuss is about and admits, "You're following the rules to a T."

Others in the campsite are not, however. One couple has pitched a tent only a few feet from the lake, far too close to prevent an impact. You must have a permit even to be here and a reservation for a designated campsite, which are all far from the sensitive shoreline. They have neither.

Another couple has sloppily left food behind in the kitchen area, neglecting to stash it in their food bag and hoist it up the pole. It could have attracted a grizzly last night. The Belly River ranger very kindly educates them and imposes no fine. He feels it's his job to teach out here, not simply be a law enforcer. He goes on his way without incident, and we know now what we've suspected all along: they've been watching us.

As we leave Elizabeth Lake, I say to Bob, "Only sixteen more days left to hike. Isn't it going quickly now?"

"Would you be upset if I stayed only until the Canadian border?"

"Only one more day! Would my getting upset affect your decision?"

"No," he smiles.

"Oh, Bob," says Sierra. "I want you to stay a hundred more days, not just one."

"What gives, Bob?" I ask.

"You need some time alone."

"We need some time alone, or you need some time alone?"

"The kids have been getting to me a little bit," he whispers.

I feel bad. We really try to keep peace and meet needs and ensure that everyone has as good a time as possible. Bob thinks we spoil the kids. I do pick "the red and green things" out of some of their freeze-dried suppers. Back home, I make them eat whatever I put in front of them. Out here, Todd and I both tend to be a little more lenient. They're doing a great deal for us—battling wind and cold and all kinds of foul weather and being troupers about it. Is picking out a few green peppers too much of a simple thank-you? But that's not the issue.

Bob thinks we need to bop Bryce when he does things like poking people with sticks. But since we discovered that he's bored with riding and truly loves to hike, his behavior has improved. I never was big on hitting. I know any kind of misbehavior occurs because of a deeper-seated problem. It seems wiser to address the cause, not the effect. It isn't always easy to parent out here. And it isn't easy to have someone looking over your shoulder all the time. We have to learn different skills and techniques, just as we had to learn the lifestyle. Anyone out here with us for any length of time must go along with our trial and error and feel our growing pains as well. You can't divorce yourself from the community experience. But I suppose it can get tiring, even if you're simply watching and listening. We have to respect Bob's need for privacy and space. We'll miss him. He's a real part of our family.

Among his many gifts, Bob takes super pictures of our family and of me. Taking pictures is such a big part of my trip. I need them to illustrate the magazine and newspaper articles I write; I draw from them to illustrate my books; and I create slide presentations to share with audiences. The children have always been excellent models, moving a foot or two to the left or right, smiling on demand, walking down the same stretch of trail half a dozen times, patiently waiting for the sun to come out from behind a cloud. Their father, on the other hand, sees shooting photos as a hindrance and rarely takes the camera from me. If it weren't for Bob, my audiences would think there are three in "the Llama Family" instead of four.

Sierra enjoys taking pictures with the thirty-five millimeter "point and shoot" camera Bob bought her. Atop Red Gap Pass we see four snow-white mountain goats clicking along on the rock cliffs. They are a striking contrast to the rusty red of the soil and rock, caused by iron and other minerals. She points and presses the button. "Got it! It was great!" she shouts, after taking each picture. I try to explain that you never really know if it's a great shot until the pictures are developed back home, but she has all the confidence she needs. She wears her camera around her neck, inside her fleece coat. She happily tells me that I can have copies of any of her shots that I like. I hope my children will enjoy at least one or two of the things that give me reason for living, though not necessarily with the same passion. Just to share it on any level is a gift.

From Red Gap Pass, the wide-open plains are once again visible through the gaps in the peaks. Before long we'll be whizzing through them on our way down to Butte to do the last leg of this summer's hike. We've been hiking northeast, and it's remarkable to see how much drier the country is than the interior of the park. Storms, normally coming from the west, have lost their punch once they get here.

Since we left Many Glacier three days ago, we've been following not the official CDT but the Chief Mountain route. The Ahern Drift on the Highline Trail is a permanent snowbank that is steep and hazardous to cross until a good path has been cut. All stock parties must avoid it and follow the Belly River, which is really a beautiful alternative.

Sometimes you don't realize something has been missing in your life until it reappears. Away from the higher alpine areas, we suddenly discover a profusion of birds. There are feathers everywhere on the trail along the Belly River. We regard each bird as a treasure, even though many are common gray jays. To the Native Americans, they symbolize spirit. The alpine country we've been traveling in is so different from this open broad river valley, an ideal habitat for birds. Their songs fill the air.

The view from the Belly River ranger's cabin is one to die for. The log building is nestled in a lush meadow of tall, billowing grasses. Beautiful, spirited horses gallop back and forth behind the wooden fence, the wind in their manes. And the peaks of the northern park seem to rise straight up from the meadow. I believe your days here would be filled with pure gratitude simply to walk out your door and see. Just seeing, that's all, would be enough.

The ranger who approaches us, however, doesn't look happy. "Could you come up to the cabin for a moment? There seems to be a problem, and I'd like to talk with you about it."

On his porch, he continues, "I got orders from my boss to fine you before you leave the park." We are two miles from the border.

"He said he was up to Morning Star Campsite and measured how far out your llamas grazed, and it was beyond the distance that they should have been."

"You've got to be kidding! He went up there with a measuring tape? A ranger was right there, and she saw how we had them tied and never said a word about moving them, which we would have done immediately."

"Well, I'm not comfortable fining you for something that I didn't see myself. It's not in my district, and I don't believe it's my responsibility. I feel like they're passing the buck. I couldn't find any fault with your behavior in my district. I'm not going to write you a fine, and I'm going to call him on the radiophone and tell him."

Todd and I look at each other and feel terrible. "How much is the fine?"

"Twenty dollars."

"We could pay the fine. It's not the money. We don't believe we deserve it. Could you lose your job over this?"

"Perhaps, but it's a matter of principle. I think what he wants me to do is unethical."

He calls his supervisor, our old friend Ranger Hedd, and says, "I've found no problem with this party, and I don't believe it's my place to be judging them for something that's out of my area. I'm not going to give them a fine." There's a long silence. Since it's a radiophone, only one person can talk at a time. We wait in suspense.

"All right," Ranger Hedd replies. "I respect your decision. Have them call me at the customs office when they get to the border."

We are amazed. Two miles before we're out of the park, Ranger Hedd tries to get an uninvolved ranger to head us off and give us a fine for something we're being blamed for doing sixty miles back. Does this man have something out for us or what?

There's no way we're paying $2.50 a minute to call that guy from the cell phone at the customs office. We pile into our truck and ride back to the village of East Glacier, where Todd calls from a pay phone.

It's 8:00 at night. We're starving and exhausted from hiking all day. The children and Bob and I sit in the truck cab while the ranger interrogates Todd for half an hour. I can tell the verbal abuse Todd is undergoing because of his body language. He constantly shifts his legs and arms. He runs his fingers through his hair and barely says a word. The person on the other end is doing all the talking. When Todd returns to the truck, he looks sick. "He says we're under investigation. He'll be speaking to us later about it and will inform us of the outcome."

"That's horse shit. Those other people at Elizabeth Lake who violated the rules get 'educated,' and we get a fine. I don't think so."

The ranger does call us at home over the matter, as we learn from our house sitter, but we won't be back there for another few weeks, and we have no intention of returning the call. I knew from the get-go that we'd be locking horns, when he took it upon himself to call us before we left and try to talk us out of coming to Glacier, but I wouldn't have believed it would go this far.

Horses are the traditional stock animal here and the symbol of the West. But llamas are new in the backcountry. Some horse people think of llamas as exotic fluff balls, incapable of carrying the same weight as a horse or a mule and hence inferior. They have no use for them and would rather not share the backcountry. They certainly don't want to make any changes to accommodate their unique needs. Some see llamas as a threat—they could compete for space, clients, and permits in the future. The "multiple-use" concept can break down user groups the way racial tension does in the city, where one ethnic neighborhood is in conflict with a different one. So it is in our very small public lands and parks. But the area is too small, and we need to work together. There are different types of people with different needs. We believe llamas have a real place on the trails, not only because they have much less of an impact on the environment, but because they provide a way for families with small children to get into the wild. For this prejudice to percolate into the bureaucracy of our public lands in unjust and inappropriate.

It's a five-hour drive back down to Butte, where Bob will drop us off on the trail and shuttle our vehicle to the next town stop. The children are not naughty in the truck, they're just a little fussy. We have to consider that we haven't been immobile, or in such an enclosed space, for weeks. We have no story or music tapes to occupy them, radio reception is bad, and the books and drawing supplies are all buried in the back. The three adults sit crowded in the front. Because there's a stick shift on the floor, Bob's clunky hiking boots and muscular legs compete with mine for space, along with rolling water bottles, trash, maps, and two camera cases on the floor. We stop at Burger King and, because we're pressed for time, decide to eat while we drive.

I hand back french fries, chicken tenders, juice with straws, napkins, pieces of our hamburger that the kids want to try, ripped-open ketchup packets, and wet napkins to wipe their faces. My armpit is in Bob's face, and I'm sure it has smelled better. I help Todd with his lunch—get his food out of the bag, fold back the wrapper, and hand him a napkin and his drink when he's ready for it. I struggle with a salad in an unruly plastic container, trying to squeeze dressing packets and deal with that big flapping lid. My large cup of coffee, which is too full, and Todd's soda, which is not stable, spill all over my clothing and the towel we're sitting on.

Bob looks at me and says, "This is an experience. This is just what I needed to convince me I'm making the right decision about pulling out of the hike." I look at him and stick out my tongue.

Anaconda-Pintler Wilderness
AUGUST 26, 1995

We need to have people who mean something to us, people to whom we can turn, knowing that being with them is coming home.
— BERNARD COOKE

IT WAS SCARY to see the mining city of Butte, Montana, up close. It sits on the edge of the huge, mile-wide open Berkeley pit where metals were extracted until 1983. Now it has the distinction of being one of the nation's largest Superfund sites, part of a federal program designed to rid our land of hazardous wastes. Our Montana friends call Butte the armpit of the West. The press calls it the ugliest city in America. At one time it was called the richest hill on earth, when it produced more than $2 billion worth of gold, silver, copper, and zinc. The hill is gone, and a crater remains. We stare at it as we travel south on the CDT from Homestake Pass. One stretch of trail remains. Bob said his good-byes after shuttling us to the trailhead. He'll tool around in his motor home for a while before heading south to his Colorado home. Our route will first make a seventy-mile half circle around Butte before entering the Anaconda-Pintler Wilderness. For the next miles, we'll mostly be walking roads around the city.

From our camp tonight, high above Butte, we stare at the lit-up city and mine and that strange, horrible pit. Trucks work all night long. The steady banging of machinery sounds like drums that never stop. The main pit has been filled with water, creating a toxic lake as minerals and chemicals leach into it. Any waterfowl that touches down on it dies. Sound-making devices around its rim make eerie, robotic noises that echo over the landscape to deter waterfowl. The whole place gives us the creeps. We're looking at unfettered human greed. What a contrast to where we've been, Glacier National Park, and where we're heading, the Anaconda-Pintler Wilderness.

Butte is said to be one the cheapest places to live in the West. We can understand why. Actually, Butte is a melting pot. The mine drew thousands of immigrants in search of a living wage. The labor union was strong here, making this the most militant union town in the nation. We're eager to meet some of its residents in the days ahead.

Walking on a road is rarely much fun. It's often in the hot sun, and dust and dried sweat stiffen your face. Gas fumes linger behind passing vehicles, and conversations revolve around how much you'd be willing to pay for ice in your water bottle. As we head into Butte on a wide dirt road, seven loose horses run back and forth at top speed. They thunder around the sage flats on each side, then cross our road and abruptly stop in front of us, curious about the llamas but nervous as hell about getting too close. When we almost reach them, they hightail it away. About this time, a man comes running out of his split-level home swinging a camera. We chat a few minutes and pose for a picture. Then he tells us to wait while he disappears into the house and returns with ice for our water bottles. Angel number one.

Angel number two doesn't look like an angel. A spent-looking old man yells to us across the road, "Could you come over here for a moment? We've got a bet going." He's a toothpick in tight jeans, high-heeled motorcycle boots, and a belt buckle so large it looks as if it could injure him if he bent over too far. A black miner's hat sits on his head.

"I bet my niece here that you folks sold your home and all your belongings and are walking across the country."

"Not exactly," I say. "We're hiking a section of the Continental Divide Trail, and I do this for a living."

"Damn!" he says. "Come on up for a cold beer." Their old motor home is pulled off at a picnic area on national forest land. You can camp anywhere for free on these federal lands. It looks as though they've set up shop. Baby toys are strewn about in the dirt, along with a filled diaper, an empty can of Spaghetti-Os and the soiled saucepan on its side. A baby with red curls and an absolutely filthy face brings a ball over to Bryce to play. Bryce hides behind my legs. The baby's rough-looking mother is extremely young, with bleached hair and tight pants.

"Did anyone ever tell you that you look like someone?" the old man asks Todd.

"Yes," I chime in. "He's been told he looks like Jesus Christ, Abraham Lincoln, and, when he has a rough day, Charles Manson."

"He don't look like Charlie," he responds immediately. "Charlie's face is much fuller. I done time with Charlie."

We almost choke on our beers.

After road walking for another hour, we come to a shady park and playground with a creek to water our llamas. As we're relaxing, a family pulls up in a long boat of a car from the 1950s. Three pretty sisters come over and sit down at our picnic table and begin asking question after question. They all wear their long dark hair in sexy hairdos. They sport lots of flashy jewelry and makeup and low-cut midriff tops showing a generous amount of cleavage. They all have tattoos somewhere, and they're all chewing gum, loudly, with their mouths open. But sweet!

They offer to buy us cold juice and ice cream bars. When they return with the goodies, they refuse our money. Since Bryce doesn't eat chocolate, one sister gently picks off the chocolate coating. In exchange, we give the one sister's son a ride on Berrick, take his picture, and copy down his address to send him a picture. A whole family of angels!

As our day winds down and we draw closer to setting up camp, another angel pulls up alongside us in her car. She's very interested in what we're doing, asks tons of questions, and confirms that there is a national forest campground up the road. Although the campground is now defunct, we can still stay there.

She invites us to her neighborhood's potluck dinner tonight. "There will be plenty of food, and everyone would love to meet you." In the next breath she remembers it's tomorrow, not tonight, but adds, "So take the day off tomorrow. Come up to our home. Take a shower. At least come for breakfast in the morning."

After giving us directions, she says good-bye and motors off, but she soon returns carrying a large plastic bag of just-picked red raspberries and two "good" beers.

After dinner, a Forest Service truck slows down to study us and comes to a halt. Oh, no! Our last experience with rangers in Glacier left a bad taste. We expect to get reprimanded for something, but all the driver wants to do is tell us how to get off this hot gravel road in the morning and onto a side jeep trail with no traffic. "There will be a 'No Trespassing' sign posted that the county put up, but disregard it. It's federal land and open to the public." We talk a while longer and he leaves, wishing us a good trip.

When Todd and I crawl into our bags and lie in each other's arms, we feel warm inside from all the Butte angels we met today. The city of Butte looks ugly, but its people have some of the most beautiful hearts anywhere.

This is a land of cattle guards and fences and holding down wires so the llamas can step over. It's a land of sun and lip balm and sunscreen and swabbing foreheads with wet bandannas. It's a land of dry chaparral and sagebrush everywhere and filtering water from stock tanks and searching for anything green for the llamas to eat. At night it's a land of yipping coyotes and stars so abundant that if you are a little boy and wake up in the middle of the night, you stand and stare with your mouth open and your head tilted way back, and you pee on yourself because you just can't believe how many stars there are in the sky. This is the kind of country my friend Beth Ellen Pennel from Michigan is stepping into. She will be hiking with us for the next 150 miles, until the end of this summer's hike.

Beth is not originally from the Midwest. She has a mug that reads, "Born in Maine. Living in Exile," for that is where her heart remains. That is also where we met, sixteen years ago on the Appalachian Trail. She hiked most of the last hundred miles of Maine lake wilderness with me, climbed "the greatest mountain"— Mount Katahdin, where that famous footpath ends—and celebrated as I finished my first long-distance hike.

In recent years Beth had drifted away from long-distance hiking, but at a trail reunion last year I showed slides from the Colorado Trail and it pulled at her heartstrings. She decided she would never again stay separated from her loves: hiking and high mountains. She invested in all new equipment, trained for months, and bade good-bye to her husband and young daughter to come out here and join us for two weeks. We're to meet her at Deerlodge Pass, on I-15. There are absolutely no services at this interchange. "Ranch access" is all the highway sign says. It's a "highway stop" for her bus—a lonely place to be dropped off, not knowing when or if your party will make it there.

We emerge from the woods on a dirt road and can see the interstate a full four miles before we reach it. Our eyes are glued to the overpass as we walk, looking for a bus or a person. Soon a bus pulls up and leaves someone off. A figure wearing a red pack walks back and forth across the bridge. "I bet that's Beth!" After a bit, a motor home pulling a white stock trailer stops at the interchange. The figure goes over to it. "Don't tell me that's Bob? It's got to be him! How many motor homes pulling a white trailer need to stop at this lonely exit?" We're still miles away, but in this open country we can make it all out with our naked eyes.

After a while the figure begins running toward us. It *is* Beth. She hugs our sweaty bodies and excitedly talks about her trip here, and yes, it is Bob. He knew our schedule and came looking for us.

We camp by a pull-off on the dirt road we're traveling on so Bob can drive his rig up close. Out come folding chairs, chips and salsa, dark beer, and the fixings for our dinner—burritos. Bob's own dinner selection is a low-calorie Healthy Choice entrée. "I'm trying to make the weight I lost come back slower," he says.

Come morning, the aromas of coffee and microwaved croissants waft through the desert air. We set whipped butter and black-berry jam on the ground, since there's no breakfast table. I sit back and sip and look at the far ridges we just walked over from Butte. I hear the llamas' bells tinkling while their big soft lips gently pull at the grass. Beth sits at my side—my hiking friend of sixteen years. Who would have thought, back in Maine, that we'd be making a Montana memory?

As Bob cleans up the dishes, I go in to say my good-byes. "When are we going to see you again? Will you meet us at the next road crossing?"

"This is it!" he cries.

"I really do love you, Bob. You're one of my best friends."

He proceeds to get very flustered, putting things in the wrong drawers, hitting his head on the cabinet doors. "Now you've got me all worked up!" he says.

I feel touched that he put all this effort into finding us. It's only been a few days since we last saw him. Bob has his way of showing how much he cares.

An alternative shortcut to the Anaconda-Pintler Range takes us from Highway 274 through historic Mule Ranch and across some of the most beautiful open land in Montana. It eliminates miles of highway road walking. When we arrive at the ranch, however, we're surprised to a see a metal gate blocking the entrance with a sign stating, "Authorized Personnel Only." Our guidebook didn't mention this. The sign is posted by Montana Fish and Game, the overseers of the abandoned ranch. Todd isn't one for deviant behavior, and he's inclined to set a good example for his children, but there are shades of gray here. The CDT is far from being secured and built. In the past there have been only a handful of long-distance hikers going the long haul, the entire trail, who don't want to skip anything, even the unpopular sections. A single backpacker, with sound wilderness ethics, can slip through a small area that is closed to the general public, and the owner doesn't even have to know. Our guidebook often tells us to cross these occasional pockets of private land. To cover himself, the author usually suggests getting permission first, but it isn't as if you know who the landowners are, where they live, or how to get in touch with them. As the CDT is built, however, and more and more folks walk it, their growing numbers will necessitate that the route go entirely on public lands or roads.

We see that the gate is held closed with one small piece of twisted wire. Even with our entourage of strung-together llamas, the highway is so deserted and lonely, with only an occasional passing vehicle, that it doesn't feel very naughty to slide through. The wooden buildings are in excellent shape; their tin roofs look very sound, and we imagine the ranch bustling with miners and mules. This was a resting spot for the beasts as they hauled ore out of the high mountains. We follow the old wagon road, looking ahead for the faint ruts. Sometimes one rut is much higher than the other, and we think of the wagons tilting as they roll by. We walk across wide expanses of grassy plains, buff-colored and dry this late in the summer. The wall of the Continental Divide provides a dramatic backdrop to what finally feels like Big Sky Country. There is so much land to look at. So much sky. The wind blows unceasingly as we follow handmade wooden fences. They snake for miles and miles, following the lay of the land, rising up on the heights and dropping down into the depressions. Sierra is captivated. She rides for hours, never asking for a break or to be entertained.

I notice Beth walks with a permanent smile on her face lately. She's unwinding from her supervisory job as a statistical researcher. This reprieve into Montana's high country is just what the doctor ordered. With each day that passes, she drops her high-strung ways like a snake shedding its skin. She feels so at home on the trail in the mountains that being separated from her family is not a hardship. When our route takes us up to the open ridges of the Divide, however, she pops out her cell phone and calls home. Tonight is her husband's birthday. It wasn't too many years ago that you had to get yourself to a pay phone to call home.

We've never carried a cell phone or a radio while we hiked, although we considered it; but we've never had a medical emergency either. The use of cell phones has led to an enormous influx into the backcountry of people who have come unprepared and then, faced with the reality of the wilderness, demand immediate help. Cell phones and global positioning systems will never replace outdoor experience and training. But Beth's phone supplies an important emotional link to her loved ones back home. Without that, she probably wouldn't have come.

Bryce and Beth have taken to each other. He hops off his llama to walk every chance he gets and joins Beth in the front. She's still adjusting to the altitude, so they make a good pair. A hand-holder by nature, he automatically raises his little arm and slides his hand into hers. She shortens her telescoping hiking stick to fit his height. They sing songs and ask each other questions, and he tells her the most detailed, lengthy monster stories you ever heard. It keeps him moving for miles. Then I hear him say,

"Beth, do you like to poo in outhouses or in holes dug in the ground?"

"Well, outhouses are usually stinky, so probably holes."

"Would you rather poo in outhouses that don't stink or in holes?"

I smile. He's thinking about our stay at the defunct campsite the other night, which had a smelly outhouse. I gave him the choice of where to go to the bathroom. This decision is high priority for a three-year-old. So often we eliminate choice for our children. It takes time, and parents often think we know best. But what seems like a small thing to us is causing him to think and evaluate what he likes. He's getting to know himself, and in order to really know his new friend, he needs to know what she would choose.

We're on our way to Lower Seymour Lake and the entrance to the Anaconda-Pintler Wilderness. At the lake's campground, we are to meet my friend Timmy Lebling and his girlfriend, Ann, who will hike this last stretch with us. Together with Beth, we'll have quite a grand finale party this season. That's the way I like it: good company and good times, especially if the weather turns nasty, which it easily could as we cruise into September.

SOME PEOPLE in our lives feel more like kin than our blood relatives do. They're our soulmates. Timmy is such a person to me.

We met last year, 1994, when he was a through-hiker on the Appalachian Trail. A mutual friend picked him up and brought him to our house for a meal and a rest. As soon as he walked in my door,

I knew: This one's a keeper. His personality is like the sun. He is the happiest, easiest person to be with. My kids and I immediately fell in love with him. He stayed for nearly a week, unable to pull himself away, and when he finished the trail in Maine, we drove up so I could climb Mount Katahdin with him, cementing our friendship as nothing else could.

He's driven all the way from Alaska in his beat-up, rusty red Ford pickup to be with us and share in our family's adventure. When we spot the red pickup driving toward us on the road, kicking up a cloud of dust, we all scream, "It's Timmy!!!" The truck barely comes to a stop before he's out of the cab and hugging. He and Ann brought two half-gallons of ice cream and a bag of ice to keep it frozen until they found us. We sit in the shade of the truck, laughing, stuffing our faces (Todd with a soup ladle that Tim found in the back of his cab), and telling stories—really only fragments of stories, for there's so much to share and we're so excited to see one another that no one can get out a whole story before being interrupted.

Tim is twenty-six. As an instructor for NOLS (National Outdoor Leadership School), he takes people into the wilderness of Alaska in the summer and to Baja California in the winter to teach them sea kayaking and how to survive in the backcountry. Ann just graduated from Dartmouth College and is hoping to get into medical school. What Ann lacks in trail experience, she makes up with her good attitude. Like Beth, she's a trouper.

We have seventy miles of wilderness travel ahead of us, through two ranges, to reach the Idaho-Montana border at Chief Joseph Pass. The Anaconda Range has spectacular sheer peaks rising abruptly from forested valleys. The CDT follows the Divide's craggy crest through much of the range, past high mountain lakes and parks and drainages full of deer and elk. We'll conclude with the Pintler's trails, which are more gentle, with tree-covered rolling mountains.

Some people's presence makes your life easier. The conditions you're living under don't really influence it. It's chemistry. When you're together it works, mostly because we're all working together and helping one another.

We all help to unload the llamas when we get into camp and take off their saddles. Ann heats a large pot of water on her camp stove for hot drinks for everyone. Tim helps Todd stake out the llamas in the evening and brings them in to saddle come morning. Everyone tells stories to the kids while we hike and reads to them in camp. Not everyone is at the same performance level when it comes to hiking. Some may be experiencing blisters, headaches from the altitude, or general fatigue from the strenuous exercise. Todd and I take weight out of their backpacks and put it in our own. When I see Ann dragging behind on a steep climb and get an "I'm coping" answer when I ask how she is, I hike with her and ask her questions about herself to keep her mind off her discomfort. It feels as if we're living with an extended family, as if the children have aunts and uncles along to care for them. At mealtimes everyone shares food, passing pots around to sample, swapping spices, making community desserts. We all use Beth's soy sauce, Tim's sugar, our Parmesan cheese.

Todd usually gets to clean up Beth's leftover freeze-dried dinner, but tonight he's having trouble getting it down. "This freeze-dried beef stroganoff looks and tastes like dog food. The meat is gristly. It looks like someone already chewed it. Those llama pellets are beginning to look better. Add a little water and make a green slurry. What if you puked from this crap in Glacier National Park? Would you have to pack out your puke too?" The kids won't even sample Beth's freeze-dried applesauce. Our whole family is suffering from freeze-dried burnout.

Timmy comes to the rescue and begins making meals for us. He carries flour and yeast in his monster pack and mixes up bread dough that rises under his shirt by his warm belly. Next he rehydrates home-dried veggies and mixes them with spaghetti sauce and mozzarella cheese to make calzones in his special baking pan. Come morning, he mixes more dough to bake an apple cake. Another day it's fudge brownies.

When it starts to rain and hail, Tim breaks out his harmonica and plays cheerful tunes. His gives his spare to Bryce, and they make music together on breaks. Tim calls himself Trail Hand and talks to Todd (Trail Boss) as if Todd were his master and he the willing slave. At breaks, he entertains the kids by putting dried apple rings in his eye sockets and slitting others to make earrings and a nose ring. We all laugh more in his presence. Even Todd has begun to forget that this trail life is supposed to be hard, serious work. I find the two men walking together in the rear a lot, having discussions and talking and laughing, most uncommon behavior for my husband. Tim is very good for Todd to be around. He's showing him another way. I haven't had many opportunities to be one-on-one with my special friend since he arrived. Everyone gravitates toward him, especially my adoring children. Tim and I smile at each other and wink on switchbacks, and we're happy just to be in each other's presence.

The weather has deteriorated considerably since we entered the wilderness. Today it's hailing marbles. We listen to them hit our raingear. The frozen balls build up on the nylon golf umbrellas, making them a lot heavier. Every now and then we tilt them to dump off the hail. We watch it ping the foliage by our sides, making it bounce. We walk in a line, fairly close, no one speaking. Bryce is asleep in Todd's pack, so we don't want to wake him up to add another layer since the temperature has dropped. Instead we drape his fleece coat over his shoulders and back. We walk around and above beautiful Elk Park, with its green meadows and meandering streams, white granite rocks, and scattered dark evergreens. There is so much wildlife in these mountains—elk, moose, and bighorn sheep at Rainbow Pass. The droppings we step over are profuse, for big game often use our trail.

We're camping at Surprise Lake this evening. When you're uncomfortable, the mileage to your destination always seems to be off. "I'm ready to be surprised," Beth says. "Any minute it can appear." Everyone is feeling raw, but spirits are still up. Summer has abruptly changed into fall. We saw bow hunters entering the woods on horseback today. Since it has been raining a lot lately, we set up a large tarp in camp where we can all cook together instead of being in our separate worlds in our tents and vestibules. Beth is experiencing no homesickness, since Tim keeps her laughing so hard she snorts, which is uncommon for her and makes her laugh and snort even more. When Todd comes out of the tent to eat, Timmy stumps over hauling a llama pannier and says, "A seat for the trail boss and a stool to rest his feet."

"Don't spoil him," I tell Timmy.

"Gotta take care of the trail boss," he says. "I listen for my alarm call every morning—the zipper of your tent. Then I know it's time to get up and saddle. If the tarp is off the gear, I know I'm running behind. Sometimes I think about trying to get up before the trail boss and bring the llamas in on my own to surprise him, but I can't tell what time it is. I'm liable to get up in the middle of the night to do it."

"When we work together, we don't need to talk to communicate anymore," Tim adds.

"Such male bonding," Ann says sarcastically.

"We might say one-word sentences like 'Morning.'" Tim goes on. "Mostly, we grunt, nod, use hand signals."

"We don't want to wake the sleeping beauties," Todd says.

As the days move on, we stake our tents closer and closer in camp. We don't feel the need for much privacy anymore. This way we can talk to each other while we're in our tents. Our friends hear us sing lullabies to the children and listen to them say their prayers. We hear them fart. Another sign of our growing familiarity is the shortened distance we walk away to urinate. Living together and sharing nearly everything has a way of breaking down barriers.

OUR LAST NIGHT together on the trail. Trail Creek at Gibbon's Pass Road. A campfire is in order for tonight's festivities. A fire is a treat too rarely indulged in out here. Once we get to camp, we're usually too tired or busy or short on time to build one.

We all gather firewood. We choose the best meals of what remains in our supper bags and serve them buffet style. Trying to find an appropriate dessert, we combine Cheerios, melted marshmallows, and margarine to make a version of Rice Krispies treats. Beth presents a can of imported beer she's been secretly lugging for two weeks, which gets split five ways. Tim gets the great idea to have a percussion band and play music around the campfire. We push pebbles into the opening of the drained beer can, pour raw rice into an empty water bottle, and tie pot lids together to make cymbals. Bryce uses an extra tent stake to drum on inverted pots. With his other hand he holds a harmonica to his mouth, jamming with Timmy. Sierra dances around the fire and the band like a cross between a cheerleader and a ballerina. We all nod our heads and tap our feet to the rhythm. Our llamas stand still and stare with a look that asks, "What are you doing?" As a truck full of cowboys drives by, they slow down and try to make sense of what they're seeing.

"Isn't this the kind of evening activity every American family participates in?" I ask Timmy.

"These kids will not grow up to be normal. But then again, that isn't your goal, is it?"

"Sierra will probably be a ballet dancer and live in some metropolitan area. Bryce will play at a jazz club in New York City—late nights, smoke-filled rooms. They'll both get their start on the Continental Divide Trail in Montana with their Uncle Timmy."

The kids look so happy. We all feel so good. I don't care whether my children fall in love with hiking. I don't expect them to. I want them to fall in love with life, believe their dreams can come true, work hard at making them happen, and find joy in absolutely everything, no matter where they are, who they're with, or what they're doing. Maybe this long journey is helping them learn this. Helping *us* learn this.

ON OUR WAY EAST, we stop in South Dakota to refuel. The locals sit and sip coffee at the counter and talk about the snowstorms raging across the Rockies. We got out just in time.

On I-90 in Iowa, a truck pulling a trailer loaded with cattle slowly passes us on the left. The closed-in trailer has a six-inch-wide opening along its length at the exact height of the cows' butts. They stick their butts out and splatter diarrhea down the trailer's shiny white side and over the manufacturer's logo. It says in bold letters, TRAIL BOSS. I nudge my Trail Boss, and we both burst out laughing.

Sierra is in the backseat ripping pictures out of a coloring book she picked up at Burger King and "decoupaging" them to her vinyl car seat arms with spit. They have learned to entertain themselves. I'm feeling a little displaced. Not positive about returning home.

When we stop at Beth's on our way through Michigan, she tells us her colitis is acting up again—nerves from work. It's midnight, and she's crawling around on the white tile kitchen floor in her office clothes, picking up tiny specks of dirt that only she can see. Then she wipes her white countertop over and over again. A silver coyote pin sparkles on her blouse; she bought it at the Missoula airport before returning home. The coyotes called to her on the first day of her hike and the last. She's worn it every day since she returned, no matter which outfit she has on. Her colleagues ask, "What's with the pin?" and she replies, "It's my only link with that other life."

WE AREN'T supposed to hike next year. It's supposed to be our year off—"the year of the pig." Todd's had a hankering to raise pigs organically for years. My Pennsylvania German husband craves bacon, sausage, and ham.

"I might not get a pig next year," he says.

"If you don't, how do you feel about coming back out next summer to do another stretch?"

"How would we get the money together?"

"Don't worry about that. I can save it."

I pull out the road atlas, turn to the state of Montana, and begin studying. He shakes his head and smiles.

Two little "peanuts" trucking down the Colorado Trail. Bryce longed for the opportunity to get out of Dad's child carrier and stretch his legs. (1993)

An evening stroll on the Colorado Trail with Mom through the aspens, one of our most favorite things to do before climbing into the sack. (1993)

A wet but happy little camper (Bryce) having a morning bowl of cereal in Montana. (1995)

Enjoying the sunlight and fantastic view of the Green River Lakes, Wyoming. (1997)

Llamas aren't fond of deep mud. Todd offers a little "encouragement" while Sierra naps unawares in his backpack on the Colorado Trail. (1993)

Sierra and Todd ready to cross over the hairy Jackass Pass in the Bridger Wilderness, Wind River Range, Wyoming. (1997)

Topping a magnificent pass in Glacier National Park, Montana. When we reached the high point, the children were always inspired to get off their llamas and walk over the land themselves. (1995)

Todd leading the llamas down a steep "trail" in the Southern Bitterroots, Montana. We discovered only later that we had lost the trail and were negotiating a rock slide. (1996)

In the San Juan Mountains, Colorado, we take shelter under some dense evergreens to wait out a hailstorm while the thick-wooled llamas good-naturedly brave it out in the weather. (1998)

Cindy leading Sierra on Berrick across a swift stream in the Wind River Range, Wyoming. (1997)

Bob Riley and his "boys" topping a pass in Glacier National Park, Montana, while the landscape explodes in beauty at his feet. (1995)

Cindy doing "double duty" in camp: cooking a delicious supper plus reading to the little munchkins in the Montanta sunlight. (1995)

Todd and Bryce enjoying a downhill across the New Mexican desert during the last few days of the entire journey. (1998)

Sierra and Bryce take advantage of the pathetic "shade," trying to contort themselves into the shape of a diamond-shaped road sign in the New Mexican desert. Todd wishes for a kickstand to park his long, heavy "rig." (1998)

"Thumbs Up" at the Border Crossing Station in Antelope Wells, New Mexico. The long five-year dream is finally complete. (1998)

PART THREE

THE CONTINENTAL DIVIDE TRAIL

CHIEF JOSEPH PASS TO THE

TETONS, 1996

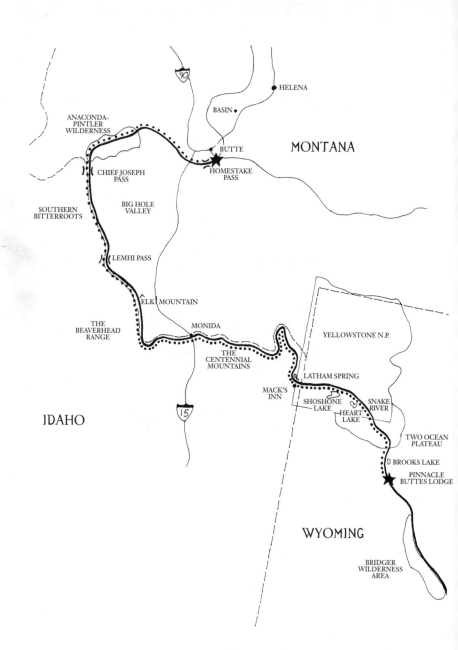

The Centennial Mountains
JULY 1, 1996

"I don't see much sense in it," said Rabbit. "No," said
Pooh humbly, "there isn't. But there was going to be
when I began it. It's just that something happened to
it along the way."

—A. A. MILNE

FOUR DAYS before departure. Todd hyperextends his ankle and can't walk on it. His face is white, and he looks shaken. A dark cloud descends over us. We are nearly packed and ready to go, but how will he be able to cross mountains leading a string of unruly llamas if he can't even walk across the floor?

The next day, it isn't much better.

"Do you really want to go?" I ask.

"Yes. But maybe it's a test to see how much I want to go, so when I get out there and it's tough, I won't be able to complain and say I really didn't want to come."

Todd has cultivated a healthy concern over the route-finding challenges in the first section of this summer's hike. Bob, who will be joining us for a few weeks, has purchased a global positioning system (GPS) to help out. I'm concerned about my husband's attitude. I have doubts about how much his heart is in this trip and how much he's going out of love for and dedication to his wife. Responsibility is an admirable trait, but it isn't enough when things get rough. If "out there" isn't where you truly want to be, you don't have much of a chance.

Two days before departure, he gets an X ray. The ankle's not broken, and the doctor says he should be able to hike. All systems are go, but tonight Sierra wakes up with a fever—tossing and turning and having bad dreams. She had been complaining that she wasn't ready to leave, asking us to put it off another week.

On the long, fatiguing truck ride out, she looks sallow. She leans her head on her bed pillow pushed against the cab window. Her lips are parted, and she's breathing through her mouth because her nose is stuffed up. Her long bangs hang in her eyes, making her look like a poor child in a Third World country. She sits up to cough and spits out phlegm.

I stare out the window and can't remember why we're doing this again.

Bryce is cranky. He throws one fit after another: over dropping his Slim Jim; over its being too gristly; over not being able to find a red crayon; over not being able to find the next number in his "follow the dots" book. Maybe he's getting sick too.

On day two of the drive, we spend the night at our friend Steve's house in Wisconsin. Bryce comes down with a fever. He's up half the night crying and coughing. I'm sick too, and when I finally get him back to sleep, I join the men in the kitchen. We sit and stare at the linoleum.

"We may have taken on too much this time," Todd says.

"The drive or the hike?"

"Everything."

"We push them. We definitely push them."

The problem is we really shouldn't deviate from our schedule if we can help it. We have friends joining us who have already bought plane tickets, and we have a permit for Yellowstone, a month and a half away. But I announce, "I will not get on that trail with sickness. We have to get better."

The next day on the road, Bryce is having another fit over his tight seat belt and how his pillow is arranged, and over the apple I peeled and sliced for him. He says the sections "aren't pointy enough." That's it. I lose it and yell, "You're making me nuts!" which causes him to fall apart.

Our internal clocks are off as we head west and cross time zones. The sun is still up at 10:00 P.M., but our bodies think it's midnight. We visit with friends and stay up too late.

I look at Todd and say, "Maybe we'll only make it a week or two. The problem is, not enough time has gone by since our last hike. We remember how hard this can be."

TWO WEEKS LATER, I'm leading my llamas down the dirt road outside the tiny settlement of Mack's Inn, rope in hand, kids swaying gently, llama bells tinkling softly. When I turn around, I see a scene that looks completely familiar. I see Todd leading his string of packers and then Bob in the rear, taking it slow. Bob smiles at me, his belly making a slight bulge in his T-shirt. Before the end of his hike he'll shed his winter fat and be a stud. He goes through this every summer.

I'm suddenly bowled over by the feeling that we never left, that the whole chunk of time between last summer and now has been compressed into nonexistence. That there's only one life, and it's the life of the trail. But the adults are a little grayer, the children a little taller. Each individual is coming into this hike with a different attitude and set of expectations that inevitably will affect the orchestration of this summer's hikes.

Todd is limping and must consciously think about where he places his feet, even on a smooth dirt road. His ankle is still tender, and one uneven step could lay him up for a week. I'm working hard to use hand signals, for the least bit of speaking sends me into a violent coughing fit. I don't have my strength back, and even flat walking at this high altitude is wearing me out.

Bob admitted he wasn't totally psyched to come out here again, for he's so busy at work that he really shouldn't have left. He literally threw his gear together at the last minute.

To all of this add the mountain range ahead, the Centennials, which supposedly will test our route-finding skills like no other section on this long trail. This summer's hike began at Mack's Inn, the northern border of Yellowstone National Park, Wyoming, three hundred miles farther south than where we finished last year. We'll follow the Idaho-Montana border north, through the Centennial Range, the Beaverhead Mountains, and the southern Bitterroots, until we arrive at Chief Joseph Pass, where our hike terminated last year. Then we'll hop off and shuttle back down to Mack's Inn, hiking south through Yellowstone, the Teton Wilderness, and the Wind River Range. Splitting the hike up this way will let us walk in the lower, drier Centennials first, while the snows are still melting in the higher, rugged Bitterroots.

When we plan our summer's hike, we take each five-hundred-mile stretch and figure out the best way to hike it, trying to minimize our difficulties. It's not usually in a straight line. We don't get caught up in thinking, like some long-distance hikers, that a linear progression is the only way. Each summer's hike is unique. This makes shuttling a challenge.

We're directed through this rolling sagebrush country on a combination of cross-country travel, jeep tracks, secondary roads, and old pack trails. Elevation hangs around 7,000 to 9,000 feet, and it fluctuates radically and frequently with the climbs and descents. No long gentle ridge walks in this section. It's a tough place to break ourselves in.

Route finding requires all of Todd's time and energy. He and Bob spend most of the day with their heads together, studying the map, compass, guidebook, and GPS. Part of the problem comes from needing to read the guidebook backward; every left is a right, every ascent a descent. The men often call a halt if they're unsure of our direction. We lose our way in the sagebrush meadows where game trails intervene and in the forest where downed timber blocks our way. The guys head in separate directions, looking for a clue like an old hatchet mark on a tree that marked the pack trail years ago, while the kids and I wait impatiently.

This first week is wearing on Todd. In addition to never knowing where we are, he hurts his ankle a few times every day. His llamas are acting like meatheads too, especially Chips (alias "chip steak," the king of meatheads). A well-trained pack string is supposed to walk directly behind one another. But on descents Chips pushes the llama in front of him, who in turn pushes the next llama, until they're jogging abreast, herding Todd down the mountainside. Todd walks with both arms outstretched to hold them back, yelling and flicking the lead rope and a stick in their faces. It's only on downhills, but it makes caring for his injured ankle even harder.

Since Todd is often physically and emotionally unavailable to us during the day, most of the burden of keeping Bryce happy rests on me. He demands nonstop monster stories, which I don't have the background for, never having been fond of them myself. And when I talk at any length, I begin to cough uncontrollably. Singing, an old standby for entertainment, is simply out of the question. To Bryce it looks as if we're ignoring him.

At our break this afternoon, Bryce keeps jumping on Bob and grabbing him, no matter how many times we ask him not to. Bob wants to rest, eat, and read the map. So he puts his elbow out to block him, and Bryce runs full steam into it, burying it in his belly. Bryce bounces off and lands on the ground, injured emotionally more than physically. He cries and cries, upset because he can't believe his friend tried to hurt him "on purpose." He can hardly get the words out between sobs, the syllables separated by gasps of air. "Bob . . . is . . . not . . . my . . . friend . . . any . . . more!" he cries over and over.

Bob is crestfallen by the unexpected outcome. He was just trying to get Bryce to stop. It takes some time to calm Bryce, but Bob says over and over that he's sorry and that he loves him. To this Bryce replies, "He's just tricking me. He tricks me a lot."

We tell him he'd better start to choose good behavior, because if this naughtiness continues till he's grown up, he could get himself in trouble with the law. We wink at Bob when we say this. This leads to an hour's discussion on prisons, criminals, inmate behavior, wardens, escaping from prison, and last, Alcatraz. Bryce is fascinated and keeps taking it to the next level. Tonight, he decides, instead of saying, "Bad, bad Brycie," as he does when he gets in trouble, he's going to say, "Good, good Brycie," because he "doesn't want to turn out bad and go to jail."

"Do you think I can turn out good?" the sweetheart asks me.

"Of course. You *are* good."

Bryce finds a totally dried-up shrew on the road today and begs me to let him keep it. It looks as though it's frozen in mid-jump, and my compassionate son's heart goes out to it. Although Todd doesn't think it wise, I let him hold it by its hard tail just until we reach camp, if he promises to wash his hands. He names it Thumpkin and sings and talks to it, telling it how much he loves it for over an hour. I'm amazed at what strange, seemingly insignificant things bring children joy and entertainment on the trail, and how imaginative they are when they're not stifled.

When I see behavior like this, I'm reminded that all young children are inherently good. These behaviors are not unique to my children. What *is* unique is the arena in which they are learning life's lessons—the backbone of the Continental Divide. That's where our challenge lies.

This week's challenge has been that the children can't jump off their llamas and hike any time they need a diversion, for the route has been so rugged and vague. They get bored; they seek attention. Being naughty *always* livens things up. On the trail, there aren't a lot of places to get away from each other (as in poor Bob's case), and there aren't a lot of tools to divert them. This lifestyle, like the land we travel over, is sparse. We have to make the best of what we have. Even Bryce knows that gifts sometime come in the form of a dried-up shrew.

With so much of my attention going to Bryce, my daughter now asks if I love her brother more than her. This year I'm leading Bryce's llama, Monty, instead of Berrick, because Monty isn't as trustworthy and skilled as Berrick and I need to be able to control him in short order. Bryce and I end up talking more, and Sierra feels left out. She's stuck with her taciturn father, directly behind her, who is concentrating on how he places his feet and where to find that east-heading, intersecting jeep track. He would really rather not discuss what she wants to be for Halloween, which is months away, and what she can use to make her costume and mask. So over the top of Bryce's chatter I also try to yell back and conduct conversations with Sierra. It makes me crazy. Between favoring his sore ankle and finding the way, I know my husband is near his limit.

Sierra, thank goodness, is easier to deal with on this trip. She seems to have reached a new level of maturity and takes pleasure in sharing small but important female things with me. We often go off to urinate together. We both seek a little more privacy, as opposed to Bryce, who whips it out no matter where he is or who is around, usually because he waits until the last possible second. Sierra never bothers to bring along toilet paper, so I end up sharing my piece, letting her go first. There's something about crouching behind a tree with your pants down that is very intimate. (In a weird way, pissing with your daughter in the wilderness bonds you!)

I teach her how to wash up in a creek in camp. We go down to the water with our change of clothing, a cook pot in one hand and the peppermint biodegradable soap in the other. I show her how to wash out her soiled underpants first, then use them as a washrag to scrub her body. I show her how to wash handkerchiefs, which are being overworked with everyone's runny noses. The snot rehydrates when wet, and we have to scrub the fabric together to loosen the now slimy boogers. Sierra twists her face up. "It's a gross job, but we gotta do it," we agree, laughing. I think of pioneer women doing laundry down by the stream.

After the chores, we both retire to our chairs and sketch the view in our journals. She puts her pen down to watch me, and I explain foreground, middle ground, and background. The wind is soft and friendly tonight. The light is low and golden. Birds are singing their evening songs, and we've forgotten the day's hardships. "I could sit here forever," she tells me. She looks at me and says, "I love you, Mom." I know it's not just for giving her drawing lessons but also for sharing my toilet paper and washing our bodies by the creek and teaching her how to clean underpants and handkerchiefs. It's for simply wanting her here in my life right now, sharing in this adventure.

I look over at her, illuminated in a wash of sunlight. This is it. These sublime golden moments are the reason my half-lame spouse

and I left our comfortable home, drove two feverish kids and six llamas for five days across the country in the shadow of the pioneers to
face a summer of hardship and the unknown in this wilderness
together.

WE LOSE our way in these Centennial Mountains about twice each
day now. Then we revert to cross-country travel. We're forced up
and down lots of steep knolls and gullies, which is fatiguing. We
pick our way through the knee-deep sea of sagebrush. The dead,
twisted gray limbs scratch our legs like claws, and the curving lower
arms that hug the ground trip us up. But because of our cross-country route, we are given a gift.

We first catch sight of two or three elk moving ahead, across
open spaces in the sparse forest. We hear high-pitched warning
whistles that sound like birds. We are driving them ahead as we
walk, totally unaware of their number. All of a sudden they decide
to herd together and change direction, sprinting across our path,
not twenty yards away. The ground shakes as cows, calves, and stags
with massive racks thunder by, close to a hundred strong. We stare
with open mouths and big smiles. When we reach the spot where
they crossed, the ground is chewed up. On the other side of the
knoll, we traverse an open area and see where the entire herd bed-
ded down in the five-foot-high swaying grass of the meadow. Oval
flat spots of compressed grass look warm and sheltered, tempting us
to curl up and take a rest ourselves. We're exhausted. It's been a
rough first stretch.

There aren't many things in our lives at home that require the
enormous amount of energy, both physical and mental, needed to
repeatedly undertake an adventure like this, summer after summer.
We count on that interim winter period to recharge and psyche us
up enough to travel another five hundred miles come summer. But
this year's hike arrived awfully fast, and it's no wonder our tanks feel
a little depleted.

Mexico is a long way off, and the kids aren't getting any smaller.
Once they weigh more than sixty pounds, they will be too heavy for
our medium-weight llamas to carry, so we are pushing to return
every summer without a year off. Fortunately for us, the mountains

have a wonderful way of feeding us when our hearts are open and willing. And as hard as this first week has been, Todd is now walking normally and we're all feeling healthy, happy, and content about being here.

To end this stretch, we have a nine-mile road walk into the "town" of Monida. Since we parallel I-15 on a service road the entire time, the kids entertain themselves by pumping their arms up and down to get the truckers to pull their airhorns.

A fascinating junkyard welcomes us on the outskirts of this once-bustling town, whose name is a combination of the two states it straddles, Montana and Idaho. Dead truck cabs stick straight up in air like planted tombstones. Goats and horses run with us on the other side of the fence. The ghost storefronts advertise ice cream and a garage, but we can find only one resident. He walks past his loose mare on the weedy front lawn, beer in hand, and greets us. He tells us the town used to be a hot spot for shipping cattle on the railroad, one of the busiest in the West. Now all it offers is a pay phone with a sign announcing, "No local calls," as if anyone were in town to call. We dial our friend Dick Reichle's number in Dillon, Montana, and get ready for some well-deserved R and R.

Dick drove a cement truck for a living until his legs were badly injured in an accident. Now he makes llama gear and equipment under the name Ollie Llamas.

Dick and his wife, Linda, feed us like kings, take us to the rodeo, repair our gear, and give us some coolers for the llamas to carry. After a few days, we feel like extended family.

15

The Beaverhead Mountains
JULY 23, 1996

Now I know the secret of making the best persons. It is to grow in the open air and to eat and sleep with the earth.
        —WALT WHITMAN

MY FEET are in Idaho and my butt is in Montana as I sit here and write in my journal. We are in the Beaverhead Mountains now and will be following the border of these two states until we hit Chief Joseph Pass, our dropping-off point last year. Many times there's a fence along the tops of these dry grassy knolls, for the two states don't want their cows to mix. We follow the fence line as we hike, snaking over the crests of this open, windy land. Mountain blue-birds perch on the wooden fenceposts. We pause to watch great herds of elk running across the lowlands. On the neighboring ridgelines, pronghorn antelope sometimes appear, silhouetted against the bright blue sky. Above us, hawks and eagles dip and soar and play in the wind. They hold themselves suspended in an updraft and just float. Every day we find at least one beautiful feather lying in our path.

The mountains are buff-colored and velvety. Trees are scarce; just an occasional bush of sage. The only bright green is way down in the draws where it's wetter. The steepness of the knolls has relaxed since we left the Centennials, and route finding has become fun. We can see far, and that, together with the never-ending friendly wind, makes it a joy to walk. The kids find themselves jumping off their llamas, holding hands and singing. We see no other hikers in these mountains, no other people at all. Maybe a cowboy in the distance, riding the fences looking for breaks. We are happy.

Beth Ellen has joined us for this stretch, along with Bob. Dick Reichle lent her a llama to help carry her gear and to train him for the packing season. But Gandalf is not doing well. He is balking badly and downright refuses to move, especially when he sees an ascent ahead. Then he visibly gets worked up and sounds as if he's hyperventilating. Pulling so hard on his lead rope makes Beth's back hurt worse than if she had carried a loaded pack. Bob spent the day walking directly behind him, prodding his butt with his umbrella. He teased, "The question is, do I open it before or after?" Toward the end of the day, Gandalf began sitting down, and Bob had to twist his long neck all the way back to his hind end before he'd get up. One time Bob picked up his hind legs like a wheelbarrow. That sent Gandalf kicking and got a good hundred-yard trot out of him. In camp tonight, Beth is pulling grass for him and feeding him out of her hand. Bob says she has a big job ahead of her.

Gandalf is fat and out of shape. He's trying to plug himself into our bad-boy team of seasoned llamas, and he can't cut it. Bob feeds him salt tablets in camp, for the poor boy wouldn't eat or drink all day and Bob's afraid he's dehydrated.

We're camping only feet away from a stock tank tonight, for it's the only flat spot around. Water is scarce this high up on the divide, so most of our water now comes from stock tanks. There won't be any wild animals or even domestic cows coming close to this tank tonight, not with all these llamas around.

Come morning, Beth announces, "Gandalf is loose." "Problem child," Bob mutters.

He must have gotten thirsty in the middle of the night from all that salt and broken free to find water. "I *thought* I heard an animal drinking last night," Beth says, whose tent is staked right alongside the tank, "but I couldn't figure out what it could be."

Now we have a big problem, catching a llama in this big open country. We've heard of loose llamas being stranded in the mountains until winter because they refused to be caught. How long would we stay here trying to catch him before we abandoned him? Would men come up on horseback with a tranquilizing gun? I envision my whole summer being wrecked because of this.

Bob and Todd have a plan. Everyone needs to help, for we might only have one chance at this. Fortunately the boundary fence is intact on the ridge. We all spread out and walk slowly up the draw. We each have a rope (picket lines) that we'll hook together and make into one as we get closer. Bob and Todd move up on each side of Gandalf and tie ropes to the fence, then swing around and close in on him. We all walk quietly toward him, acting as visual boundaries, no one looking directly at him. Todd offers him some cracked corn in a sack (llama granola) that we carry just for this purpose. He slowly grabs his halter, and we all drop to our knees in thanks.

Beth hikes with a cell phone so she can communicate with her family back home in Michigan. Todd takes it and walks eight miles out to a mountaintop where he can finally get service. He calls Dick to come and fetch his poor llama.

Beth is making it a point to join us on every summer's hike now. She always trains before coming out, but we gave her our sickness when we stopped to visit her en route. She's been struggling to get better ever since. That's why she opted to get her own llama to help with her load. But she's a trouper, and if she's having a hard time, it's impossible to tell.

She treats my children as if she were a dear aunt, and they adore her. They take turns hiking with her all day long. Bryce is always slipping his little hand into hers. She reads to them in the evenings from books she brought and carries just for them. Like Bob, she has her own family back home but leaves them to travel with us. It takes a special person to plug into this group and get along so well. As with any family, you've got to take the kids' whining and bickering along with their adoration and love.

Of course anyone is easy to live with when they're happy, and my children's attitudes have taken a 180-degree turn since we left the Centennials and entered the Beaverheads. Their parents' relaxed attitude toward the easier trail and route finding has a lot to do with it.

I watch them on breaks, running off to climb on a fallen tree or slop in a creek. They're "starving their brains out" seconds before we stop, but they immediately forget once they're free to play in the great outdoors. I watch them rip off their clothes for a refreshing swim as soon as we get near a lake. They romp naked, Sierra dancing ballet in an attempt to express her joy.

"What's wrong with us?" I rhetorically ask the adults. "Let's rip our clothes off and join them." Todd sits under a tree, his face dirty and sweaty and greasy. "I'm enjoying the shade," he says.

"Bob! Come on!" Bob is so private he won't even take his boots off to cool his piggies in a creek. He's the type of guy who considers bare feet personal, a part of your body you just don't expose in public.

Well, Beth and I can no longer resist. We tear off our sweaty clothing and dive in, whooping it up. Before long we realize we're being watched from the far side of the lake. Cowboys on horses have raised their binoculars. We rarely see anyone out here, and now we have peeping toms when we're trying to have a little fun. Beth and I laugh. Don't those cowboys ride over for a closer look! We say they're probably placing bets on how old we were. Our youthful figures may have tricked them before they saw our breasts, sagging from years of nursing.

WHEN IT'S breezy on the divide, the kids hike together and hold hands and sing Pocahontas's Disney song, "Colors of the Wind," in their sweet, off-key voices. Bryce in his beat-up cowboy hat, chewing on its rawhide cord, looks like a miniature Jethro from the Beverly Hillbillies. He wears a dancing skeleton pendant around his neck that he named Hosie. Big sister Sierra, in her pink cowgirl hat, frequently puts her arm around him and helps him learn the lines of the songs he can't remember. It's hard to imagine "growing up" on the Continental Divide, but that's what they're doing. Even though it's only two months out of each year, our days are packed so full with adventures that it seems much longer. How can it not feel like your second home after all these months and all these experiences?

Although he's doing much better, Bryce still throws an occasional belligerent fit, like the day we climb Elk Mountain. Elk Mountain is a tawny, massive 10,194-foot dome, the second-highest point on the trail in Montana and Idaho. The view from the summit is outstanding, with the Lemhi Range and the southern Bitterroots framing the northern horizon, our next mountains to traverse. We want to be able to relax up here without feeling pressured by building thunderstorm clouds. But Bryce will not budge. He refuses to hike. He can't be tired, because we've only gone a mile so far today. The problem is over the water bottle. He wants one of his own, not to share with his sister. They're supposed to drink from opposite sides of the rim so they don't get each other's cooties, but to antagonize him, Sierra licked the entire rim before passing it over. He's sitting under a small tree, crying and crying and rubbing his grubby little hands all over his wet face. Todd and I refuse to come down for him, no matter how long we have to wait on this slope.

Sierra grows very concerned and stomps down, saying, "I don't want to leave him. I won't have a little brother then." She coaxes him up by saying he can have her piece of red licorice that she's been saving in her pocket.

"You should have left me!" he sniffs once he joins us. "I *wanted* you to leave me."

Bryce has to walk more because now we're having problems with his llama, Monty. He simply refuses to carry Bryce. He sits down on the trail and won't get up. When he goes down, he scares Bryce, who jumps off and begins to cry. The men have tried all kinds of things, switching him around so Todd leads him, since the llamas don't ever test their trail boss. We've put Monty in the rear to make him move, since not many llamas like being separated from the rest of the herd. It's touchy, because they can't communicate with you and you're never sure whether they're trying to pull something. They usually don't, however, for llamas are extremely loyal. They'll work for you unless something is genuinely wrong.

Old-timer Berrick, Sierra's llama, now has to split his time carrying the two kids. Bryce cooperates by walking more. Todd will carry him in the child pack if he has to, but live weight feels heavier than Bryce's forty pounds.

Todd and Bob both watch Monty's behavior when he refuses to walk, and they wonder if there's something wrong with his conformation. He doesn't limp, but his rear legs look as though they might be too short! They wonder if he's a little arthritic, so they try smashing up aspirin and mixing it with some llama granola. Once in the morning and once at lunch seems to keep him moving.

Bryce doesn't seem to miss riding Monty. He's just as happy to walk unless he's very tired or testing his will as he did on Elk Mountain. Most of the time he's the easier of the two children to entertain.

In camp tonight, I'm busy writing in my journal about this afternoon's episode, not wanting to be bothered, when he struggles out of the willows carrying something. "I've got bones!" he says. "That's nice," I reply, not even looking up. He makes trip after trip. Huge cow bones, so big he can hardly carry them. He sits down and gets out his felt tip markers and draws monsters on the flat areas (pelvic bones are best). He's planning on putting together a puppet show for us. He disappears for more and yells to me to help him. "I can't carry them," he hollers. "It's too big!" When he finally rouses me, I discover they are still stuck together! There is dried meat and sinew on them yet! Of course, he never noticed. He was too busy having fun.

It never ceases to amaze me what these kids find interesting to play with out here. We're waiting at Lemhi Pass for our friends to pick us up and resupply us. This is also Beth and Bob's dropping-off point. The kids are playing with trash they found by the roadside. They bat a plastic milk jug around for over an hour. A gate nearby has a large pivoting pike pole; the kids swing on it and squeal when it bangs into the post. We adults just sit, looking down the road for a vehicle, feeling bored. What happens to us along the way? I have a discussion with Bob about becoming stuffy and bored with life. We examine the difference between childish and childlike, and I tease him about loosening up a bit. But it's a struggle, as it is with my husband.

Todd came up behind me this morning and hugged me and planted a kiss on me. I told him that was the first time he'd shown me any affection in weeks. It's a good thing I have the kids, or I would just shrivel up and die from the lack of being touched. A quick hug or a quick kiss in passing takes no time at all. He said, "This is the hardest job I've ever had. First route finding, then Gandalf, now Monty. It takes up all my energy."

The kids may finally be having fun and feeling comfortable out here, but Todd's work never lets up. As soon as we were rid of Gandalf, Monty became a gimp, which means Todd has to carry Bryce more. I could barely handle carrying him when he was a baby, let alone a heavy, active four-year-old. I feel for him, but I really am starting to miss the husband I used to enjoy. I seem to have left him back in Pennsylvania and replaced him with an ever-distant man.

Like any young couple in love, we used to be all over each other, having sex in every room, several times a day. Then babies, breast-feeding, and sleepless nights entered the picture. Young children's needs left me exhausted and groping for a few precious moments to myself. My poor husband's physical needs faded into the background. Pretty normal.

Add to this Todd's Pennsylvania German upbringing, where an outward show of affection ended on the child's first birthday. Then add his true personality of needing his private space, time to think his own thoughts, even though he's surrounded by a gregarious, chatty family.

Then add the challenging—physically as well as emotionally— arena of the Continental Divide Trail. Retreating into himself is truly survival for him.

But it's leaving me, a passionate Sicilian, feeling starved and lonely. I wonder if the tender daily affection in our marriage has been slowly waning ever since parenthood began, though imperceptibly until now.

The Southern Bitterroots
AUGUST 7, 1996

The second hardest thing in the world is to engage in the challenging process of living intimately and growing with another. The hardest thing in all the world is to live alone.

—UNKNOWN

MANY FEET have trod this path up to Lemhi Pass, long before it became the Continental Divide Trail. For eight thousand years it was an ancient Indian route between Idaho's salmon rivers and Montana's buffalo country and was known as the Blackfeet Road. Hunting parties passed this way, and so did Lewis and Clark, the first white men to cross back in 1804. They had been following the Missouri River for many months, looking for its source and a water route to the Pacific Ocean. When they stood on this pass and surveyed the spectacular vistas of mountains and valleys below, it looked remarkably the same as it does today. Much of the wild

201

Montana Mountains they explored remain unchanged.

There are plaques at the pass with excerpts from Lewis's journals. We read them and feel the intense pleasure and satisfaction
they felt on reaching their goal and surveying this stunning land. A
short distance from the pass is a spring and a camp that is a memor-
ial to Sacajawea, the explorers' female Shoshone guide. There on
the Continental Divide Lewis wrote, "Exultingly we stood with a
foot on each side of this rivulet and thanked God that we had lived
to bestride the mighty and therefore deemed *endless* Missouri."

We do the same. We bend down, cup our hands, and taste the
sweet waters just as they did many generations ago.

Tonight is even more special because we have neighbors, a rare
occurrence in these empty mountains. Our campmates are two gen-
uine cowboys who've spent years working ranches and wanted to
try their hand at riding the Continental Divide Trail. Two horses
named Griz and Buck are tied to the trees, along with a mule. The
men's outfits of old weathered cowboy hats with horsehair bands,
tight cotton jeans, flannel shirts, old sheepskin vests, and pointed
cowboy boots whose toes are reinforced with duct tape let us know
they're the real McCoy and not a pair of wannabes. They are sleeping in bulky cotton sleeping bags with a motif of pointer dogs and
hunters. (Like most real cowboys, they've never heard the mountaineering saying, "Cotton kills.") Our modern backpacking gear,
like a two-and-a-half-gallon water bag that we hang in a tree and
our collapsible foam Crazy Creek chairs, amazes them. They're toting a large wicker picnic basket, a two-burner Coleman stove, and
lots of cans of beans. They have a little dog called Pee Wee who can
do tricks like jump through their arms when they say "big jump!"

Around the campfire tonight, our cowboy friends tell us about
the new horse they just traded for because their old one went lame.
Seems that the horse trader accused them of being too hard on it.
We tell them about Gandalf and now Monty, how we have to feed
him aspirin round the clock to keep him moving. We both decide
that "being too hard" on your animals is relative. What we're out
here trying to do, cover a big chunk of the Continental Divide Trail
through the wilderness, *is* a really hard thing. It's hard on us too,
physically and emotionally. But in one sense our animals are very

healthy, for they're exercising every day and are in great shape. They are healthier than a lot of horses and llamas back on ranches that are fat and out of shape (like Gandalf). We know of llamas that dropped dead from heat exhaustion in the summer after doing nothing but lying around and eating and getting lazy. We suspect that our llamas love hiking from the way they run through the pasture back home when they see the trailer coming, the symbol of a hike. They literally kick up their heels in joy! They *are* pack animals, after all. This is what they were bred to do.

Part of Todd's burden in dealing with Monty (and all his trail boss jobs) has been relieved now that our dear friend Timmy has rejoined us. He pitches in with all the chores, and his ideas for child entertaining never cease. He acts like a snorting stallion when we come across an empty corral, giving the kids rides on his back. In the evenings, if we're camped by a stream, they spend hours sneaking around looking for fish and trying to catch them. He makes up stories all day long while we hike, and in camp he reads to the kids and draws them pictures. They adore him. We all do. He makes my husband happy, which is something I haven't been good at lately.

There is often a distance between Todd and me these days. We aren't connecting on the intimate level that I need and long for—there are no locked gazes, no gentle touches of the hand, no kisses thrown to one another. It's beginning to feel like a business arrangement, this quest for Mexico. I feel drawn to Tim; his light spirit lifts my heart, while Todd's often strained and cool disposition pulls me down. Todd, too, feels drawn to Tim, so the gap between us seems to widen.

The first thing Timmy does after everyone is awake is clap his hands and say, "Damn! It's going to be a great day!" This has a way of putting a smile on our faces first thing. The kids love to say it because it gives them a chance to say a "naughty word." Timmy shows us the importance of playing and having fun no matter what your age.

We've been hiking in a large arc around the expansive Big Hole Valley, the site of an 1877 rout of General John Gibbons and his troops by Chief Joseph and his Nez Percé band, who rallied after their sleeping camp was ambushed at dawn. The forest gives way to expansive vistas of the valley. It's legendary Cowbone Lake that my son's eyes are searching for. The lake was named for about ninety cattle that drowned in the 1920s, whose bones still lie on the bottom. The cattle were being driven up the long, dry Idaho slope across the divide en route to Montana. The thirsty cows spotted the ice-covered lake below them and rushed toward it. Their weight was so great that the ice collapsed. They went crashing through and drowned in the frigid water. Bryce is amazed at the gruesome bones still strewn around our campsite next to the lake. He walks the shoreline in search of more, as they eerily lie half-submerged in the silt.

This whole area is fascinating, for there are many well-preserved cabins of the Darkhorse Mine right along our route. We peer through the window openings to see broken bedsprings and parts of wood cookstoves and try to imagine living and working in these rugged mountains.

THESE DAYS are hot, and the children take off their clothing and ride in just their underpants, their bare toes playing in the llama's wool.

Sierra holds out her arms when a refreshing breeze blows and says, "I feel like I'm taking a wind bath!"

If there's a lake or stream in camp, they rip off their remaining clothes to go frolic. Sierra dances gracefully in the sunlight rays, and I run for my camera. Bryce wants to get in on the action, so he grabs a stick and pretends it's a sword, thrusts out his naked white butt, puts a ghoulish look on his face and says, "Take a picture of me, Mom." I can't keep from laughing and think to myself, How does this happen, this difference in the sexes? This isn't the behavior he's learned from his quiet, gentle dad and a life of no television. It's got to be a male gene thing.

I love swimming with my kids in cold mountain lakes. At the one we've come upon today, their naked little bodies, covered in goosebumps, cling to me as I carry them out into the deep water. Afterward we lie on large rocks that have soaked up the sun's rays to warm and dry ourselves. The kids yell across the lake to the granite cirque we sit in and it echoes their voices. The land is talking back to them, and it tells them of the largeness of their world. I feel as if this lake and these surrounding craggy mountains are all ours, for we're nearly always alone on this trail. Before long they won't be hiking with their little hands in mine or dancing nude in the sunlight for me. I will look back on these diamond days on the Continental Divide Trail and see them as the jewels that they are.

I APPRECIATE the children's intimacy with me because my husband is distancing himself more and more. After Timmy leaves us at Miner Creek, Todd's mood rapidly deteriorates. I can't remember one conversation we've had all day, not even one sentence. He didn't once smile at me or touch me or say, "I love you." When I go to hug him tonight he says he has no time for that, he has chores to do.

I feel as if I'm being punished for something. What, I don't know. For being out here on this hike? Is this something he's doing only for me, and resentment is building up? Maybe he doesn't think I'm pulling my weight with the workload. At home, with privacy and time, I can usually persuade him to open up and share what's in his heart. But I'm running out of energy too, and I can't perform my usual amateur psychologist role to help him figure what's bothering him.

Tonight he's moving the llamas' stakeout ropes a second time because they ate their grass down. They're like lawn mowers, trimming nice and close but never taking the roots. They're very hungry, for they've lost all their winter fat in the past month we've been hiking.

There seems to be something deep going on here. When I was trying to get Todd to open up and talk to me earlier in the tent, wise Sierra said, "Mom, how can you have a discussion or an argument if he's not talking, if it's only one person?"

Bryce doesn't help matters by putting on a performance when Todd takes his socks off his stinky feet in the tent. Bryce pinches his nostrils, yells "Yucky!" half a dozen times, and burrows deep into his sleeping bag, shoving himself into the far corner of the tent. Todd offers to sleep outside.

I say, "Maybe Daddy needs to know we all love and appreciate him." We all take turns saying, "I love you" and giving him a kiss, and with each one his eyes grow softer until I swear I see tears in them.

There is no privacy. We can't hide anything from the children. They look everywhere. They find everything. Their poor father really does love his solitude and *needs* it to maintain his mental peace, but he has none out here with this family circus. As he lies naked on his stomach near sleep, Bryce is singing, "If you like adventure, if you like to travel far." (We tease Todd when he's having a bad day and say, "What's the matter, Pop, don't you like adventure or to travel far?") When he gets to the lines, "All you have to do is read a book, open up the covers and take a look," Bryce leaps on his father's naked back and spreads his buttocks apart as if he were opening a book of great knowledge. As I said, you can't hide anything from children, they look everywhere!

In bed tonight, I ask Todd if he's having a good time out here, and he just shrugs. Once we get into the heart of the spectacular Bitterroot country, I'm hoping he can eke out some joy.

Our guidebook claims the scenery through the southern Bitterroots is some of the most exquisite on the entire 3,100-mile trail. Rugged mountains like Homer Young Peak with its mountain goats and black bears, the parade of granite peaks, the abundance of clear lakes, and the profusion of wildflowers (Sierra and I counted thirty kinds in one thickly laden meadow!) make this section one of the trail's most enchanting secrets.

Three days remain of this long two-week stretch before we reach Chief Joseph Pass, complete the Montana-Idaho section, and shuttle down to proceed south through Wyoming. Our food is down to slim pickings. On every break I run through the list of what remains, and they respond like clockwork, "Is that all there is?" The kids and I believe in Winnie the Pooh's philosophy: "Eat the best food first so the next best food is always the best food." Todd's philosophy is disciplined rationing so your good food lasts the entire time. At least we don't practice Pooh's other philosophy: "Let's eat all our provisions now so we don't have to carry them!"

Eating might be one thing, but when it comes to route finding, I let Todd rule. He's always been fond of shortcuts, however, and they've always scared me. Our guidebook suggests going cross-country over the saddle behind Lana Lake to the Slag-a-melt Lakes, thereby cutting off over five miles of walking. We always have to consider that the guidebook is written for foot travelers, and llamas may have a problem or even find it impassable.

At the bottom of the slope, we tie up the llamas and watch as Todd attempts to climb. The bottom part of the half-mile-long saddle is covered in long, slick, and shiny beargrass. Todd uses his hands for balance and pulls himself up with fistfuls of grass; his legs stretch wide to take big steps. The kids stand by my side, staring up the mountain and say, "I don't think we should do it, Mama."

After a while he descends and stands there without speaking. He's thinking. He needs to make this decision all by himself. When he decides to make the climb it isn't my choice, but I will support him.

Todd and I each lead our strings and instruct the children to climb on their own, stay together, and help one another. They crawl up the slope on their hands and knees. I lead Berrick and Monty, who are strung together, up the first leg, trying to stay well ahead and give them as much lead rope as possible. They leap and pull and huff and puff but make it over the worst. Down below, Todd is having a terrible time with Chips. He will not budge. His feet are planted and his long neck is stretched out while Todd pulls him with all his strength.

"Tie your guys up," he yells, "and come help me! We need to lead them one at a time." They've pulled their saddles off three times, forcing Todd to unload, resaddle, and reload while balancing on the slope. On my descent I slip on the beargrass and scream as I go flying down the mountain, unable to grab on to anything but strands of grass. When I stop, the kids frantically yell from above, "Are you OK, Mom?"

After I calm my racing heart, we lead the llamas up the slope one by one. The more time passes, the more upset Chips becomes, for we're leaving Mr. Stubborn for last. He paces back and forth on his short lead, pulls at the rope, gets tangled. We work fast, climbing quickly so as not to get run over as the llamas leap with their loaded panniers. We can't catch our breaths from the exertion and our soaring adrenaline. The kids soothe the llamas that have already been brought up. Whenever we let out a shriek when a llama runs us over, the kids quickly yell from their post to see if we're all right.

When we safely get them to a more gradual slope, poor Chips' legs are shaking. I've been through an ordeal myself. I hug my little children, so grateful for their good behavior—never complaining or whining when the going gets rough. They just do what we need them to do when they know we're depending on them. At times like this, we're reminded we're all in this together.

I feel grateful to our llamas too, who will follow almost anywhere and do almost anything we ask of them, even if they think they can't or if it goes against their better judgment. When I think of the one-foot-wide bridges or the narrow trails on steep slopes with 2,000-foot drop-offs that I've led Berrick across with my young daughter on his back, we are talking trust and loyalty. It's amazing to see these traits in an animal. It makes them seem almost human.

Todd doubted his decision very early in the climb. He admitted, "I can see this was the wrong decision," but I said nothing, just grateful no one got hurt.

That night in bed, I can't sleep. I lie awake thinking of the day and how alone I feel, even though my husband is right by my side. I wake him and ask him, "Have I done something to hurt your feelings these last weeks?"

"No," he replies.

"I don't feel a lot of love and warmth coming from you. You don't touch me. You don't talk to me. Do you think the love has gone?"

"I feel so driven," he tells me. "To get up and get the llamas ready, get us down the trail so we can finish and come back next year. I'm working harder out here than any job I've ever done. I feel as if I have no energy or time left over for any affection or even conversation."

"You probably never wanted to come out here this year, but you just did it for me, then spent all these miles resenting me. I never wanted you to come unless *you* wanted to come."

"I did," he says.

"Maybe you were trying so hard to make me happy that you forgot about your own needs and desires. I don't care about getting to

Mexico or my dream of writing a book about our family's adventure, not if it's going to put our relationship in jeopardy. We both have to hold the dream in our hearts or it won't work."

So I suggest, "Why don't we consider going home early? Leave Wyoming's Wind River Range for another time. Look at it as a compromise."

We were planning on hiking another couple of weeks through the high and remote Wind River Range in Wyoming. Our target finishing date in mid-September is getting late to be in the high mountains, with the growing cold and approaching snow (especially with young children). No access roads cross the Winds for 150 miles, increasing the risk should we run into trouble. Saving this rugged range for a fresh year immediately relieves the pressure on Todd's mind.

"But won't we have failed, then?" he asks.

"Don't you believe you need to have your heart in something or it isn't worth it?"

"What about the affection problem?" he asks next.

"I don't want tons of affection or conversation," I say. "Just a connecting smile or a pat when you walk by."

I want us to be more aware of each other. It isn't lack of time—we just aren't considering each other. We're both doing it. We used to sleep with our sleeping bags zipped together, but we stopped after we had kids. Even last year on the trail, Todd would wake up after the kids went to sleep, and we'd lie there in the candlelight and quietly talk and look at each other. Now he goes right to sleep.

I begin to cry and say, "I just miss you." I pull him close and hug and kiss him, and we go to sleep holding each other.

Come morning, he doesn't blast out of the tent to start "working" the way he normally does but rolls over with his warm brown puppy-dog eyes—the first time I've seen that out here this year—and just looks at me lovingly. We lie in bed for an hour until our kids wake up on their own, without being roused. We break camp an hour later than usual and even get lost, but he doesn't bat an eye. He relaxes on breaks, let's us eat whatever we like, and waits until *I* say I think we should get going. The change in his behavior is like night and day, and we are all happier for it.

I used to be closer to my husband before we had children. Now my children demand center stage. Most wives force their husbands into second place without even being conscious of it. Husbands tend to lose out when children enter the scene, for we women now have to do a balancing act to meet everyone's needs. The more years that go by, the easier it is to forget about nurturing the relationship; you figure it will just run on what you had in the past. It's not our fault that we begin to consider each other less. It *is* our fault if we neglect to bring it to each other's attention and do nothing to change it. There isn't much you can hide out here. This CDT stage seems to magnify every aspect of life and hold it up to be examined. It doesn't let you merely muddle through. The heart has to be involved. Anything less won't work.

17

Yellowstone
AUGUST 22, 1996

Jars of spring water are not enough. Take us down to the river.
—RUMI

WHEN WE WALK into Yellowstone National Park on the Continental Divide from the park's west boundary—along an ascending road walk from Mack's Inn, Idaho, in the valley of Henry's Fork—we seriously consider turning around. Our first view of the oldest and most popular park in America is of the utter devastation caused by the most destructive of all the 1988 Yellowstone fires.

Mile after mile of totally burned forest exposes us to the hot summer sun. When we seek shade, there are only narrow strips from individual skeleton trees, and the four of us line ourselves up back to back for a break, all shifting every five minutes as the earth rotates.

Very little vegetation has come back to this area, because the North Fork Fire incinerated all the ground cover and overstory as well. The kids hide from the sun under their cowboy hats and ask for wet bandannas to swab their faces. At four and six years old, their sweat glands are not developed enough to rid their bodies of excess heat. Todd and I lick our lips and search the draws for "green," for dampness and the presence of water. But the dry draws are clogged with forest debris, bulldozed by long-gone rushing water when melted snow and rain ran over the naked earth. This land is dying of thirst.

We flag down a pickup and ask the driver if he knows of any springs nearby.

He tells us about the less than enchanting "Piss Pot Spring," which sounds, from his directions, as if it's far off our route. And there's another one—perhaps—at an old poacher's cabin with the door nailed shut and sawblades in the windows to keep bears out. But he hasn't been there in eleven years and doesn't know if it still exists.

Latham Spring is supposed to be along our route, according to our guidebook. There is bulldozing all around the jeep road that leads to it, so whenever I see a dirt pile that's pushed to the side, I investigate it. I step over blackened twigs and dry dead grass that's so crispy it seems as if it could reignite by spontaneous combustion. Grasshoppers ping from the grass whenever I take a step. I peer into the draw and report, "Nothing. All dry."

But Eagle Eye Sierra drops lower down and suddenly yells, "I see a pool of water!" We can hardly believe it. Long, luxurious grasses grow around a pool that moves with just the slightest trickle. She is so proud, because all of us, including the llamas, want water badly.

Things like this really build a child's self-worth. In our "other lives" we parents are always reminding them to pick up after them-selves, to do their chores. They must feel as if they create more work for us instead of being assets. Even though we tell them we love them, it's important that they feel needed and valuable. Finding water for us all, especially when her mother craved it but missed seeing it, especially when we were all so thirsty, was a loud message saying, "You're needed."

We are soon stopped in our tracks, for the trail completely disappears at the edge of a very recent burn. Everything is black: the carved stumps, sculpted by the flame tongues, even the soil itself. There are dozens of small fires in the park like this one that are monitored and left to burn small areas of two to three acres. The land looks as though it's still in pain, as if it had burned only yesterday.

Todd suddenly realizes that our llama, Jerry, is hurt. He is limping badly, and we surmise that one of the sharp branches from the many downed trees has bruised his leg. We divide Jerry's load among the other llamas and pull our kids off so the llamas have less weight to carry. They are expending too much energy trying to leap over the downed trees.

A ranger later tells us that a severe windstorm came through a few days ago, forcing trail crews to clear up to 250 trees in any given five-mile stretch of trail. The standing dead wait for the freeing winds to knock them into their graves. The trails leading directly to popular areas are the first to be cleared. The low-priority trails, such as the boundary trail we are on, may not get attention for years.

By the time we reach Summit Lake, we feel like refugees in a war. Our hands and faces are black from rubbing up against the charcoaled trees. Flushed, hot, and exhausted, the kids and I rip off our filthy clothes and head for the shallow warm waters of the lake. My water sprites dance and sing, sunlight shines on their glistening bodies, and all our hardships melt. We are disappointed with Yellowstone. We tend to equate "scenery" with "greenery," and we've seen little of that in these first miles. Gifts can be given only if the receiver is open to them, however. Yellowstone is a changing park, and if we don't change our attitude, we'll miss out on an unparalleled opportunity to witness nature operating on a scale rarely seen anywhere on earth. In the next days we'll discover this.

After Jerry hurts his leg, we talk about going home. On breaks, he can't seem to find a comfortable position. He walks like a chicken, bobbing his head with each step. Stopping only makes the leg stiffen up. We feed him even more aspirin than Monty. Yet no one feels ready to go home yet, even though the going has been rough.

The kids can't ride through the blowdowns. It's too hard on the llamas to leap over fallen trees with them on their backs. Bryce's cream-colored cowboy hat is all black on top from ducking under burned tree trunks. These kids are working hard. They don't always take the most direct route around the blowdowns, thereby adding more miles to the day, but they're good sports and rarely complain.

When they can ride, they take turns listening to story tapes with a Walkman (two tapes each per day). Their cowboy hats perch precariously on top of their headphones, and they stare, mesmerized, as they listen. When the rabbit in *Alice in Wonderland* sings out, "I'm late, I'm late, for a very important date," and the Seven Dwarfs sing "Hi-Ho, Hi-Ho!" the kids can't contain themselves and belt out the lines along with them, their voices echoing through the Yellowstone backcountry. I can't help but laugh. They're making the best of a not-so-ideal situation.

Yellowstone is most famous for its hydrothermal features: its brilliantly colored hot pools, steaming fumaroles, terraced springs, bubbling mud pots, and over three hundred spouting geysers, all volcanically produced. To the Native Americans, the Yellowstone region was known as the Land of the Evil Spirits, and most tribes avoided it. Certain precautions must be taken even today, although most of the thermal areas have safety catwalks. Many people have been seriously injured by falling into scalding hot springs.

Because of the danger, we shorten up the lead ropes on our llamas. Llamas are very inquisitive by nature: they peer into the steaming, spitting, belching holes that are only inches from the trail and seem to say, "What's in there? Is it alive?" Sulfur stench rises, and they flare their nostrils and snort when they catch a whiff. Todd's string gets so worked up that they jump off a catwalk, wanting to be on the ground, which to their brains seems safer.

Back in the 1800s these hot springs kept alive a man named Everett, who was doing some mapping in the Yellowstone area. He fell off his horse, which promptly ran away, broke his glasses, and found himself alone for thirty-six days. To keep from starving, he ate a spiny-looking thistle that grows up to eight inches wide, and he sat in the hot springs to keep from freezing. After he was rescued, he was in such rough shape from constipation that they fed him bear grease and named the plant in his honor. We imagine munching these "vittles" as we walk by and suddenly feel blessed with our boring beef jerky and dried fruit.

After visiting Black Sand Basin thermal area, as we're hooking our boys together, Berrick suddenly begins to sound his warning call. We jump and peer in the direction the llamas are all staring, trying to see what the fuss is about. Buffalo! If I were a three-hundred-pound llama, I'd consider a two-thousand-pound bison a threat too. Half a dozen of them are walking across the blacktop road at the painted crossing like obedient tourists and are heading right for us!

You don't want to get too close to a bison. Though they are generally docile creatures, they are unpredictable, and these are wild—the last wild buffalo on earth. Yellowstone's herd fluctuates between about 2,500 and 3,500, depending on how hard the winter is and whether they venture out of the park in search of food. Our llamas try to walk forward while looking backward, shoving each other and us in their fright. The kids won't ride them when they're flipping out, so Todd puts Bryce on his back in the child carrier. Because the meadow we're crossing is marshy, Sierra can't make any time. Todd adds her to his shoulders, making ninety pounds of extra weight. For a mile, the bison follow us through a long meadow heading toward Old Faithful.

We escape into the developed area around Yellowstone Lodge, and as we drink cans of soda in the cool shade of a maintenance building, someone finds us fascinating. "Last year President Clinton was here with all his Secret Service men," a park worker says to us, "and now this year it's you!" We're surprised that our new friend puts our visit to Yellowstone on the same level as that of our nation's president, but I suppose our company of gypsies including six beasts of burden is quite an oddity. Todd leads four packers, and I lead the way with my two kid-carrying llamas. The kids sit up there with their cowboy hats pulled low, singing, laughing, or chattering, swaying to the rhythm of their beasts. Bells dangle from the llamas' necks to alert any grizzlies. On road crossings, we often turn to see what stopped all the cars and what people are photographing, but it's often just us. If there's no wild game crossing the road, I suppose we're a good substitute.

We look wild enough. Every now and then I see myself in a big mirror, like the one in the bathroom of the maintenance building, and I'm shocked. Dark brown, sunbaked skin; red, weatherbeaten face; charcoal smudges on my skin and clothing. An office worker visits the john and politely asks, "Just starting out on a trip?" I can't help myself, and laughingly reply, "Do I *look* like I'm just starting out?" This is part of backcountry living, however, and you realize how far you've strayed from the rules of society only when you reenter it.

On the trail to Shoshone Lake today, my eyes feel opened for the first time to Yellowstone's new type of beauty. We see tremendous examples of forest regeneration. Pine saplings two to three feet high grow in lush green grass that a llama would die for. They are backlit with sun, and their new growth appears almost incandescent with light. It is so encouraging to see the forest coming back. In other places, pearly white everlasting flowers grow in bunches among the stark black stumps. I'm amazed at how much beauty there can be in a burn.

The shallow bottom of beautiful Shoshone Lake is sandy, and the water is exceptionally clear. We walk out hundreds of yards into the vast blueness. It feels so refreshing to wash away the soot from my body and, with it, my preconceived notions about fire and beauty.

From Shoshone Lake on, magic seems to happen daily as we wind our way through the park. To begin with, after a day or two of serious limping, Jerry is miraculously healed. We don't have to go home yet! Moose follow us for two and a half miles over a ridge above the swampy meadows at the far end of the lake. One night we hear wolves howl, part of the new pack that was successfully reintroduced to the park in 1995. It sends a shiver of excitement through us to sleep in a wild place. In the morning mist, a pair of tall and retiring sandhill cranes circle our site. Another time we hear the blast of the formerly endangered trumpeter swan. And there are grazing herds of elk with their blond rumps and huge racks. In the full moon over Heart Lake, we hear loons calling. One far in the distance wails mournfully as though calling for its lost mate. The one close by does the more excited staccato call, as if frantically saying, "I'm here! I'm here! Find me! Find me!" I feel as though Todd and I have made some progress toward finding each other again, but we have to keep working on it. The best marriage can't function on autopilot under the easiest conditions, let alone in the challenging arena of the Continental Divide.

WE'RE FOLLOWING the Heart River out to the park boundary and then into the Teton Wilderness. Fall seems to be advancing faster and faster. The water shimmers in the sunlight, and our view is clear through the burned trees to the winding river below. The ground is covered with blazing fireweed, which has now put on its autumn dress. It's fascinating to see how the fire came so close to the river and then petered out, unable to burn the trees and the land when the moisture content became too high. In these days we've learned to "think" like fire. We've observed its patterns, its personality, and learned its story by the mark it has left behind on the land. We have more respect for it and more gratitude to the earth itself for knowing how to heal without our interference.

Our postcard image of what Yellowstone and wilderness should look like has changed. We wanted Yellowstone "fixed," and we wanted it done quickly. But nature works on its own schedule. It scars and heals on a scale of centuries with no regard for our human shortsightedness and selfish desires. Perhaps one of Yellowstone's most important lessons is to help us broaden our perception of wilderness beauty and to teach us the humility to allow nature to work at its own pace.

18

The Teton Wilderness
AUGUST 28, 1996

There is only one world, the world pressing against you at this minute.
—STORM JAMESON

WHEN I FIRST hear the eerie sound in the wilderness night, I am the only one awake in our tent. I finish recording the day's happenings in my journal by candlelight, blow out the flame, zip up my sleeping bag, and close my eyes.

Suddenly my eyes fly back open at the sound of a high-pitched scream. It reminds me of children's voices at an amusement park, only muffled and far away. Todd snores softly by my side. The kids are hunkered down in their bags, hats on, for it is late August and already quite cold in the Wyoming mountains. Bryce's thumb is poised by his parted lips; it slid out when he fell asleep. Sierra clutches her teddy bear.

There it is again. I listen with my eyes wide open, as if they

218

could help me hear more distinctly. Now it sounds like whistles, some far off, others close up. Why, it's elk bugling! They're calling for mates! I rouse Todd, and together we lie on our backs in the darkness, smiling, listening to the symphony. All night long they call from all sides of the forest. We feel like privileged guests in their wild world.

When fatigue finally overtakes me and I fall asleep, I'm awakened by another strange sound, a ripping noise right by my head, followed by a more leisurely chewing sound. I rustle my sleeping bag, and whatever is out there bounds away. In a few minutes it is back. I call out, and once again I scare it away. Todd is too tired to care. In the morning the mystery is solved. A deer had been eating grass and small plants by the tent right where we had all urinated before turning in for the night; it must have been attracted to the much-needed salt.

We're sleeping right by the wooden sign announcing our entrance into the Teton Wilderness–Jim Bridger National Forest in northern Wyoming, first established as a primitive area in 1934 and boasting 585,468 acres of roadless country. Yellowstone National Park butts up against its northern border. When you enter a wilderness area by trail, the sign at the border is the only apparent change in the land, at least until you get into the depths of the wilderness. But the animals here have ways of letting you know before the sign's announcement.

We had seen subtle changes miles before we reached the official border. Until this point the sandy trail had been covered with various-sized boot and sneaker tracks with a huge variety of swirls, lines, and tread patterns, heading in both directions. Abruptly, deer, elk, and bear tracks replace them, covering the trail in the same profusion as the people tracks. Suddenly we feel we are in *their* country.

When you enter the Teton Wilderness from the north, you follow the Heart River downstream and the Snake River upstream. Following a river elicits a different mind-set than hiking through other kinds of terrain. It's never static. Your mind doesn't drift as much. We watch the Snake River as we walk along its bank. We look for waterfalls and deep emerald pools and listen to its gushing roar. When we are high above it, watching how it curves and snakes, how the bank on one side is steep and greatly eroded, we understand why the trail was built up here safely above it. We look down the river's course to Mount Sheridan, which stands guard over Heart Lake, our campsite a few nights ago. We look at the width of the gravel bars and are moved with respect as we realize how wide the river can get in high water and snow runoff season. It can be a raging, churning wild animal, impossible to ford. It is much friendlier now, about one-third its capacity. For practice, we study the channels, watching for places we could ford, and we look for game going to the bank for a drink.

Few humans are here. The heart of the Teton Wilderness is virtually undiscovered by hikers and backpackers. For the most part the trails follow the drainages and valleys and open bottomlands and avoid the more exciting craggy skyline. But these glacier-scoured valleys are very handsome, with abundant water, good campsites, and feed for the llamas. The trails are easy, and they are safe. Ninety-six percent of the use here is by horse packers, and they widen the trail to twelve feet in some stretches and groove the meadows with up to sixteen parallel tracks, evenly spaced like plowed furrows. If you're here in the wet season, you see firsthand how horses' hooves can pound the soil into mud. But now, in late August before hunting season begins, the trail is dry, the packers are resting, and we have the country all to ourselves.

There isn't a lot of wind in these protected valleys compared with the ridges right on the Divide. Up there it never seems to cease, but in these Teton valleys all is calm. The sun is warm, and you want to soak up these last golden days of summer. Todd is now leading Sierra on Berrick; we think the long-distance hiking has finally done the old boy in. He's going on fourteen and is still able to pack, but he's developed an attitude this summer. He emits a deep throaty moan on climbs and stops to urinate about half a dozen times on each ascent. He only lets out a little squirt each time; it must be his way of taking a breather. When he stalls I lag too far behind, so Trail Boss gets him now, since our llamas can't say no to their master.

"What do you want to talk about today, Daddy?" Sierra asks Todd. "If I had my pick," he replies, "I would rather be quiet. If I *had* to talk, it would be about building sheds back home—finishing the hay barn, putting a porch on Mom's writing cabin, building a pigpen and a solar shower."

I think my husband might be just as happy homesteading and working on our land, whereas his wife's wanderlust grows more passionate with each year. Being the more assertive of the two, I often get my way simply because he's easygoing and doesn't care as much. And his heart is so big and good that he always puts me first. Perhaps Todd learned this summer that when he has strong feelings he needs to speak up and take care of himself. This summer may have been a time when we should have leaned more heavily toward Todd's needs of staying home than toward my need for adventure.

As we climb out of the lowlands to Two Ocean Plateau, a patch of open country 10,000 feet high with outstanding views in all directions, the wind picks up. Our guidebook advises an overnight stay in clear weather, recommending a nearby pond as a water source. The water level is very low, and we must walk out far until the cracked and dried dirt turns to squishy mud by the water's edge. Here in the mud a story is written of every creature that lives on this plateau and visits the watering hole for a drink. Very large, very fresh bear tracks sink deep from the animal's weight, and Todd puts his own paw down to compare the shape and size. "Black bear, no grizz," he says.

The llamas are spooked. Their sensitive noses can discern the individual animal scents, while we humans detect nothing. They look around nervously, as if expecting to see a local resident lumber over a knoll and find us in his home. We feel like trespassers, as if we're peeking in someone's refrigerator or dresser drawers, snooping into their private lives and habits. We fill our water bag and go over a knoll, out of sight of the pond, not wanting to bother any animals that may come for a drink tonight. Within the Teton Wilderness all food and beverages, as well as scented and flavored toiletries, must be hung out of reach of bears, but it's hard to find a good food-hanging tree on the plateau. Many campsites have food storage racks already constructed. One of the kids' favorite treats in camp is a homemade swing. Todd throws two ropes over the horizontal pole, ties them to a length of firewood, and folds a Crazy

Creek chair over it as a cushion. Since the food poles are twenty feet off the ground, this makes for a very long swing and a very high ride. But no screams of delight will be heard on the plateau tonight, for there isn't a food pole in sight. The view and the immense beauty of this place, however, are worth the search for a food-hanging tree.

It takes a long time for the llamas to settle down to eating and chewing their cuds. There is so much land to check out, so much territory to scope for movement, for danger approaching. But we are in heaven. We carry our guidebook and compass up different knolls and read aloud about the views and mountain ranges that surround our spot on all sides. The mountains in the east are shrouded by a scrim of forest-fire smoke, with long orchid and mustard-colored waves rising above the peaks. In the west, the jagged skyline of Grand Teton (13,766 feet) towers over Jackson Lake and looks flat and ethereal, as though it's been cut out of light blue construction paper and pasted in the sky as a backdrop. The beauty of being up here is that you can see where you came from, trace the drainages and understand how the land is formed, and see where you are going. It's like running your eyes over a huge relief map. Mount Washburn and Specimen Ridge, gateposts for the Grand Canyon of the Yellowstone River, are visible beyond the flat expanses of Yellowstone Lake and the Hayden Valley.

To the south lie the sheer cliff of razor-edged Soda Mountain and the Soda Fork Valley in front of it, tomorrow's destination. We watch the sun go down, and because we are high and in the open, we are all up early enough the next morning to see it come up on the opposite side of the plateau. When our children study the solar system at home, they make planets and the sun out of balls of aluminum foil and hang them by strings in shoeboxes. But it's all beginning to make sense to them out here, where they can see the horizon, understand the roundness of the earth, and witness the circle of the day from a place like Two Ocean Plateau.

Down off the side of the plateau lies a very special place called the Parting of the Waters, where the grandness of the thing rattles us and fills us with wonder. The Blackfeet Indians of Montana called the Continental Divide the center of the world. It is the central point not just for North America but for South America as well, for it splits the river systems of two continents from the Bering Sea to the tip of Patagonia. No other divide separates drainages in such continental proportions, sending rivers not only in two directions but to two oceans.

And here at Two Ocean Creek, a small stream so gentle and friendly you can ford it by merely rock hopping with your boots still on, you can see the Divide at work. A small spit of land, a tiny tongue of a peninsula, big enough for only a few people to stand on, rises from the creek, pushing up the land, splitting the stream in two. One tiny tributary goes off to the Pacific Ocean, 1,353 miles away, while the other, Atlantic Creek, must roll 3,488 miles before reaching its resting spot in the Atlantic.

The children slop in the creeks barefoot, uninterested and unable to grasp what is happening here. Todd and I stare at the sign and try to visualize these two tiny streams on their long journeys, growing wider and picking up volume as streams are added and the miles roll by.

When we walked on the Divide itself, when the Rockies were gentle and the tread easy, you knew the backbone you traveled on split the country's watercourses in two. But on the summit, you don't usually see the waters, at least not actually dividing and going their merry separate ways as they do here. We stand in the creek, straddling the tiny peninsula, the water pouring over our left feet going home, the water over our right feet heading to California. We feel like titans, with our feet in different oceans and our heads up in the clouds. We are striding along the spine of this continent, drinking from mountain streams and using rocks for pillows. As I watch the sparkling rills, I remember that I am 65 percent water. I have more in common with this quicksilver stream than with the rocks, boulders, and clay that are holding me up. I toss in a stick, and as it heads toward the Atlantic, where we'll be returning soon, I send along a silent prayer for our loved ones on the East Coast.

Our guidebook says that the north fork of Soda Creek could be hazardous to ford early in the season because of snow runoff. We don't expect any trouble in late August, when there isn't a snow patch in sight, but as we stand on its bank and look at the swift, rolling water with peaks indicating the boulders lurking beneath, we are a bit shaken.

"How do you want to do it?" Todd asks. We have some options, and a situation like this call for an evaluation. Todd will carry Bryce on his back, and Sierra will remain astride trusty Berrick.

I cross first with the pack string of four, moving cautiously yet swiftly. You don't want to dilly-dally; the llamas are always eager to have it over, so they step lively. The ones in the rear get pushy and upset the first ones into going quicker than they should. Since I'm in their way, I get the same treatment, so I walk with my arms spread out trying to keep them back. At the same time, the icy water pushes against my upper thighs. I grit my teeth and seek out a flat spot between the boulders with one sandaled foot before placing the other. Part of my brain concentrates on the river, the other on the animals breathing down my neck. Once across, I bound up the bank and jump aside, for the llamas always leap out of the water after a particularly hairy ford, with no regard for their leader. Todd, with his longer legs, greater strength, and well-behaved llamas, has little trouble. This is our last ford in this country of many crossings, and I'm not sorry to dry my feet for the final time.

As we draw near the end of our hundred-mile stretch at Brooks Lake and the highway to Dubois, Wyoming, the horse packers are entering the mountains. Bow-hunting season opens in a few days, and they're coming in to set up camp. The first and last rider in the string look like real cowboys, with old cowboy hats stained with sweat and weather, worn for protection, not for the image, and having a content, at-home look. The guys in the middle wear baseball hats and sweatshirts silk-screened with university team logos and cotton-lined nylon windbreakers embroidered with their softball teams' names. They're probably from back east, out for the hunting trip of their lives. They could be our neighbors. After they pass the air smells of horse urine and manure, grassy smells of meadows recycled as the smells of the West.

With the arrival of the hunters, so too comes autumn—or perhaps I should say winter, for the mountains often skip a season. Just last week in Yellowstone, we were swabbing ourselves with wet bandannas to stay cool. This morning our water bottles are frozen. We wake up cold in the night and have to put on long underwear and hats. "Any day it could snow," we say as we watch the mare's tails or angel hair clouds high in the atmosphere—cirrus clouds (or "serious clouds," as we call them), the forerunner of an icy front. We want to get out before the snow flies. When the thermometer dips low, you can really burn up the food trying to stay warm. But very little appeals to us anymore. After two months of traveling in the backcountry, we're craving homemade food. We're putting mustard on everything these last days, even granola bars and dried apples, for it's the most flavorful thing in our sack. We think about our decision to call it quits after the Tetons, and we feel it's the best thing we could have done.

Once we finish, Todd is planning to hitchhike back to Mack's Inn to get our truck. I teasingly say, "He should get a ride unless he looks too scary."

"He could take a bath," Sierra suggests, "and wash his hair, and you could comb it for him, Mom, 'cause I don't think he knows how."

How well these children know their father. I don't think he has combed it for two months; it's a good thing he had it cut short before we started this trip. On the trail, appearances don't matter. There is no "society" out here to pass judgment on you. That's one of the luxuries this lifestyle affords. What it costs in inconvenience, it gives back in other ways.

Upper Brooks Lake, a gorgeous blue eye of the earth, is just the kind of place to spend the last night of a long journey. You'd expect it to be crawling with boaters, campers, and fishermen, and it would be if it were close to a road. But the area is wild, and we have it all to ourselves. After our last trail dinner, the kids lead me through the laurel thicket maze down to the high grasses by the lake. We lie on our backs in each other's arms, watching the clouds race by overhead. "Tomorrow we head home," I announce. "This is home," replies Sierra. Her response takes me by surprise, for although I know our kids enjoy the wilderness, children of this age usually equate home with comfort and security. Here they must do without their toys, their regular beds, their pets, and all the things they're used to. As adults, we're not much different. How can such a wild, unknown place come to feel so familiar? A place can't feel like home if you just observe it from a scenic overlook. You mustn't be distant from it. You must live in it. You have to immerse yourself in the sylvan streams, the sunrises and sunsets, the sound of the bugling elk. Living with the Tetons makes them yours. It's a different kind of ownership, a different kind of home, and it's perhaps more lasting.

AFTER SPENDING a chunk of time in the wilderness, reentering can sometimes be a shock. This summer we don't even reach our home state before we get yanked back to reality.

In Wisconsin, we get off the interstate and stop in a tiny town for a break, looking for a park with a playground. We park our trailer of llamas, their curious heads poking out the openings. It looks as if there's an adult softball team picnic going on, and I pass near folks on my way to a picnic table. I try to make eye contact, but no one looks at us, nods, smiles, or says hello. It's obvious we are travelers passing through. I suddenly feel terribly sad. I want to say to them, "Our family has just been walking the Continental Divide, across the rooftop of our gorgeous country. We saw where our great rivers begin. We followed them down from their heights. The beasts that carried our children are just over there in the parking lot. You have llamas in your town, and you aren't even interested. You have an adventuring family right here in your picnic grove, and you won't even make eye contact, let alone share a small pleasantry. We aren't any different from you, for we're all travelers on this planet. You might be adventurers in your own lives—fighting cancer with a parent, starting a new business."

I felt less alone when we were isolated from the closest human by miles of wilderness. It breaks my heart that after two months of living in the mountains with nature and wild animals as our companions, here I am, back with my own species, and there is no connection. It's as if there's been a break in the line.

PART FOUR

THE CONTINENTAL DIVIDE TRAIL

Through Wyoming, 1997

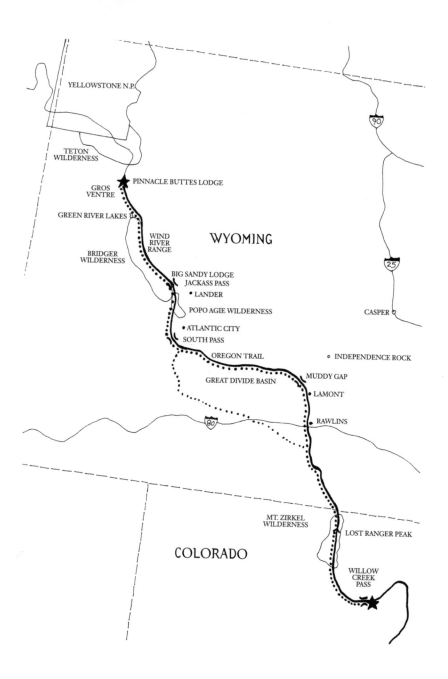

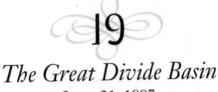

19

The Great Divide Basin

JUNE 21, 1997

A rough road leads to the stars.
—FROM THE LATIN

SOME SAY there's nothing in Wyoming's Great Divide Basin, but I beg to differ. It's devoid of what we're *used* to seeing—telephone poles, electric lines, pavement, buildings, and people. There *is* a lot of sky and sage and antelope and wind and sunlight, and I like it this way.

In central Wyoming, the Continental Divide splits to form the rims of a basin a hundred miles wide. Since this bowl is so huge and the soil is so porous, all the water running into it sooner or later dries up. The dry land is vast and open; it is not entirely flat but has gently rolling hills covered with sparse, sweet-smelling sage. Wyoming is our least inhabited state, and this Great Divide Basin is the least inhabited place in the entire country. What a place to begin this summer's hike!

During the day, we watch lizards scurry at our feet and prong-horn antelope run on the plains. No matter which direction you look you see the antelope, dozens and dozens in a day. By afternoon rain clouds build up, and off in the distance you can see the rain falling through the sky in great gray sheets. But the air is so dry that it absorbs all the moisture before it ever hits the ground.

We are busy route finding all day long, looking at the map and taking compass readings. There are so many jeep tracks that to keep your bearings you must hold the lay of the land constantly in your mind—anticipate that gulch coming in from the right or that willow-lined gorge running out to the left. You have to be aware of passing time, your pace, and how much ground you've covered so that you're ready for that jeep track intersection, for there could be three west-traveling tracks within half a mile. Todd fluctuates between knowing exactly where we are and being extremely pleased with his route-finding performance and feeling completely lost. No one else is with us this first stretch, so I help him as best I can.

There are many cows out here on the open range, grazing on public land. The kids entertain themselves by trying to identify them. They look for pregnant cows, wondering when they'll drop their calves; they try to decide which calves belong to which moms and how old they are; they especially like to look for bulls, scouting for their hanging testicles, wondering if size is in direct correlation with meanness. We aren't afraid of them, for they rarely even acknowledge our passing, but it's fun to speculate. Passing close to these "bad boys" always sends a shiver up Bryce's spine, as if they'd charge him and liven up his day.

BEING IN this wide, open land with all this sky has a way of exposing you. This sparse country makes me feel raw and very emotional. I don't feel like myself this summer. I feel lacking, incomplete, restless. Maybe it's my age and the time of life I'm in. Part of my heart is at home, and I search the landscape for answers to questions I'm not sure I have the right to ask.

My Catholic faith of forty-two years has left me wanting. After our hike last year, we returned to our church and a priest who is fond of preaching hell and damnation and sin. After one Mass, Sierra said, "We leave here feeling worse. I feel closer to God on the trail. Why do we go?" And I started to wonder that myself.

My work as a travel writer has begun to feel stilted and unfulfilling. Stories come out of me like rote formulas, and I long to write about the heart and soul of my life and to find the courage to look at the dark places inside me, the questions, the things that move me.

Last year's hike was hard on my marriage. I was drained from the effort to get Todd to give me more affection and attention when his plate was already overflowing with responsibilities. This summer's hike will be no different, with its many challenges vying for his energy, and it worries me. A good enough marriage doesn't feel good enough anymore.

In the Great Divide Basin, you can walk the rim and hug the true Divide. Or you can drop down into the basin and follow alternative routes. There are choices, but they don't seem monumental because they all come together at the end and lead to Mexico.

But it's said that there are only a few truly crucial junctures in any life. Take a misstep at such a moment and it will shape the rest of your journey. I raise my head to the sky, blink back tears, and try to quiet the needs inside me that crave more.

ALTHOUGH NOW this trail is empty, between 1841 and 1869 nearly a half million people followed this route across the continent on the Oregon Trail. For the next few days we will be following parts of the Oregon, Pony Express, California, and Mormon Pioneer National Historic Trails. For two thousand miles and six months these pioneers crossed prairies, forded rivers, and battled storms, Indians, mountains, and sickness. They were the restless ones, the determined ones, the ones looking for a better life, and I can't get them out of my mind as we retrace their steps.

The trail is dry and dusty, and it's easy to imagine the wagon trains rolling over this land, eating clouds of their own dust. The trains, sometimes twenty wagons long, plowed through three inches of dust as fine as flour, obscuring even the mules pulling them. When there is occasional moisture in this arid land, the mud quickly

dries, cracking and curling the soil into large chips. We often come
to a water source (with appetizing names like Stinking Spring
Draw) and find the banks lined with crusty white alkali deposits.
Sierra knows, from her *Little House on the Prairie* books, that this is
what killed so many of the pioneers' cattle. Although our thirsty llamas strain on their lead ropes, we pull them away and continue.

When we reach "reliable" water sources, they are usually large
mud puddles that are completely overrun and trampled by cows.
Bryce happily obliges as he finds a sagebrush stick, then runs and
yells to chase the cows off. We have to clear the slime away with a
stick to get to the water, which usually resembles cow piss. It's not
appetizing, but it's all we have.

These puddles and pools are the kids' greatest source of fun, so
we usually let them go into the larger, clearer ones and just close
our eyes. They dump water on their heads and soak their shirts to
keep cool. They smell like cows, of course, but they don't seem to
mind. We're grateful to find any water we can, no matter how
muddy. We are fortunate to live in a such a prosperous land, where
clean water is considered a right rather than a luxury. It's hard to
comprehend that throughout the world unclean water is among the
top ten causes of mortality, leading to dysentery and cholera, until I
look at our passage through the Great Divide Basin.

From this open country we can see rock towers on the tops of
the highest knolls, marking the way for the sheepherders. Since the
cairns all look a little different, a herder can tell exactly where he is
as he and his sheep travel eighty to a hundred miles in a season. We
spot a shiny metal sheepherder's wagon way up on a hillside.

In the far distance sit the snowcapped Wind River Mountains.
This magnificent 12,000-foot range will be our next destination
after we traverse the basin. We're buying time in the desert while
the snow melts. The pioneers didn't have to cross this formidable
range. Instead, they aimed for South Pass, which they called Uncle
Sam's Backbone, a gentle ascent in the Great Divide Basin where
the trail crosses the Continental Divide. The broad, grassy plain is
twelve miles wide, with the Oregon Buttes landmark flanking the
south side coaxing the pioneers through.

At least twenty thousand people died along the Oregon Trail, many from cholera, gun accidents, or drownings. That's ten deaths for each mile. Still, despite their hardships, the pass ahead filled their hearts with hope. Many celebrations occurred there, for it marked the halfway point of their two-thousand-mile journey.

Nearby sits the restored town of South Pass City, and we take a half day off to tour it. In the old jail, Bryce is fascinated by the shackles and the metal bars on the tiny windows. I stare at the alphabet painted on the wall of the front room, for the jail was converted to a school. All the rooms in the hotel are decorated in period furniture, and all have chamber pots. Woe to the poor hired girl who had to empty them every day. Very few rooms had heat. Travelers had to share beds with total strangers, many of whom had not bathed in days. Sounds like trail conditions!

This is also gold country, and Sierra has contracted gold fever. Todd buys her a pan, and she swirls the black silt around in every stream, trying her luck. So far just flecks, but even that she finds thrilling. Both kids are obsessed with finding a pioneer artifact half buried in the Oregon Trail. They convince themselves that everything they find along the way—an old sock, a piece of rope—was left behind by the pioneers. They look on the ground for bones and skulls of cows that didn't make it. They look for cactus. They also keep their eyes open for agates, since the guidebook says they are plentiful. Every time they find a halfway pretty stone, they pick it up and grill us: "Is this an agate?"

"I don't know, it could be."

"But do you *think* it's an agate?" We end up telling them what they want to hear. "Yes, absolutely, it's an agate," and their pockets get stuffed and grow heavier.

Other things that keep the kids occupied across this long traverse are word and alphabet games like "I'm going to Grandmother's house, and I'm bringing apples." But mostly they just look at the land. At home after a summer's hike, I notice how taut and streamlined my face and neck are from all that far-reaching looking. It's a different way to spend your day than looking at a computer screen.

Evening is when the magic creeps into the desert. Color returns to the land, the breeze is cool, and the sun is low. Shadows are long and dramatic. The kids and I climb onto a rock pinnacle near our camp; we spot wild horses off in the distance, hear coyotes howl to the setting sun, and watch an eagle soar above, riding the currents.

I look down at our llamas' jaws moving as they chew their cuds, and I bring up my unanswered questions to chew on again. Todd delivers a bucket of water to a llama and waves up to us. Is it fair to ask him to be someone he's not, even when we're away from the CDT and he has the extra time and energy? If not, what am I supposed to do with my needs? Stuff them? Who should I be true to? To my husband? To myself? Can I be true to both at the same time?

Women on the Oregon Trail didn't give their own needs or even their own happiness much thought. They did what they had to do to survive. We modern women have choices about the kind of life we want to live. But with these choices come conditions and complications, and we have to be willing to accept them.

I like clarity, and I want to have answers rather quickly in life, but perhaps I should consider what Rainer Maria Rilke wrote in *Letters to a Young Poet:*

> Have patience with everything that remains unsolved in your heart. Try to love the questions themselves, like locked rooms and like books written in a foreign language. Do not now look for the answers. They cannot now be given to you because you could not live them. It is a question of experiencing everything. At present, you need to live the question. Perhaps you will gradually, without even noticing it, find yourself experiencing the answer, some distant day.

AFTER NEARLY a week of crossing the Great Divide Basin, a serious problem occurs. One of our kid-carrying llamas goes lame. Since we retired Berrick after last year, we borrowed a very large, gentle llama from our breeder friend, Stan Ebel. Stan provided our very first llamas on the Colorado Trail, three years ago. Dominique has been carrying Sierra with no trouble until the past few days. I'd noticed he was pulling on the rope a bit, but I figured he was just hot. Our guys all had their midsections sheared before we left this summer, to keep them cooler, but with 450 llamas, Stan can't possibly shear them completely.

The real problem is he's footsore. We've noticed that he drags his rear feet slightly when he walks, and this has apparently worn down his pads. The skin is pink, translucent, and very tender. Todd pulls out a Cordura nylon and leather llama bootie made just for this purpose and fastens it with Velcro around the worst foot. The other foot needs protection as well, but we only have one bootie.

It's still forty miles to the town of Muddy Gap, where our truck sits. We can board Dominique at a ranch where he can take some time off to let it heal. We're all feeling depressed, wondering if we have to abandon our hike. Todd can carry Bryce more, even though he's miserably heavy; Bryce can also walk more, and Fun Run, the llama who has been carrying Bryce, can alternate between the two kids. We're not ready to go home after only six days and fifty-five miles.

A few hours after we discover Dominique's sore feet, we "happen" across a blown-out truck inner tube lying right alongside the dirt road we're walking on. In all the miles of road walking in our hiking career, we've never come across one of these. It couldn't have arrived at a finer time. We take a break so Todd can figure out how to fashion a makeshift bootie, and he says, "If only we had scissors."

I reach into my pack and pull out a Swiss Army knife I "happened" to find yesterday on our road walk that just "happens" to have a pair of scissors in it. The road doth provide! We duct tape the rubber bootie around Dominique's leg, and once he learns to pick his feet up, he's walking along happily.

The longer we traverse the basin, the hotter it gets. There's no getting away from the sun. We crawl under sagebrush on breaks to escape. When I get undressed to wash up at night, Todd says my "hiker's tan" makes it looks as though I have clothes on. When we sit still in the sun on a break, because there is no place to avoid it, it feels as though my flesh is being cooked.

We take what shade we can get—in ditches, curled up under sage like lizards. We looked fried. Our lips are cracked and bleeding, even though we smear lip balm on every time we take a sip of water. I have painful lip blisters from the sun, and my chest is covered in a prickly heat rash. We continually slather our exposed skin with suntan lotion, yet we are windblown, leathery, and burned. I tuck cotton bandannas under my rucksack's shoulder straps so they hang down to shield my red, tender skin. When Sierra rides, she drapes a set of bandannas over her upper thighs, where the sun hits most directly. The kids' eyes are bloodshot from the bright sun and its reflection off the light-colored soil. I can't get either of them to keep their sunglasses on; they claim their hats push on the earpieces so they hurt their ears. At the end of the day, Bryce's blue eyes take on a glazed look as though he has the beginning stages of snow blindness. Besides looking fried, the kids have contracted some funky rashes from playing in the cow slop water, and Sierra has conjunctivitis. The desert is beginning to lose its charm.

Just when we think it can't get worse, Bryce's llama begins limping! Two kid carriers down for the count! Todd lifts up his hind foot and discovers a half-inch crack in his tough, leathery pad. The dry air and arid soil must be the culprits; it's a big difference from the spongy soil in a forest. Having to carry both kids and rarely getting a break hasn't helped either. Now the poor kids are forced to walk even more, across a desert, of all places. I can already imagine the stories our grandchildren will hear: "When I was your age, my parents made me walk across the Great Divide Basin desert."

We are pushing hard, hiking fifteen miles a day to get to Muddy Gap and our truck. We talk about options. About taking turns day hiking the remaining forty-five-mile stretch from Muddy Gap to Rawlins or maybe finding bikes to ride it. No one wants to quit, regardless of how difficult it may sometimes seem. When we get into camp at the end of the day and the kids find a running stream, even if it's eight o'clock, they're building dams and bridges and forgetting how hard the day was. Tonight they're putting on a dance performance in camp with their opened Rugrats umbrellas. "Costumes" are merely *Lion King* and *Beauty and the Beast* underpants.

The kids are also learning valuable lessons. If nothing else, they have come to love and revere pure, clean water. Sierra says that water is her best friend, followed closely by shade. To find refreshment and entertainment in mere mud holes is a gift. You can't truly appreciate something until it's taken away; to our children, tall sagebrush and a mud hole are reasons for delight.

At a jeep intersection, a car just "happens" to pull up with a mountain bike perched on its roof, and its driver cuts the motor. No doubt he's an outdoor enthusiast wanting to chat. I greet him with, "Now that's the way we ought to be crossing this basin, on a bike." I introduce myself as "Cindy" and he follows with, "Cindy *Ross*." This is the only person we've seen for over a week on this "trail" and the guy knows my name! He's from Washington state, and we've never met. Bert tells us he belongs to ALDHA, the Appalachian Long Distance Hiking Association that Todd and I are also members of. He saw my llama slide show at a hiking conference a few years back and fondly remembered us. Even a place as seemingly inhospitable as the Great Divide Basin holds friends. And what a strange "coincidence."

We were going to follow this particular jeep track for only a quarter of a mile. One minute later, and our paths wouldn't have crossed. We sit right down in the middle of the road to visit, knowing full well this is all the traffic this road will see today. Bert was hiking the entire Continental Divide Trail himself until he hurt his knee. Now he's riding the basin stretch on a bike. We share our idea of boarding the llamas in Rawlins so they can heal and cycling the rest of the way on our own, and he strongly recommends it.

"In fact," he says, "when you get to the Colorado–New Mexico border next year, trade your llamas for mountain bikes and ride that entire state to the Mexican border. Water sources are forty miles apart in the desert, and the trail is nearly all roads." Hiking forty-mile stretches with pack animals and children is not even remotely possible. We make mental notes for our trip next year, thank him, and go on our way.

A MOTEL in Rawlins, Wyoming: the kids are lying on the bed, under blankets in the too cold air-conditioning, staring at the TV, yelling at Todd and me when we walk in front of the screen, not wanting to get up for anything, even a tissue or a drink. Could this be that "normal" life we're depriving our children of?

In the shower, you have to scrub each small area of your skin, leaving brown handprints on the white washcloth.

Besides resting and cleaning up, today's mission is locating a bike so we can take turns to finish this section of the trail. One cycle shop will sell us a bike for ninety dollars and then "consider" buying it back when we're through. Another option is a secondhand shop, but it's closed and the tires on the road bikes displayed out front have dry rot. If llama pads blow out on these abrasive roads, surely a bike's tires will.

I'm just about to give up when I blurt out my dilemma to a woman on the street. "Try the police department," she suggests. "They're loaded with stolen bikes."

So I burst into the station and unload my saga to Tracy, the secretary. Although her boss, the police chief, is very nice, he's concerned a kid will come in to claim her bike and it won't be there.

"I just 'happen' to have a bike you can use," Tracy kindly offers.

"I'll gladly rent it," I say.

"Oh, no, but can I get you to give me your driver's license?"

"How about my credit card?" She laughs and agrees.

On the way to Tracy's home, Sierra asks why I would do that, and I explain that it's a matter of mutual trust. Tracy could charge all kinds of purchases on my card, or I could take off with her bike. This way we both feel confident that neither of those things will happen.

At the motel tonight, who just "happens" to get the room next to us but our new friend Bert, who offers the use of his helmet for the next few days.

Todd drops me and the bike off fourteen miles from Muddy Gap, in the town of Lamont. A sign announcing it reads "Lamont. Population 3." Not a popular place to live, this Great Divide Basin. But Grandma's Restaurant in Lamont is a very popular place to eat. A permanently fixed Open sign swivels on its hinges. Grandma (evidently one of the three residents) comes out in her polyester pantsuit uniform with "Grandma" embroidered over her ample bosom. She delivers coffee to ward off the chill wind that is sweeping across the basin this morning. I'll cycle this stretch back to Muddy Gap while Todd drives the truck, then he'll take the bike and do the reverse while I drive. That way we'll both ride the trail.

We don't believe in skipping part of the trail, for as Todd explains, "Where do you draw the line before you're missing large chunks and using the excuse that some parts are inconvenient?"

First you skip a mile or two, then ten. It gets easier and easier, and before you know it, you've missed out a whole section. Our goal is cover the entire distance from Canada to Mexico, ideally on foot, but we will make an exception like this if we must. Neither of us wants to miss even a mile. Some of our friends back home think this is an obsession, and in a few years we may agree, but we love the idea of covering the *entire country* from top to bottom. Then we'll feel that we know it in its entirety and know it intimately. We collect long-distance trails, like cherished friends.

WHEN I go over the rim of the basin and drop into the flat bottom, it reminds me of a great dried-up sea. Dry alkali beds, white as snow, stretch off to my sides. A hunk of retread lies by the road, patched with duct tape. Signs tell motorists to keep their headlights on when crossing the basin. Because the land and the road are so flat, it plays tricks with your eyes. Optical illusions make it difficult to tell how far away an oncoming vehicle is and how fast it is traveling. If a motorist decides to pass, it's like playing chicken. Wooden crosses mark the spots where fatal wrecks have occurred, and I wonder how many of the unfortunate ones were cyclists like me. One thing that strikes me as strange is that all the billboards, on *both* sides of the road, face the oncoming traffic. All I see is their framework. Not a single message is delivered to me. Then I realize why. They're for motorists heading into Rawlins. I'm heading directly into the basin, no-man's-land. There's nothing to advertise (except Grandma's).

The wind gusts are so violent today that they blow the grasses completely horizontal. When I see this happening ahead, I apply my brakes and creep to a near standstill. But the gust hits me broadside and throws me onto the asphalt, ramming my elbow and grinding gravel into my palms and knees. I pick the stones out of the bloody mess and think, Oh, Lord, this could get dicey. I watch the grass, and the next time I see the wind blowing it violently, I hop off and walk. But this time the gust lifts the bike completely off the ground and throws it over my head, with me still holding the handlebars in a death grip. All I can think of is Miss Gulch (the Wicked Witch of the West) riding her bicycle in the tornado in *The Wizard of Oz.* This happens several times before I make it to Muddy Gap. I am not thrilled about Todd's going out there, because the direction the wind is blowing will throw him into the line of traffic, and there are a lot of vehicles, not to mention big trucks thundering by. I'm not ready to lose him.

"When the wind blows like this," the owner of the Muddy Gap store tells us, "nobody goes out. The kids get ear infections and croup from all that dust."

High winds in the Great Divide Basin are considered inclement weather. You can't open both doors of your vehicle at the same time or the wind will sweep out everything that is on your seat, floor, and dashboard. We decide to put off the rest of our cycling until tomorrow, when the forecast is for fifteen-mile-an-hour winds as opposed to today's eighty miles an hour!

But what's this? Our truck is dead. Todd never turned the headlights off while he was waiting for me. The store owner comes to our aid and calls her neighbor Frank, who just "happens" to be home and owns a set of jumper cables.

A new challenge hits us come morning; one of the bike's tires won't hold air for longer than a mile or two. The road, now gravel, is rough, with corduroy ridges, and before long both tires are going flat. Evidently the bike's inner tubes are not in great shape, although the bike looks new and barely ridden. We didn't think to buy a spare tube or a patch kit, thinking a thirty-five-mile ride wouldn't be a big deal. We need to use our time wisely and cover the distance before the end of the day, for we promised to have the bike back. But because we both have to ride the trail, the truck must drive the trail three times to shuttle the bike riders, eating up a lot of time. We fear it's not worth the half-hour drive back to Rawlins to find inner tubes, so we just do an incredible amount of pumping.

Amazingly, the kids are doing just fine through all this driving and waiting. They happily sit in the truck cab, listening to children's tapes, drawing, and eating an entire large jar of their beloved Polish gherkins. They've had enough of the desert experience and don't mind giving up this section.

On each stretch, the rider hopes to make it to the truck before the tires go flat, but we usually have to walk the last quarter mile.

On one stretch Todd isn't paying attention and watching in the rearview mirror, and the tires go flat long before the anticipated spot. I flag down a pickup and say to the driver, "Tell that guy in the white truck that I have a flat tire and to come back for me."

"I'll give you a lift," he offers, but I turn him down, saying, "No, I can't. I'm doing the whole Continental Divide Trail, and I can't skip anything."

When he catches up to Todd, he delivers the message but gives him a puzzled look and says, "She wouldn't take a lift. Said she was doing some continental thing." We both laugh at how absurd it must have sounded to him.

Just when I'm growing weary and feeling as if this crazy day will never end, a cyclist just "happens" to approach us from the opposite direction. We stop to chat, and he decides to turn around and keep me company. Although Charlie is seventy-five, he must slow his pace down for me. The last miles click off, thanks to good company and good conversation.

A GOOD part of the day, I wonder about the overall sense of what we are doing—all that shuttling and all that tire pumping. It takes us all day, from 9:00 A.M. to 6:00 P.M, to cover this last section of the Great Divide Basin. We drive back to Rawlins, buy the last two inner tubes in the store, and return the bike to Tracy, who tries to pay us for the tubes. We're so grateful, and we feel confident that because of this positive experience she will be even quicker to help the next person who needs her.

When we look back on our entire crossing and all the adventures and misadventures we had, we come away not with feelings of discontent, but of gratitude. It seems that just when we needed help, it arrived, whether it was a truck inner tube, a new friend on a jeep road, good company on a road bike, a neighbor with battery cables, or a generous secretary. When you are hiking a long-distance wilderness trail, you are in a more needy situation than back home. We truly do depend on the kindness of strangers. This seemingly very tough stretch has taken on an aura of magic because of all the angels who "happened" into our path and helped us on our way.

This has been especially good for Todd, who tends to get mired in depression when something goes wrong. He tries to prepare for every contingency (like bringing a spare bicycle tube), and feels he lets us down in the face of problems he did not expect. We are both beginning to see that you cannot possibly foresee everything that the world will throw at you. The best way is to do a reasonable amount of planning, stay flexible and resourceful, and accept help and kindness from others with grace and the expectation that you will be called on to help others. This time Todd didn't lose faith so quickly; he believed it would work out, and it did.

When you think of our ancestors who crossed this Great Divide before us, the problems we struggle with seem minor in comparison. We're not freezing our feet off like the Mormon handcart pushers, or burying our dead spouses and babies, or having our children carried off by Indians, or delivering babies in rickety wagons. The basin puts it all in perspective.

At Independence Rock, the pioneers climbed the 136-foot bare sandstone rock that looks like the back of a great whale and carved their names in the stone. Some signatures have dates, the places they came from, their ages; they were so hopeful at that halfway point. After examining the names, I grasp my little son's hand. The wind whips our clothing, and I think of those women, long skirts flapping, holding on to their bonnets and *their* children's hands, the wide-open desert stretching on all sides. Their hearts had to burn with longing: for a comfortable place to give birth; for something to fill the huge hole left after burying their children; for a home and a better life on the other side of the Continental Divide.

Here in the Great Divide Basin I'm beginning to realize it isn't who your husband is, or where you are, or what your job is, or what church, if any, you attend that will finally make you happy. Out here we are so close to heaven that we can reach up and scrape it with our fingernails. Yet this place isn't the answer to my questions either. I look down from Independence Rock at my husband and realize that heaven is under my feet as well as over my head. It's inside me and all of us. This is one of the reasons I have come to love the Great Divide Basin, with all its harshness and desolation. It has made me feel. A place this big and open and devoid of man-made things rips your heart wide open—for there is no place to hide—and then fills it back up with hope.

20

The Wind River Range
JULY 21, 1997

Wherever you are, it is your friends who make up your world.
—WILLIAM LARRYN

THE MOSQUITOES are horrendous. We swat as we hike, which eats up energy. We wipe them off our shoulders and arms, getting half a dozen in one swipe. I can see fifteen directly in front of my face. We make fires in camp just for the smoke. We slather on bug dope every half hour, but it seems to work for only five minutes. When we peel an apple for the kids, it tastes like insect repellent. Knowing the color red bewilders the insects, I try hanging a red bandanna over my face. This seems to keep them slightly at bay. We crush them on our scalps and pick them out of our hair. They fly into our mouths when we take a bite of food. They buzz in our ears and get lodged in the wax.

From the depths of the Great Divide Basin desert to the lofty

heights of Wyoming's Wind River Range, the contrast is so
absolute that we feel as if we've been dropped onto another planet.
We shuttled north in the state to begin a 150-mile traverse of the
range. We plan on staying in the mountains for sixteen days, our
longest time yet in the wild. We'll have supplies brought in with
friends. Chuck Eckenroth from back home in Pennsylvania will be
with us the entire time, and later we'll be joined by Beth Ellen from
Michigan. Chuck is an art student at the local university where I
work part time. One of my jobs for the past twenty years has been as
a life drawing model for artists, and it was in class that we first met
and became friends.

Nothing about this bug-infested hell feels good. We can't enjoy
each other's company. The children hang out in the tent, but it feels
like a sauna in there in the middle of the day, even with the tent fly
off. They lie around naked and draw and read. When they must go
out to take a pee, it requires fast reflexes and teamwork. Someone
works the tent zipper while they blast in (or out). Still, dozens of
bugs fly in. We wait until they land on the tent wall and then smash
them into the nylon with our thumbs. If they're filled with blood,
they make a dark red stain. Mosquito carcasses litter the inside of
the tent. The kids say it's really gross.

The llamas have it especially hard. Though not many parts on the
hairy beasts are exposed, the few that are become sacrificed to the
bloodthirsty insects. Jerry's penis has red welts and sores all over it.

Chuck feels as if he is in hell. He has never experienced anything
like this. We say, "We hope you came out here for more reasons than
having fun, like building character, or you're going to be greatly disappointed." We use him as a source of entertainment. They do gnaw
on his legs more than ours for some reason. The backs of his knees
are solid red welts. But we get tired of hearing ourselves complain.
At the most, every now and then we say, "Damn bugs."

The bugs are so bad because in this area the snow has just
melted. As soon as the ground warms up the mosquito larvae hatch,
and for a few days this is what you must deal with. As we climb
higher the bugs calm down, but there's another challenge.

The trail is buried under snow. Under an evergreen canopy it
doesn't melt uniformly but remains in large drifts or mounds,

sometimes many feet high. We have to climb up them and slide down the other side. We sink a few inches with every step, and our boots slide as if we're walking on butter. It's very fatiguing. The jeep track we're on surfaces only every now and again. We have to be aware if it's going into a turn when it disappears into a snowbank and guess where it will come out so we can stay on course. The llamas are exhausted because their feet frequently break through the soft snow and they have to leap (with their gear on) to get out. Only the children are having a blast. They spend their time glissading on their boot soles, delighted that in the middle of summer they're playing on snow.

I'm fascinated by the way the earth comes back to life as the snow recedes. The newly exposed ground is buff-colored, looking pale and lifeless. The grasses are matted and compressed from the weight of the snow, which was just recently weighing them down. The ground appears to green up in mere hours after being uncovered and warmed by the sun. Glacier lily buds are the first to push through. The tender bright green shoots poke up through the brown mats and explode into sunny yellow blossoms.

When we finally get on a clear trail and leave the jeep tracks behind, after following them for weeks, I realize what has been missing this entire summer—the trail. A narrow trail is far more intimate than a road, for it immerses you in the land where you are traveling. Walking along even a double-tracked jeep road seems to separate you from your surroundings. It's interesting how something like the presence of a trail can buoy your spirits.

Chuck is good for the kids. He's twenty-two, and he plays with them just like Timmy does. He entertains them in camp by drawing pictures. During the day, he tells them stories. Sierra is smitten with him, for besides showering her with attention, he is so pleasing to look at. His classic features, chiseled jaw, and broad forehead are framed by beautiful brown hair gathered in a ponytail that Sierra loves to pull. It is always interesting to plug another person into our little family unit. Your behavior all comes out in the open. For a short while you can make believe that you don't lose your patience and yell at your kids, but not when you're living this close for such a long time. Just the simple chore of trying to keep kids clean in the wilderness is exasperating, especially a kid like Bryce. His hands usually look as though "dirt juice" has been poured over them and dried, so it seems like his actual pigment. When he separates his fingers the skin between them is lighter. He's been in the tent now for over an hour, moaning and crying over cooked carrots. I made two different freeze-dried dinners tonight, and they both had cooked carrots in them, which he hates and refuses to eat. I peek in to see if he's ready to calm down and eat, and his face is filthy from rubbing his grubby little fists all over it. He is overtired. Chuck just watches.

Sierra has been a joy this year. She helps Todd with the llamas every night, staking them out and feeding them a bowl of "llama granola" (chicken scratch or rabbit pellets) as a treat. Sometimes she understands the way her father thinks better than I do. The other night Todd and I had a tiff over selecting a camp spot. No one was taking the responsibility of choosing a place, so I picked what I like best—good views of the hulking mountains. Todd quietly acceded, although I discovered later that he wasn't happy with the amount and quality of grass for the llamas. He went off and sulked. I began to feel depressed about his lack of communication, so Sierra decided to help him stake out the llamas and talk to him. He returned smiling, and she reported, "I talked to him in little bits and slowly got him excited over trying to fish with his drop line and got him happy." How can a seven-year-old already understand her father and know how to handle him better than his wife of fourteen years? She is more like him than like me. She knew that working by his side and giving him support would help. Not pestering him by talking about the problem but taking the circuitous route is the best way to change his mood. But after all these years of struggling to get him to communicate, I get tired and adopt the attitude, "Oh, go blow it off!" Even now, after years of struggling, I still try to get him to communicate the way I think he *should*. Sierra is clever enough to communicate the way he *does*.

Chuck observes and listens to all of this, mentally gathering information for future reference—on marriage, on child-parent relationships, on sibling behavior. Since Chuck arrived, I've been spending a lot of time with him. We often walk together, sharing feelings and thoughts. He is young and new to all this and is eager to talk about it. I see Todd's dark eyes watching, questioning.

Part of the reason I'm drawn to Chuck is that my husband appears to be unavailable. He's "taking care" of us in the most fundamental way, keeping us safe, found. But I want him to pet, stroke, and emotionally take care of me. How much can I expect from him? And how healthy is it to look for it elsewhere?

In camp, Chuck and I stay up late by the campfire, talking about life and dreams. Todd, exhausted from the day's demands, collapses into sleep. Or maybe he's awake worrying, since he sees me enjoying Chuck's company so much.

For the past few days, we've been approaching the Wind River Mountains through the Gros Ventre Wilderness. It isn't until we arrive at the Green River Lakes that we begin to penetrate this stunning range and enter the Bridger Wilderness. For one hundred air miles, the "Winds" rise above the plains like a sheer wall. They form a squadron of more than forty 13,000-footers, with glaciers and snowcapped peaks. The emigrants called them the Shining Mountains because of the way the light shines on their white granite faces. This range has been compared to California's Sierra Nevada, but happily it's a better-kept secret. The only place you really see many people is at Green River Lakes, the best access point into the high country.

OUR FRIEND Beth Ellen joins us there, along with a party of twenty fishermen. Beth will be with us for ten days until she leaves at Big Sandy, the only other dirt road access in the entire range.

The fishermen play leapfrog with us the entire day, around the two lakeshores, past the enormous granite plug called Flattop Mountain, which looks more like a gigantic rock tree stump, and along the Green River until we arrive at the most formidable ford of the summer. Todd read about the Green River ford last winter when he began planning this trip, and his concern has been growing ever since. The guidebook warns, "The fifteen-foot crossing requires considerable caution, especially since the water may be over six feet deep and the current strong." We also learned that the "permanent bridge" has been washed away and that the replacement, a cluster of lashed parallel poles, is long gone. We quiz the hikers we meet on the best place to cross. Flagging ribbon marks a course, but after careful consideration we choose a wider and shallower spot with a gravel bar in the middle of the river. We find two sticks of lodgepole pine on the bank and push on through the thigh-deep water, holding hands and planting our feet securely before each step. When our group is safely across, we look back and see the first of the fishermen getting ready to start. We tell them the best way to cross and they venture out, looking really nervous. I can tell by their stiff, jerky movements, tongue licking, and lip biting that this is something they don't often do.

"We should help them," I say.

Todd disagrees. "They'll be fine. They'll figure it out." But Beth looks at me and whispers, "Go help them."

I ford the river and say, "Could anyone use a stick or a hand?" Half of them take me up on my offer and hold my hand with such a death grip that I can tell they're terrified. I show them how to plant each foot securely in the riverbed before taking another step, how to angle upstream and use the pole as a third leg. They warmly express their gratitude once they're on the far bank and set up camp near us for the night. It's so refreshing to find grown men with egos strong enough that they can accept help from a woman, and I mention this to Todd.

The guys are mostly in their forties, with three father and son teams. Every year they go on extended backpacking trips. I tease them and say, "You owe me big time for that crossing. What do you have to trade? What kind of dessert is on the menu tonight?"

They eat communally from a huge pot, taking turns cooking. "Freeze-dried blackberry cobbler. You're more than welcome to have some."

We sit around the campfire sharing cobbler and stories. A sixth-grade natural history teacher is scraping the hair and flesh from an elk skull he found.

"You're not going to use that knife to spread your peanut butter, are you?"

"Oh no," he chuckles. "This is only used for stirring the cobbler. Actually, it's my roadkill knife."

Another eyes our boys grazing in the meadow and asks, "How much does a llama cost? My pack was feeling awfully heavy today."

"Eight hundred to a thousand for a good packer."

"I could cover that right now with my school's charge card!"

I ask where their women are, and they say it's not that they weren't invited.

"Is there something wrong with them that they don't enjoy this?" I ask. They reply, laughing, "We were wondering the same thing!"

I love the attention, the company, and the great conversation, for I'm still feeling a little deprived from my people fast in the Great Divide Basin.

My husband teases me and calls me River Queen for the rest of the evening when no one can hear. Todd seems to be relaxing more over sharing my company with Chuck or even a group of strange men. We are different people with different needs. Although he is out here doing such an extremely nonconformist thing as leading his family along the Continental Divide, he feels comfortable with boundaries. He likes structure and seeks it out. At this point in my life I'm more attracted to flexibility and fluidity, and I am searching for a way to get my needs met yet still take care of my husband's heart and our marriage.

The very next day we're faced with another challenging ford, Pole Creek. At fifty yards wide, it looks more like a river than the Green River does. It has very little current, but still we end up in trouble. Beth volunteers to test the river's depth by going first. It's a bit unnerving, because the way the light is hitting the water, we have no idea how deep it is. It rises to her waist, and that's enough to tell Todd the kids should not be on their llamas' backs. Once the llamas' panniers begin to float, they're thrown off balance and get upset, which is not safe for a rider. Bryce goes on Todd's back in the kid carrier, and he leads the kid-carrying llamas across minus the kids. This leaves Sierra and me and Chuck and the pack string. Chuck volunteers to lead the llamas while I tend to my crying, frightened daughter. She's decided to wade across with me. She takes off her clothes except for her T-shirt and underpants and slowly walks into the river, holding my hand. As the cold water creeps up to her chest, she cries and cries. I realize the river bottom is sandy and smooth, so I hoist her onto my back and cross like Saint Christopher.

Chuck remains on shore with the boys, who grow more upset with every minute they are separated from the rest of the herd. It's as though they get support from just knowing the others are near by.

Chuck struggles to keep the llamas behind him and not get run over, but they're pushy, and Chips, the leader, begins to run in circles around him in the middle of the river. Chuck is afraid the rope is tangled, so he drops it. They bolt across the river and run up the steep bank, loosening a pair of boots that were loosely draped over Chips' wooden saddle horn. They bang against his belly and he goes ballistic, pulling the others along in his frenzy. Beth comes to the rescue and manages to grab the lead rope, while disgusted Chuck is swearing and calling, "Stupid llamas!"

I can only imagine what these poor loyal llamas are thinking when we ask them to do something that must seem threatening to them. There are lots of large snow patches lingering in the high country. When we have to go from a rocky area onto a snowfield, we get worried. Boulders absorb the sun's heat and melt cavities around them, hidden below the snow's surface. The llamas' legs break through into them and can get pinned between two boulders. This is a great way to break a llama's leg. The llama in the rear more often gets in trouble, since he's being hurried along. He might not be paying attention, or the lead llama might decide to leap, leaving those in the rear without time to think about where to place their feet or how to get them out from between two boulders. After a few days of this kind of travel, all the llamas have at least one leg with the hair scraped off and bloody scabs on their shins.

We also have snow bridges to cross in these Wind River Mountains, where a flowing stream runs under a snowfield and hollows out an arch underneath. Even after we examine the thickness of the bridge and a brave soul goes out and tests its strength by pounding a hiking stick on top, we never know how stable the bridge is. The llamas are heavier and could break through, but they follow faithfully.

Todd is the guardian of our animals, and me, and our children. Our friends who join us, like Beth and Chuck, help out a lot. When

Bryce goes off climbing some rocks in camp and gets caught in a narrow chimney, Chuck runs to his rescue. Afterward he teaches him some of the basic principles of rock climbing so he can do it safely. Beth is always up bright and early to help Todd bring in the llamas and deliver saddles to him. Chuck often scouts ahead to see if the llamas can get through questionable terrain. He clears the trail of debris so the kid-carrying llamas don't have to leap, which the kids find frightening. We take them down whenever a situation looks hazardous, which is about twenty times a day. My arms get tired from lifting them back into the saddle, so I try to lead them through as much as I can get away with. The kids sit up there just looking around, lost in thought or conversation, and then whammo! They're flying in the air as if they're on the back of a bucking bronco, though it's usually only one buck. They never hold on when they ride, so their arms flail and their necks get whiplash. It's different when you're riding a horse, actively watching where you go and steering around obstacles. I can prevent the first llama from jumping by pulling his head down with the lead rope, but I can't do that with llama number two. Inevitably it's Bryce, the second rider, who gets thrown around the most. He has a chronic bruise in the small of his back from hitting the wooden saddle.

Todd says I'm supposed to turn around and watch, anticipate what the second llama will do, and then react quickly while still watching where I'm going. But the llamas are sentient beasts with independent thoughts and fears that we cannot anticipate. I usually cross my fingers and keep going, hoping the llamas won't leap or that the kids will be ready if they do. Todd says I push it, but that's the story of our lives out here.

I realize the extent of the kids' wilderness skills when we cross two interesting passes today. The first is a no-name pass that funnels us narrowly through two jutting crags. We feel as if we're walking through a hallway between the peaks that sail off in the distance like a row of granite ships. The views from the passes take our breath away, and we always walk those last steps anticipating the whole new world of mountains about to burst upon us. On the other side of this first pass is a long tongue of snow that funnels us into the valley. We can't see how far it goes or whether it gets steep and drops off, but there's no other way to go. Beth and Chuck go first, cutting steps in the snow like little ledges or platforms to place our feet on. The kids bop after them, totally confident, unlike their parents. They scramble across the snow like mountain goats and negotiate the thirty-foot drop down to dry trail as though they've been mountaineering all their lives. Todd and I smile proudly.

At Lester Pass, the guidebook warns, "The slope on the south side of the descent may be convex, with cornices, and should be treated with respect. It may be possible to find a safer route."

We creep around the edge of the gigantic snowfield that smothers the pass and, sure enough, there's the hairy cornice. So we travel down the ridge about a quarter mile and the kids ask if they can lead. The country is open, but you have to look ahead to see if the piece of meadow you walk on will drop off, turn to boulders, or safely lead you to another strip of dry ground. It's like a chess game where you are constantly planning two or three moves ahead. But we follow the children closely and are amazed that their direction of travel is exactly what we would have chosen. It's the same with choosing rocks when hopping across a stream. They're not afraid of the rocks' being shaky or worried whether they can stretch far enough. They have excellent balance and make good choices. They plant their feet with skill and float across with agility and grace.

We don't know how much is seeping into their subconscious just by doing it as they follow us all these miles. It's not as if we sit down and actually teach them wilderness skills. They might not be adept at manipulating a computer mouse or finding the Old Navy or Gap stores at the nearest mall, but they've sure picked up some other skills along the Continental Divide.

Are knowing how to negotiate a mountain pass and how to ford a stream considered worthwhile skills? Will they need these to get through life? Doubtful. It's what the experience and the knowledge are doing to their personhood—building confident people, so they can go on to do anything their hearts desire. There are not many finer gifts we can give our children.

EVER SINCE we rose above Green River Pass, we've been immersed in a world of jumbled peaks, spires, and domes. The mark of the glaciers is particularly evident in the multitude of beautiful lakes carved into high cirques. Today we hike around thirty lakes and ponds within ten miles. The trail remains at 10,000 feet for close to twenty miles, never dropping out of heaven. We dip in and out of tundralike plateaus that resemble the Arctic. The views around each corner are more stunning than the last ones. We have this remote paradise all to ourselves.

It isn't until we travel farther south in the range toward the aptly named Sheep Creek that we begin to see other people. These are not your typical backcountry travelers but are Basque shepherds from Spain. The rugged land of peaks has given way to a high plateau at the edge of the Wind River Mountains where open meadows abound, perfect for sheep. Sheep grazing in this area dates back to the turn of the century and is still allowed in the Bridger Wilderness. The section of trail that we travel on, the Fremont Trail, is a major stock driveway. We see flocks of large herds with their guardians on horseback, accompanied by the traditional sheepherding dogs. These black-haired, dark-skinned natives of the Pyrenees speak very little English, but they approach us, smiling, wanting to take a picture—a picture of Beth and me, that is. One shepherd hands his camera to Todd and puts an arm around each of us. We dig back through the cobwebs of our high school minds to resurrect what little Spanish we can remember.

As we approach the Big Sandy access road and the Big Sandy Lodge, visions of food dance in our heads. Todd is hankering for grease in any form. Gourmet Beth would be thrilled with a plain hot dog. She's treating us to a cabin for the night and to dinner and breakfast before she departs. Chuck has three days left.

It isn't long after Beth leaves that we traverse one of the most exciting passes we have ever negotiated and lay eyes on some of the most thrilling scenes in our entire hiking career. Jackass Pass, the fabulously horrific entrance into the famed Cirque of the Towers, is where we are heading. We climb north away from Big Sandy and across the high wall of the Wind River Range for the last time. We're taking a side trail through the Popo Agie Wilderness so we're closer to the town of Lander. Our truck is parked there, and it's also the home of the Lander Llama Company and their Bunk

House Bed and Breakfast, where we'll take some well-deserved R and R.

The fun begins as we try to skirt Shaft Lake on the way up to the pass. The stock trail is steep and dead-ends in the lake, forcing stock to swim through four feet of water—OK for horses but way too deep for llamas.

Hikers coming from the opposite direction tell us the hiking route is "really bad." They aren't even sure our llamas can make it—it's hand-over-hand climbing. Todd ascends to check it out and returns with the verdict: "They can do it, but we have to unload them and lead them one at a time."

Todd tries to coax Chips up, but he will not budge. He braces his body against a rock and resists with all his might. Todd has to get under him, take each shaking leg, and place his feet on the boulder above while I pull on his lead rope. We work hard and we work quickly, hauling up heavy panniers in our arms, being careful not to slip. Thunder rumbles, and it begins to rain. We stop our work to put on raingear, telling the kids, "Point your toe! Hold your cuff!"

"We're hungry!"

"Shove some cookies in your mouths," I tell them, "and have some candy."

"Can I have a whole Milky Way bar, Mom?"

"Sure! Just don't make yourself sick."

We're dealing with high stress, high-energy work in cold and rain—perfect hypothermic conditions. Only sugar will do, and we mentally add the "caloric intake" variable to the increasingly complex equation of survival in the outdoors.

We tell them to make the climb and descent on their own and wait for us at the bottom. "Be careful!"

We continue, with Chuck's help, leading each llama up the steep boulders and then cautiously down the other side. Todd and I feel wired as we watch the storm approach, but we work together, moving swiftly and smoothly.

A hiking party stops to watch, and I pause to ask, "Do you think we're crazy?" I'm thinking how we must look, with the kids and all, let alone the llamas. I sometimes wonder if people regard our parenting as strangely abusive or as just plain loco.

"No," one replies. "I find it interesting."

When we arrive at Arrowhead Lake at the head of the pass, we have two options. The lower route crosses a large boulder field; the higher route, recommended for stock, is buried under a long, steep snowfield. The lower route looks well worn so we go for it, only to retrace our steps when the boulders increase to the size of compact cars.

The rock pinnacles loom above us like silent stone sentinels as we climb. When we turn around to take in the view with the Temple Peaks dominating the scenery, we see ominous clouds moving in. The thunder grows loud. Our only choice is to continue upward.

Once we reach the snowfield, Chuck volunteers to go first and cut in steps for the rest of us. The children follow, but since the sun has never shone the whole day, the snow is icy and hard and Chuck's steps are too shallow. Both kids slide, but they don't get hurt. Todd and I have our hands full with our pushy, nervous llamas.

Atop Jackass Pass, the view is extraordinary. The Cirque of the Towers is a colossal curved amphitheater carved out by the glaciers. An arc of 12,000-foot peaks with their east faces sculpted into near-vertical walls provides the backdrop for Lonesome Lake, our camping spot for the night. The weather looks much better from this side, and the kids dance down the switchbacks a-hootin' and a-hollerin', so damn happy to have made it off that treacherous pass and so happy to be here in these mountains.

I *love* to hear my children exclaim over the beauty of nature. It tells me they are amazed. It tells me they are moved. It tells me they are feeling deeply, even after all they've seen in these thousands of miles. I am always comforted by these realizations, because it reassures me that we are neither abusive nor loco. Then I know this trip, despite all the hardship, has had a positive effect on them.

SCOTT AND TERESE WOODRUFF have been running Lander Llama Company for over fifteen years, leading wilderness pack trips. We can hardly wait to get to their Bunk House Bed and Breakfast and take a break; it has been a long, tough stretch. When we emerge from the forest at the trailhead and see our truck parked by the

Woodruffs', we are overjoyed. With so many challenges facing us on the trail, at least we don't have to worry about getting in and out of the mountains.

There are so many llama folks who have helped us on our journey. They've shuttled our truck, boarded our llamas, welcomed us into their homes, taken us to buy groceries, and on and on. Most of them didn't know us before we hiked into their lives, but we left feeling as if we were reunited with long-lost family. We could not have done this long journey without their support.

Chuck has distanced himself from us more and more as we got closer to Lander and the end of his trip. It's part of the separation process. He's spent the past sixteen days being woven into our family. Days before you actually leave, your thoughts begin to drift to that other life. After Todd and the kids exchange warm embraces with him, I drive him to the bus station. We relive the highlights of his hike and talk about his experience of living so intimately with our family.

I tell him, "It's really more intense than a marriage because we're together twenty-four hours a day and we can't escape to a job or anywhere else. Sixteen days is a long time to be together, but it worked great. Everyone got along, and everyone helped out." I thank him for all his help and the kindness he's shown my children. "I learned a lot out here," he says. "I learned tolerance—of mosquitoes and of the kids."

These last weeks we have all shared a very communal lifestyle. In the evenings, we've sat together under golf umbrellas in the rain, warding off the cold in fleece coats and hats, waiting for water to boil and watching the peaks drift in and out of the clouds. We've shared our meals and heated water for each other's tea. We've gathered at sunset almost every night to watch the sun go down and marvel at the light show that follows. We've shared llama chores, and we've all done our part to help entertain the kids. After fording rivers and crossing snowfields together, Chuck feels like a member of our family, thanks to this rich time spent in the Wind River Mountains.

21

The Mikulsky Boys

AUGUST 8, 1997

If there is no struggle, there is no progress.
—FREDERICK DOUGLASS

WHEN I LOOK behind me on the trail, I have a hard time believing what I see—my brother-in-law John Mikulsky and his ten-year-old son Ryan, my nephew, with backpacks. All our married life, Todd and I had wished *someone* in our family would join us out here. Besides sharing some memories, they might understand why we do this and, with any luck, come to love it too.

It would not be difficult to love hiking this particular evening. The fresh wind blows gently and is a perfect temperature. The low-angle sunlight is gorgeous. We have an easy two-mile walk to our campsite, which is smothered in wildflowers. In camp, John leans back in our Crazy Creek chair and says, "I love this."

"It isn't always like this," I tell him. "It rains sometimes, but the other types of weather bring a little variety."

"I don't need variety," he replies.

Their first full day of hiking, however, produces more variety than he and Ryan care to experience. We are following the quiet ridges of the divide along an old stock driveway. This was a ranchers' backcountry freeway in days gone by as millions of cattle were driven along this route. A wide swath has been cut through the trees to allow the passage of these large herds, and the ground is denuded on both sides of the trail. Every now and then an old yellow sign that once read, "Center Stock Driveway" lets us know we're on the right path. Since it hugs the Divide, the trail runs us straight up and straight down some steep stuff, with lots of loose rocks churned up by the animals' hooves. I give my nephew tips on ascending; how to lock his extended knee for a second and take a quick break. When the trail veers away, you have to consult a map and compass. Our guests find themselves following us down drainages, bushwhacking across meadows, and searching for old hatchet wounds on the trees, the primitive blazes that mark the trail.

I watch Ryan and see him walking on the sides of the trail instead of on the trail bed. This causes him to go up and over humps, stumble over rocks, step onto downed trees. He says he's very tired, and no wonder—he's expending much more energy than he needs to. We take his pack, which holds two foam sleeping pads and weighs all of five pounds, and he says, "That is so much better!" Ryan is a big ten-year-old, but I know this has less to do with physical ability than with attitude. When he plays around on breaks, throwing sticks and exploring, I tell him to park his butt and rest so he can make it through the rest of the day.

It begins to rain. We ask Ryan if he is warm and tell him to put up his hood, zip his coat, drink water, and eat a snack. We all put a lot of energy into taking care of him, energy that would normally be spent on hiking forward.

In camp he and his dad complain of headaches and Ryan throws up, most likely from the altitude, which hovers around 10,000 feet, high enough to make a flatlander sick.

When Ryan takes off his socks, his father says, "If I'd known they were wet, I would have had you change them."

"Wrong!" I brusquely say. "If you do that, all your socks will be wet in no time. Even if the rain stops, the water falling off the bushes will run down your legs and soak another dry pair, or they'll wick the moisture from the inside of the wet leather boots and get soaked." I probably sound like a dictator to Ryan.

John packed their sleeping bags on the outside of the llamas' panniers in coated nylon stuff sacks. Lining the stuff sacks with plastic garbage bags and storing them inside the panniers helps ensure that the sleeping bags will stay dry. But John thought this way was good enough, and although Todd questioned it, it's not his personality to push the issue. As a result, one of the sleeping bags got very wet and the other damp. So they are wearing all their clothing to bed and using the damp bag as a blanket.

John is very quiet as he sits and eats his freeze-dried meal. When he's away from home, he's usually in a motel or in the comfort of his hunting camp. He's used to central heat, central air, clean bodies, and dry socks.

"Don't think of this week as a vacation, John. Think of it as an adventure, an experience, a challenge. Thinking of it as vacation, you end up rating days as 'good' or 'bad,' setting yourself up for disappointment and missing half the experience."

The next day is not much better. It rains again. In camp tonight, the kids collect wood for a fire in hopes of drying stuff out, but three times they have to abandon the fire and dive into the tent when the skies open up with a torrent of rain. Seven pairs of kids' socks and five pairs of wet underwear hang smoking on sticks, then get tossed over a nylon cord at the roof of the tent. John is determined to cook split pea soup from scratch, so he sits out there in his raincoat and somberly stirs.

"I'd like to have a *little bit* of fun," he says to me.

I laugh and say, "When backpackers plan to go out for a weekend, they just stay home if the forecast is bad, or they bail out early if they don't like the weather. On a serious trip like this, we keep going. But the longer you are out, the greater your chances of experiencing different kinds of weather. The sun does come out after a while."

"It would be nice to just hole up until the rain passes," he says.

"We can't do that. We have to keep to our schedule or we'll never accomplish anything. This is a long trail, and if we skipped hiking every day that it rained, we'd still be in Montana. And we have to hike the miles or you won't get out in time to catch your flight."

"I thought Todd might be slave driver," he laughs. Quite a few people in our family look at the relationship between Todd and me as though I'm the dominant one and make most of the decisions. Some of them feel sorry for him, thinking he has no say, which I always find amusing. But it's a different ball game out here. Trail Boss is in control, and I find it very interesting to see my usually headstrong brother-in-law being submissive to Todd, as is everyone who joins us.

The rain stops long enough for John to go down to the spring and wash up, for he's feeling he needs a bath. In the meantime, I'm able to hold his sleeping bag by the fire and dry it out completely. He returns with a big smile; he feels like a new man and saw "the most incredible sunset while he stood there completely naked." His soup is also ready, and it tastes fabulous. He can't wipe the smile off his face. Looks as if he's finding that little things like sunsets and split pea soup are enough to bring you joy in this existence.

It rains hard the next day, and John says, "I'll tell you what this weather does. It makes you go into yourself and pull out your inner resources so you can deal with it."

It's fascinating to watch our friends learn to cope with things out here. We are so used to these rough conditions that we tend to take things much more in stride. You can learn so much about a person when you live this closely and go through hard times together. After being in the same family for two decades, I find we don't know each other until we walk in the rain together.

We have to peel apart the individually wrapped mozzarella string cheeses for the kids, because they have mittens on. Bryce holds his dill pickle and soaks the wool with pickle juice. Ever since the Great Divide Basin, we have to leave every town stop with a one-liter bottle of pickles. They're the snack of choice now. Our kids take this kind of weather in stride, of course. It's all what you're used to. Bryce holds my hand, and begs me to sing the lines from the John Denver song, "For Baby," about holding a child's hand while they walk together in the rain.

Sierra and Bryce sing all the time. They skip ahead and make up songs about the trees, the rocks, and the mountains. The two of them are forever playing make-believe. Bryce acts like a baby squirrel, hunching his body and holding up his "paws" as he speaks to his sister in a squeaky voice, pretending to be her pet. Ryan just looks at the two of them. He asks them to be quiet when they're singing or to stop talking when they're jabbering happily. I say to him, "Ryan, do you know who is the only person who can make sure you have a good time out here?" "Me." "That's right." Part of it is his age. He's nearing adolescence, and he might view my kids as childish. (They are only five and seven years old.) And ten-year-olds sometimes need to be reminded how to play and to forget themselves. He spends most of his time walking with his head down. I can barely get him to give me even a half grin for a picture. When I try to joke with him, he doesn't find anything funny. I'm wondering if he hates this.

But even if his aunt and uncle and cousins are driving him nuts, he's sharing some special times with his father. In a family of three children, it's a rarity to have such one-on-one time. John holds Ryan's hand a lot as they hike, and it is heartwarming to see a preadolescent boy comfortable doing that. I think it's the wilderness. That wouldn't be happening back home on the suburban streets. Thank goodness there is a place like the trail, away from society, where our children can feel secure enough to share moments like this.

On day five of the Mikulsky boys' trip, the sun finally comes out. John is so moved that he sits on a rock in the middle of the meadow and watches the sun shine on the ice crystals that cover every square inch of vegetation. He sits for over an hour, happy to see the sun.

Meanwhile, Trail Boss is busy packing up and doing chores: taking down John and Ryan's tent and packing it up, taking down the frozen wash line, cleaning John and Ryan's pots from breakfast, saddling the llamas, packing and loading the panniers.

Todd grumbles to me, "I'd like to sit and meditate too, but I've got work to do. If he wanted a guided trip, he could have paid thousands for it!"

We have been doing a lot of baby-sitting for our relatives. I've put up their tent every night, cooked their dinner, and washed their dishes. John does not naturally move like a house on fire, so it takes him a long time just to do his personal things. If we didn't help with their chores, we wouldn't break camp for another hour. Then there have been the additional troubles they've encountered. The tent pole broke and had to be repaired with a slice of aluminum can and duct tape. Then the tent zipper broke and let in bugs one night and rain the next until that was duct-taped closed.

I just smile at Trail Boss and say, "He might be doing the best job he can, but if you want more from him, you need to open your mouth and tell him. If you don't want to confront him, then do his jobs happily and without resentment." This part of our hike has been very good for our relationship. Todd has felt compelled to seek me out and discuss my relatives instead of going internal, which is his true nature, to work it out on his own.

Sharing frustration and searching together for a solution bonds us. Our commonalities have been magnified instead of our differences. As the focus has shifted off ourselves and our personal challenges, that has brought us together. We feel like a team.

Part of what eats up John's energy and time is taking care of Ryan. They are both novice backpackers. Ryan has never gone backpacking before, and John hasn't gone for fifteen years. These rugged western mountains can be overwhelming, especially in inclement weather. John doesn't know what he can handle, let alone predicting his son's ability. He sometimes loses his patience with Ryan if he feels he isn't taking care of himself. He worries about his safety more than he needs to because he lacks experience himself. (Plus, Ryan's aunt and uncle are looking after him.) John is doing everything he can to hold himself together and deal with the altitude, the rain, the cold, and the fatigue, besides caring for his son's needs. There's a lot on his plate. He doesn't have much left over to help out with chores.

We've never had any greenhorns with us before, certainly not children. Everyone who's joined us in the past has had to have a wealth of wilderness experience and the ability to take care of themselves if our children and llamas consume all our energy. But we made a huge exception to our rule because they are my relatives and I so badly wanted them to experience what I love to do.

Of course my nonconfrontational husband decides to keep his dissatisfaction to himself. But the shining sun and the beautiful country we are traveling in makes the issue lose its importance. After many days of rain, everything is right with the world when the sun finally comes out.

Once we left the stock driveway after the first few days, our route took us past lush marshy meadows, across frequent stream crossings, and through numerous bogs. We followed the border of the Zirkel Wilderness, teasing us with views into this gorgeous country but not quite getting close enough. Not until we approach Lost Ranger Peak does John begin to see the magnitude of the beauty of this place.

Lost Ranger Peak is the highest elevation we've yet attained anywhere along the Continental Divide Trail, from Canada south through the Rockies. The summit tops out at 11,932 feet, and our guidebook describes a spectacular cliff, with its edge along our trail. The panorama of mountain chains is supposed to be breathtaking. John can hardly wait to gain some elevation. "This is what I came for," he tells me.

I agree and say, "When we get up on the ridge and walk across the mountaintops with all those fabulous views, it will be like nothing you've ever experienced. It's the reason I keep coming back. It's what gets me thorough the rain and all the tough parts."

But the night brings a new twist to our plans. Another storm comes barreling through, with thunder so loud it hurts Bryce's ears and brings tears to his eyes. The lightning is so intense that we can see the flashes through tightly closed eyelids. When I get up to relieve myself in the night, I am happy to see the stars, but the wind is howling like a monster. And it's gotten very cold.

John awakes and packs up with zest for a change. "Let's do it, Cynthia," he calls to me. But Todd and I are not so positive. We dress each kid in two expedition-weight fleece coats, two pairs of fleece pants, windsuits, two hats, and two pairs of mittens. Even so, it isn't long into the climb that they complain of being cold, and Todd and I begin to have serious doubts. When we reach the krummholz, the stunted spruce trees that grow in clumps above timberline, the wind attacks with a vengeance. The children look at me with fear in their eyes as they remember that windy saddle years ago where we had to crawl to safety before the rainbow appeared. They know how bad it can get. They have a reference point with wind that few other children have. I promise them we *will not* do anything dangerous. We will turn around before that. I tell them to get off their llamas and walk to keep warm.

I hold their hands, and Bryce hangs on to me for support. The llamas' saddles begin to blow off, and John helps Todd reposition them and strap them down with ropes looped under their bellies and around the panniers. The kids have to lie flat when they take a break and wait for us. They can't even sit up, the wind is so fierce.

"I love this!" John yells to be heard above the roar. That's all well and good, I think to myself, but we have small children and llamas to consider, and we have to do what is safest.

It's six miles across the ridge to the safety of the trees. If this wind doesn't let up and the kids have to walk the entire way, they will never make it. Especially with a cliff on one side of the ridge. We cannot risk getting blown off.

So much energy goes into bracing ourselves against the wind that it's hard to move forward. The children have much less strength and mass, so it takes even more effort for them to hold their own. The clouds hit the ridge and whip over our heads at a good eighty miles an hour. The sun is going on and off like a strobe light as the clouds race across it.

When it takes all our strength to stand upright and not get blown over, when walking forward cannot be done and Sierra begins to cry very hard, I turn to the men behind and say, "That's it. We're turning around."

A lot of elevation remains until the summit, and it will only get worse. We're not in the full force of the wind yet, and Todd and I know from experience how bad it can get. That cliffside trail sounds incredibly dangerous in this wind. Our children could not struggle against the wind for the six miles it would take to traverse the open ridge. And there would be no other options to bail us out once we got up there. We'd have no choice but to head to the side trail by our campsite and descend.

John is disappointed, and I don't blame him. It's hard to turn around, to abort, knowing there are fabulous views up there and we'll probably never return to see them.

We abruptly reverse direction and branch off on the side trail to Red Canyon. This turns out to be the better choice; soon after we make our decision, bad weather moves in. A sheltered canyon is a better place for rain than an exposed ridge. But the exquisite scenery also helps make up for our loss, for our walk past the Red Cliffs and colossal dirt slide is so interesting and picturesque that we have a hard time watching where we walk. Then we descend into a glorious grove where dark conifers grow among the aspens, something we don't remember ever seeing before. They create a startling contrast, dark green against pale green. Six-foot-high ferns grow among the trees, and we swim through them. The children disappear on the trail. We are gnomes in a rain forest. John is beside himself with the beauty.

It's a hard day despite the gorgeous scenery because we've had to add more miles since our reroute. Tomorrow the Mikulsky boys are flying home, and we have to get them to their prearranged pickup point where a local llama outfitter is meeting them. After that, one and a half days remain for our family until we are done for the year too.

This morning is the first time in a week that John contributes to morning chores. I make Ryan open his own oatmeal packages. Todd asks him to help fetch water, and I ask John to come help with the panniers. John looks at his watch and marvels that we're out of camp by eight o'clock. I laugh and say, "That was our normal departure time before *you* joined us, not nine o'clock!"

As we walk the road to their meeting point, John shares: "I understand now why Todd pushes so much. You'd never accomplish anything if you didn't. When I think of all we experienced this week, it's hard to believe so much has been packed in. I want to join you next year."

I grin mischievously and say, "Ask Trail Boss. I don't think he's going to want anyone to come who can't pull his weight and help."

"Oh, I'll help," John promises. "I'll help more. This is really fun."

I said, "Well, it isn't always fun. You found that out. But it is always worthwhile."

THE MIKULSKY BOYS had a tough stretch, but nothing like what we encounter our last day out.

Because we had to detour around Lost Ranger Peak, we're no longer on the "official route." We must cross private land to get back to our truck and conclude this summer's hike. We cut across an old logging road and head up a meadow until suddenly we are stopped in our tracks. Beavers! The meadow is completely flooded. There's no telling how deep the dark water is. There could be steep drop-offs or oozing mud. The llamas are getting nervous just looking at it.

We struggle for hours, crossing four-foot-deep canals (tested with a stick) that we have to swing the kids over and force the llamas to leap across. We detour around hummocks and chewed-off branches. We hit dead ends and have to backtrack. We wade through swamps with laurel thickets that reach way over our heads. The kids follow, yelling for us to wait up. We only see the branches waving as they plunge through, giving new meaning to the term "bushwhacking." We can't send them out ahead where we could keep an eye on them, because too many decisions have to be made on which way to go. At least after Todd and I and the llamas go through, the path is a little more defined for them.

"Don't worry if your boots get wet and muddy. Clean socks in the truck tomorrow!"

Todd finally sees an orange sign, a fencepost, and a muddy logging trail—all desirable signs of civilization at this point. But to get to the trail we must cross a recently timbered area. I try to push through, stepping over logs and breaking branches, but I run into a dead end—a huge stack of brush up to my waist. I yell to Todd to take his boys in another direction, and he successfully does, but as soon as my llamas see his on the other side, they decide they're going through! I watch them actually get on their knees and crawl over the limbs, with panniers on! A leg punctures through the brush, a face gets poked, but I have no choice but to get on my knees and crawl with them.

Once across, we sit down by the muddy logging road and enjoy a well-deserved snack. We feel grateful not only because this is behind us, but also because it's Sunday and the loggers aren't working, so we won't be in trouble for being on private property.

We follow the skidder trail for a few miles until we reach an old cabin and a spring and decide to quit for the day. There's a ranch a few miles beyond, and we're hoping we can walk through in the morning without anyone noticing. Property is so expansive and spread out in this part of the country that there's a good chance the route Todd selected won't go anywhere near a home.

Suddenly we hear motors, and two four-wheelers come ripping around the corner. Luckily for us, we hadn't begun to set up the tent. These guys do not look happy to see us. They shut off their motors and we play dumb, saying we're lost and need help. One guy asks to see a map, and when Todd shows it to him, he sheepishly remembers he highlighted this exact location in brilliant yellow marker. We're right where we want to be!

They're looking for a lost steer. They warn us that tomorrow more than four hundred cattle will be herded out of the hills and trucked to the stockyard. We ask the best way out, and they tell us about a two-day walk to public land as opposed to a half-day walk to where our truck sits. We ask them to help us get the landowner's permission to cross his land, and although they consent, we're feeling as if we're a big inconvenience. They tell us they'll be back with an answer, but they advise us to "pack up and start walking a while."

As we hike, Todd and I discuss what we'll do if the answer is no. Do we turn around and hide until dark, then try to walk through in the night? That would make tired kids really cranky.

In about half an hour they return with permission granted. When we ask about camping, one says that in a few miles we'll walk right past the owner's home and can ask him ourselves. It's getting late, the temperature is dropping, we're very tired from a hard day, and we don't want to walk miles before we sleep.

The ranch house is crowded with pickups, horse trailers, kids getting crazy on four-wheelers, and friends and relatives of all ages milling around. I weave past their staring eyes to find the owner, feeling like a Martian. As a rule, cowboys are not fond of llamas.

Many look at them as sissy and faddish compared with the "American horse" that is credited with founding the West.

This is somewhat ironic, for although the horse is believed to have originated in America, the only horses that made it through prehistoric times were the ones that crossed the land bridge from Alaska to Asia. No horses survived in America. Horses were unknown to the Native Americans, who were in awe of the ones reintroduced to the wilds of America by the murderous Spanish conquistadors in the early 1500s. Like the horse, the Camelidae, ancestors of the llama, also originated in North America about forty million years ago. One branch of the family followed the horse across the land bridge to Asia about three million years ago, evolving into camels, while a smaller variety emigrated to South America, evolving into llamas, guanacos, vicuñas, and alpacas. Like the horse, the camelids that remained in North America died out about ten to twelve thousand years ago. Both animals were domesticated at roughly the same time, about five thousand years ago. And although the ancestors of the llama did not stray as far from their land of origin as the ancestors of the horse, llamas were not reintroduced here until much later, when they were imported to American zoos in the late 1800s.

I explain to the landowner that we got blown off Lost Ranger Peak—that we had not planned on coming this way but now need a place to put up our tent. Does he know of any spots? He says the next landowner down the valley would not take well to finding us on his land, so he directs us to a grassy spot by the creek and leaves us with these instructions: "You've gotta be gone by 7:30, for there's 450 cows coming through here, and we don't want them spooked by them llamas." No problem.

Come morning, truck after truck of bawling cows passes us as we walk out his dirt road. We laugh at the irony of it all. Of all days to pick to "secretly" cross private land and try to slide by unnoticed. We're wishing the Mikulsky boys could have been along for this last eventful day. It would have given even greater meaning to the words "hardship," "challenge," and "adventure." It all has to do with your reference point. Our truck and the end of the journey have never looked so good.

PART FIVE

THE CONTINENTAL DIVIDE TRAIL

To Mexico, 1998

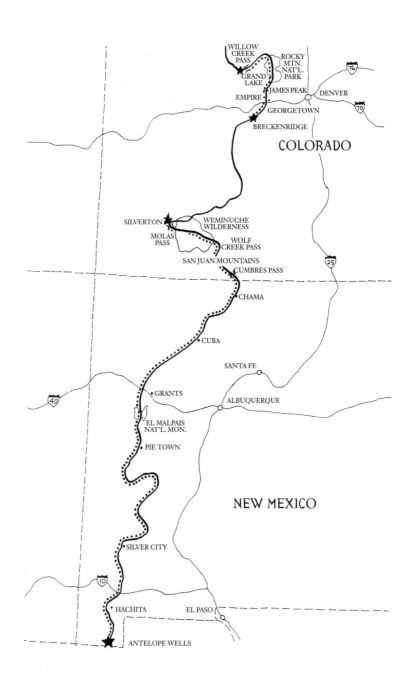

Northern Colorado
JULY 28, 1998

We do not quit playing because we grow old. We grow old because we quit playing.

—OLIVER WENDELL HOLMES

ON THIS last drive west, the kids scrape the meat out of their Slim Jims with their teeth and use the transparent casings to play doctor, making believe they are Band-Aids or pieces of skin for skin grafts. Sierra paints her toenails with colored markers. They draw, write, listen to story tapes, and chew bubble gum. They have a "morning piece" of gum and an "afternoon piece" and they can't get the first before nine o'clock or the second before noon. If they complain, they wait an additional five minutes for every whine. Sierra saves her chewed pieces from previous days on her window, and by Iowa she has one tough wad to chew. She's just learned to blow bubbles and pop them, and this is a great pastime. They've learned how to entertain themselves in the truck. We don't even know they're

271

along. Crossing the country feels "normal" and comfortable by our fifth year in a row.

As we speed farther from our Pennsylvania home, I think about all the people I've left behind who love me. I feel them thinking of me, and they never seem far away. It's as though a silver thread connects us. They'll be with us as we cross a very high stretch of mountains in northern and southern Colorado. We'll top out at the highest point on the entire trail at 13,000-foot James Peak. Once again we will be back in some of the worst areas in the world for lightning strikes. When we get to the border of Colorado and New Mexico, we'll trade our llamas for the tandem mountain bikes that are bolted to the roof of our Ford pickup. Riding across the desert pulling trailers of gear will be a whole new thing for us. Why, it's enough to get an adventuring family excited!

Todd reaches across the truck seat to brush my face with the back of his hand, and I kiss it. "Try to remember me this summer," I tell him, and he nods with emotion in his eyes.

Over the winter, he expressed his fears that this long journey may be taking its toll on our marriage. "Out there I've got six animals, two kids, and a wife that I'm leading across snowfields and raging rivers and rock slides that the rangers claim are impassable, and I'm supposed to think about how I'm going to caress my wife and how I'm going to connect with her on top of it. It's often more than I can handle."

But I don't feel guilty about this need that I have. In *A Woman's Worth*, Marianne Williamson says, "Women keep talking about human connections because we are coded to do so. We came into the world with the memory in our soul that this is our function here. It is not our weakness, our neurosis, or our addiction. It is our strength." I will not settle for anything less in my marriage. I look back at Todd across the truck cab and respond, "And I will try to go easy on you and allow you to be who you are and remember that you are doing the best job you can."

Marriage isn't linear or static, any more than the Continental Divide is. There are different ways to cover the distance and different directions to go to get to the end. The important thing is that we don't quit: we keep trying, we keep going, and we don't let our fears paralyze us.

"THE LAST first day on the trail," Todd announces as we walk away from the road. Within a few hundred yards, the children grab hands and skip and sing. In a few months, all the happiness they find on this Continental Divide Trail will be over. Border bound. For years we've been pushing for it. This is the year we will make it to Mexico. Bob "Reliable" Riley is with us for the first stretch, along with Chuck Eckenroth. Bob has shuttled us every summer, sometimes numerous times involving dozens of hours of driving and covering hundreds of miles.

This 150-mile stretch that we're doing in northern Colorado will dump us onto the Colorado Trail. For a while, the Continental Divide Trail and the Colorado Trail are the same. Where they are distinct, long-distance hikers have the option of going either route. Because of this, we have opted to not repeat this middle part of the state and will hop down to southern Colorado and the San Juan Mountains when we are through up here.

It's late July. The entire country is experiencing a blistering heat wave, but it's not hot up here in northern Colorado at 12,000 feet in the Never Summer Mountains. We are dressed for winter in layers of fleece and long underwear. It is also raining as we climb steeply, thousands of feet into the clouds. Todd and I both are experiencing altitude sickness, with dull headaches and nausea, a first in all these summers. We aren't yet acclimated to the altitude on our very first day. The llamas are dragging. Chips' legs are shaking, and Bob's llama, Mountain Man, lies down when he's supposed to be moving. Jerry has punctured his pad and limps. Grassy suffers from a saddle sore that developed after only a few days of rain. To lighten the llamas' loads, we've taken the kids off and asked them to walk, which they do happily. They're just rolling along, thinking kid thoughts, lost in their world.

Bryce is singing to himself as he holds my hand. "You're happy, aren't you honey?" I ask.

"Yep," he answers.

The clouds lift, revealing green grassy meadows stuffed with five kinds of just *yellow* flowers, let alone dozens of others. I hear Chuck hoot from the beauty. I think to myself, "This *is* enough."

After a few days in the high mountains we descend to the town of Grand Lake, where Bob bails out. He can't get Mountain Man to walk, and it's not fun pulling a fat llama across the mountains. He's going to miss the crown jewel, James Peak, at 13,294 feet one of the highest points on the entire 3,100-mile trail. He'll return in a week to hike a stretch of the San Juan Mountains in southern Colorado.

Devil's Thumb in the Indian Peaks Wilderness awaits, requiring a 2,290-foot ascent. The rugged rock monolith slowly takes shape against the eastern sky like "a giant stone troll on the horizon." Bryce is in heaven with this guidebook description, thinking up all sorts of devil-related stories to go with the landscape. The clouds blow across its face, hiding it, then revealing it. It's raining again, but we don't have the luxury of cutting our day short, for we must set ourselves up for the big climb of James Peak tomorrow. We meet a ranger who says that no one has been able to climb all week on account of the weather. We're hoping this stretch of rain breaks before we have to haul our llamas and children across it. The rock cairns that mark our route disappear in the fog, but fortunately the guidebook gives compass bearings so we are able to find our way down to Rollins Pass.

After the pass, we decide to walk an alternative route on a dirt road that traverses the mountain just below the exposed divide. The weather is deteriorating rapidly, and we have to make some miles. I'm pulling Bryce's llama, Fun Run, along at a good clip (three miles per hour), and it's making him bounce. Bryce can't hold his umbrella and hang on to the wooden saddle horn at the same time, so we forgo the protection of the umbrella and batten down the hatches of his rainsuit, hoping it will keep him dry. I keep asking him if he's OK, and he says he's having fun watching the hail collect in the llama's fur. Sierra walks with me, under her umbrella. I sing nonstop, trying to occupy the kids' minds.

Other climbers bail off the ridge, their vehicles competing for space on the road. They slow to a near stop, roll down their windows to snap our pictures, and exclaim from the warmth and safety of their cars, "Oh, you look so cute."

"I don't feel so cute," I reply, as the rain pelts down harder and thunder booms and lightning cracks. Up on that ridge is no place to be now.

After a few miles Bryce says, "I know you're going to be mad at me, but I have to poo." He knows we're trying to hurry and get to a place to camp, and these open meadows on both sides of the road are not a good place to hide. Sierra is walking but lagging far behind.

"What's the matter?" I yell to her. She refuses to answer, but when she catches up to Bryce and me, I can see she's been crying. She is having a hard time.

When I pull down Bryce's three pairs of pants he says, "I feel like an ice cube." I slide my hand up his back and discover that his three layers are soaked from his neck to his waist, despite his raincoat. He looks up at me and says, "I feel like I'm in a dream."

I scream to Todd and Chuck, never minding that the kids' ears are two feet away, "Find a place to camp right now!" I don't care where we are. This child is in the beginning stage of hypothermia. We set up the tent, strip the kids of clothing, and tell them to climb into their bags. They wiggle down to the bottoms, giggling and delighted to be warm and dry and not moving.

No matter that I badger everyone about how they're feeling: therein lies the danger of hypothermia. You often don't realize you aren't doing well. The reasoning part of your brain shuts down in the initial stages. Todd and I have been in the beginning stage numerous times, and we have also come to the aid of over a dozen people who were in the advanced stage. Some were sleeping in the snow with full packs on, just wanting to catnap. Fall asleep while hypothermic and you die, since your body temperature will continue to drop to the point of no return. We've watched a wet, hypothermic hiker walk over to an empty fire pit and strike match after match trying to start a fire and get warm, without a single stick of wood or even a piece of paper. After we helped him out of his wet clothes, got him into his sleeping bag, and put some hot food into him, he was fine. It takes someone else paying attention to the signs and then acting immediately. To have this happen to my children sends a shiver down my spine. I feel as if I am not doing a good job of taking care of them. I feel terrible. We have to be more vigilant.

There are only a few mountains like James Peak on a long trail—in your life, really. The guidebooks say this about James

Peak: "A rope is not needed but use extreme caution scrambling around the boulders of granite." "Those with a fear of heights may be a little squeamish here as the trail hovers 1,500 feet above the valley floor, then climbs another 1,300 feet to the steep summit of James Peak." "Large fields of talus pose an impossible challenge for pack stock."

Todd obsesses about this last one. It keeps him up at night worrying. But the day dawns crystal clear, and we are grateful the bad weather is gone. The trail is superbly engineered as it traverses around some ominous-looking rock pinnacles on its way to the summit. The treadway is narrow but safe, even though the rock slides and steep fields of talus drop off mere inches from our boot soles, enough to make us feel dizzy and nervous. We marvel at the dynamited trail; because of an excellent trail crew, we are able to negotiate this safely without rock climbing and without risking our lives. Chuck hikes directly behind my two children on their llamas and tells them stories to distract them from the steep drop-offs. This is exactly the kind of trail I love: exposed and exciting.

At one or two spots the trail has been washed out, forcing us to unhook the llamas and lead them across the rock slide individually. The monstrous north face of the hulking mountain lures us up; there's not a cloud in the sky, and we are happy. On the last pitches, Todd angles away from the talus and winds up narrow swaths of grass that snake between the rocks, making it easier for the llamas to walk. The kids can't ride, and at one point Bryce resorts to crawling on his hands and knees. The steepness and the altitude, 13,000 feet, make it hard to breathe.

We look for the circle of rocks that marks the summit and wedge the llamas' lead ropes between boulders, for there are no posts up here to tie them to. We are on top of the world. Mountain ranges march off in all distances, some buried in snow. The sun is warm and the air is calm, posing no threat. We lounge on rocks and relish being this high in the heavens. In the tundra grass, nestled between the rocks, are fragile pink Arctic flowers.

We've earned this reward. In this lifestyle, it eventually evens out. You always wish for a clear, calm day when you have to be up this high. And for extra special mountains like James Peak, you wish for a stellar day. I'd suffer through weeks of rain for one summit day like this, anytime.

FOR THREE THOUSAND FEET, the trail drops us out of the sky to Loch Lomond, a beautiful mountain lake at the base of the peak with a snow-white waterfall cascading into it. On an adjacent dirt road, a jeep pulls up and two people approach. Debbie and John Dehyne live near the town of Empire, our destination tomorrow. They tell us about a fabulous restaurant called Jenny's that serves excellent inexpensive food in ridiculous portions that can't even fit on the plates. Not ridiculous for trail appetites, however. They know a woman in town who also has llamas, and they'll call and set up boarding for us. Debbie also generously invites us to stay at their home. "There are beds enough for everyone," she says.

I can hardly contain my joy as we descend into town. I have Jenny's on my mind. Our own tired lunch food does nothing for us at this point, not even the candy bag.

Todd works his map and compass as we descend on mining roads. This area boasts seven thousand mines in a mere twenty-mile radius, not including test pits. The miners dig holes and dynamite them to check on the type of rock. Some of the shafts are twenty feet deep with vertical sides; the guidebook warns to not venture off the trail. The mountainsides are covered with ocher-colored tailings. This is the sulfur in pyrite (fool's gold), which turns this color when it comes in contact with the air.

Two smiling people stand outside Jenny's when we arrive. The restaurant owner and the waiter greet us personally and show us where we can feed the llamas a meal of lush grass while we indulge in our own feast. Debbie called the owner (who happens to be her sister-in-law) and told her we were coming.

Jenny's is named after a mule that accidentally ate dynamite on the site of the restaurant. The inside is decorated with antique mining memorabilia. The food is mouth watering. Thick steak fries flank colossal sandwiches. Bowls are heaped with golden brown onion rings. Bryce can't control himself even though he doesn't like onions. We guzzle large pitchers of ice water, relieving our dehydration. We roll out of there, satisfied for the first time in weeks, and down to the Dehynes.

John is a hard-rock miner who loves his occupation. He shares his extensive rock collection with Sierra while Debbie and I talk over the kitchen sink, washing lettuce and slicing vegetables like longtime friends. Her older daughter braids Sierra's hair, and Bryce and her son swap favorite books. They invite the whole neighborhood out to play flashlight tag that night, and Debbie hands us the keys to her van so we can run errands the next day and tour the Phoenix Gold Mine, a real working mine. We give our new friends a hug goodnight and tuck ourselves into our comfy beds. This is just what the children needed. They've have so little contact with other kids on this hike, and they're thrilled to be playing with people their own age.

We descend from the mountains, meet complete strangers, and find ourselves welcomed into their home and their lives in a matter of hours. Only in an adventuring lifestyle does this seem to happen to us. We have no idea there are so many angels walking this planet until we put ourselves in a position of need.

Timmy Lebling has joined us again for a few days on this last summer of fun, after making that long drive down from Alaska. His first night on the trail turns out to be one of those moments that remain with you the rest of your life.

My eagle-eyed daughter is the first to spot the beaver, silently gliding in the pond near our camp by Peru Creek. She watches only a few seconds before running wildly back to our tent to tell us, so excited she can hardly speak. We've spent enough time in the backcountry to know that beavers rarely show themselves to humans, so we all drop what we we're doing to follow. I grab the binoculars, Todd and Sierra grab cameras, and we all troop back to the pond.

Creeping toward the stick dam, we watch as the beaver chews a willow branch in two with its sharp teeth. Then, sprig clenched in its mouth, it swims to the dam and disappears. We wait, scanning the pond and trying to guess where the beaver will resurface. The kids gasp when the slick, round head parts the water and the dark, beady eyes reappear. Sierra isn't happy until she sneaks barefoot through the mud to stand closer to the dam, where for an hour she watches the beaver swim back and forth. Timmy puts Bryce on his shoulders, and we all watch that beaver, whacking and slapping his tail so close to Sierra that she gets soaked. She clicks picture after picture, yelling, "Got it!" every time. Not until evening falls and her beaver friend retires for the night does she skip back to our campsite. "Mama," she says, "today was one of the happiest days of my life."

While we are watching the beavers, a small summer shower moistens the land, bringing a brilliant double rainbow that stretches right over the beaver pond. A golden eagle soars above us, its mighty head glowing from the setting sun. I look at my family and dear friends, and we exchange a glance that clearly says, "These are the times of our lives. This is what we leave home to find."

Since Timmy can hike for only a few days, he's loaded his monster pack with fresh food to cook us fabulous meals. He raises dough under his shirt next to his warm belly for filled calzones. He bakes apple cake in a reflector oven. While he cooks, he wears a tall white chef's hat silkscreened with a bottle of vinegar and half an avocado. "I have a game," he says, while he stirs. "Everybody look down. When I say, 'Look up!' pick someone's face to look at." I don't know why, but we all find it hysterical, catching each other staring with silly looks on our faces.

Fun is contagious when Timmy is around. The kids find a big old box spring lying in the woods; there are old mining cabins up and down this valley. They spend half an hour bouncing on it, having a blast until Sierra's butt hits Bryce's jaw, causing him to bite his tongue. He cries for only a minute until Sierra climbs a tree and tells Bryce to throw up his shoe so she can try to catch it. After a while I say to her, "Come down and let your brother up. It's his turn to catch shoes." As soon as the absurd command is out of my mouth, we burst out laughing, for this simple game sounds so silly yet is bringing them so much fun.

After dinner Timmy finds a stick, takes the kids' foam ball, sets up bases with pot lids, and divides us into baseball teams. One team is called the Blue Ribbons and the other, the Box Springs. Sierra is so excited she is screaming silly things to distract the other side and cheer her team on to victory. Bryce is dead serious, competitive male that he is. The Box Springs lose by a hair, and Timmy yells, "OK, Box Springs, it's back to spring training!"

We ascend to the town of Montezuma, at 10,000 feet, named after the gloriously rich Aztec ruler. This authentic Colorado mining town was rich in the 1800s too, for there was abundant silver tucked in seams throughout this area. The population swelled to eight hundred back then, but only seventy-five eclectic folks hang around today. We've heard rumors of an eating establishment, so we walk down the middle of the one street in the quiet town. A plywood sign sits propped in a metal barrel right in the middle of the road. The layers are beginning to separate, but the words "4th Street" that are painted on it still work as a road sign.

A purple-painted place called Soup and Whiskey is not open, but the Soulhouse is. The tables are old doors, and each chair is different. Old upholstered furniture lines the walls, inviting you to pick up a magazine from their stack and read while your food is being prepared. Healthful vegetarian fare is on the menu, and although Bryce had his heart set on a cheeseburger, we all happily fill up to the tunes of Bob Marley and the Wailers.

As WE DESCEND into Breckenridge, I am pulled right back to that day five years ago when we walked this same route on the Colorado Trail. Bryce was a year old and in diapers, riding on Todd's back since he was too little to ride a llama. Sierra was just a peewee herself, three years old, and riding her trusty steed Berrick. We had borrowed llamas for that first trip and thought it would be one summer and done. But it was on this very road walk, after completing our first week on the trail, that we realized we had fallen in love with this crazy nomadic life.

And here we are, five years later. Tall and lithe, eight-year-old Sierra is riding confidently and happily, talking about riding horses when she outgrows llamas. Bryce, six years old and hiking along at two and a half miles an hour, loves hiking with a passion. Both of them are comfortable in their wilderness home. And then there are my husband and me. How have we changed over the past five years? We're learning to honor who we are, rejoice in our differences, find the courage to ask for what we need, and put forth our best efforts to take care of each other.

"Taking care of each other," we've found, involves so much more than leading our family from Canada to Mexico. Just as you can't get sloppy or apathetic out here in the wilderness without jeopardizing your safety, neither can you afford to take each other for granted in marriage.

Five summers of living and traveling on the Continental Divide, with the end growing closer in sight. We've come full circle.

23

The San Juan Mountains
AUGUST 15, 1998

Heaven is under our feet as well as over our heads.
—HENRY DAVID THOREAU

WHEN YOU top a pass in the San Juan Mountains, you can usually see the trail stretching before you—a tiny line winding, contouring, climbing over grassy ridge after grassy ridge. It's as if the mountains were made of bright green modeling clay and you took a toothpick and scratched the trail over the tops. We'll look up at a ridge's horizon line where it scrapes the blue heavens and think, "What a wonderful place to walk," and to our delight the trail will head up there. With binoculars, we can follow the trail for the entire day's walk ahead. To see how you are going to move across the land for the next ten miles and eight hours, and even where you will make camp for the night, is very exciting.

282

We have entered the Weminuche Wilderness in the San Juan Mountains, a vast, remote land where the trail rarely dips below 12,000 feet. At 488,544 acres, it is Colorado's largest wilderness area. It was designated back in 1975 as a place "where the earth and its community of life are untrammeled by man, where man himself is a visitor who does not remain." Walking through these mountains is said to be the most breathtaking experience on the entire Continental Divide Trail. It is so secluded, with beauty so rare reaching to such incredible heights, that a visitor cannot help but come away with a feeling of great humility and reverence. We are thrilled to be back here again.

For much of the next week, the trail will hug the Divide, never drifting more than a few hundred yards from the crest. There are some craggy peaks, but our trail tends to stay on the grassy, rounded ridges with gentle saddles and lush meadows that beg you to walk across them. It's one of the longest stretches with no interference of any sort from civilization. There are no roads or power lines anywhere, and it is rare to see people. Once you enter, there are no easy ways out.

It's no wonder this segment is considered the last best hope for grizzly bear habitat in Colorado. The last grizz was killed back in 1951, but in 1979 a rancher saw three huge bears that he swears were too big to be black bears. Researchers and wildlife advocates are making a concerted effort to find conclusive evidence that the grizzly exists in Colorado. Our chance of seeing one, however, is slimmer than our chance of getting struck by lightning, which feels very possible.

There is a feeling of buoyancy up here. The sun is bright and warm. The clouds are always changing, growing, expanding. Some traverses are airy and hair-raising as we cross steep slopes that fall away into secluded valleys far below. These extreme drop-offs of many thousands of feet go down to creeks to lakes to meadows. A *drainage*. That geological term is becoming embedded in our minds in these San Juan Mountains. Little freshets trickle down the steep slopes, converge, and turn into a stream. We can see the waters of the Continental Divide being born all around us.

Because we are so high and so exposed, lightning is a real danger. We must always have one ear cocked for distant thunder. Sometimes dark clouds build at ten in the morning, rumbling like a giant's empty stomach. Traditionally a mountain climber should be down by one or two o'clock to be safe from afternoon thunderstorms, but weather happens anytime in these mountains. Either we suit up the kids in raingear four to five times a day or we start them off in full uniform first thing in the morning. This is both an attempt to stay dry and a good luck charm to ward off inclement weather. Not much can dampen our good mood these last days, however; not even pea-sized hail that the wind drives stinging against our bare legs. It just adds a margin of heart-thumping excitement to this gorgeous country.

Bob Riley has returned for this memorable stretch, as has Beth Ellen from Michigan, one of our annual "regulars" who hates to miss a year with the Llama Family. It's only fitting that we end our last hiking experience in the San Juan Mountains, the best of the best.

IT'S ON THIS stretch that I come to appreciate the extent of my son's ability to focus on a world beyond the Continental Divide—the world of his imagination.

The storytelling continues. He makes up rhyming poems about Bonemen and tells extremely long stories about goblins and ghouls. I try to look around and be in the moment, but the wind is blowing, the llamas' bells are tinkling, and as he concentrates his voice fades until I can hardly hear. He might ask, "Doesn't that part give you the shivers and the quivers?" I can easily answer "You bet!" without paying attention, but when he gets sidetracked and loses his place, he quizzes me. "Where was I?" I try to repeat his last few words, hoping that's enough, but often he's wise to me.

No one else can even speak when he's in the middle of these stories. If I yell "Which way?" to Todd at an intersection, his feelings get wounded. Sierra competes to get a word in edgewise. She'll say, "Mom! Mom!" and I turn around to see her blowing up her cheeks with air and sticking her index finger in her mouth as if she's ready to barf, she's so sick of the stories. He turns around, sees her, and starts to cry.

When he tells me stories on the trail, he often hikes ahead of me, spending as much time turning around and looking at me for a reaction as going forward. It gets annoying to vary my pace, slowing down and speeding up as he moves through the story. Sometimes it would be nice to hike and not have to think about running into him. I decide to make a point and bop him on the heel with my foot, pretending I got too close and tripped on him. But he's on to me; he turns around with a stricken look in his face and says, "What kind of mama would kick her little son on purpose? On purpose!" I can't help laughing at my little actor, which pleases him even less.

If he's telling me a story in camp, he follows me around while I do my chores, from the llamas' panniers to the tent to the kitchen area.

The most amazing behavior, however, is when he creates these stories in his head as he hikes and all we see is the playacting. He finds a stick with a few branches broken off that looks like a crude gun. For half an hour he pretends he's a robber, shooting and making all kinds of mouth sounds. Or he finds a horseshoe and holds it with his shirtsleeve pulled over his hand pretending he's Captain Hook. For an hour he imagines he's a pirate, using a deep voice to make up poetry about pirates. He does all this while he's walking his normal pace of two and a half miles an hour, but he doesn't walk on the trailbed. The trail is frequently in a ditch, eroded by horse hooves and hiking boots. He crosses back and forth from the trailbed's ridge to the ditch, to the other ridge, and back down again. He stumbles over tufts of grass and rocks, putting in far more miles than necessary going back and forth. I say to him, "Bryce, stay on the trail. It's easier. Bryce, stay on the trail," but it only lasts a step or two. He's oblivious.

He's also oblivious to what's happening inside his boots. I never see his sock tops, just his lily white ankles. At breaks I take off his shoes and find fabric bunched up around his toes and jammed under his instep.

"Doesn't it bother you to hike like that?" I ask.

"I never even feel it, Mama," is his smiling, honest answer.

THERE IS a huge rock notch on the Continental Divide, a unique formation known as the Window, that the shepherds used to consider haunted. They referred to it as the Devil's Window because of the violent thunderstorms that hang around it. They never even ventured close to the hundred-foot vertical walls of the Window, and they certainly didn't go through it. Very close by on the ridge is the Rio Grande Pyramid, a perfectly pointed symmetrical cone that creates its own nasty weather. Both the Pyramid and the Window are prominent features of the Weminuche Wilderness, noticeable from every point of view for many miles.

We watch the Window and the Pyramid draw closer as we wind deeper into the wilderness, always keeping our eyes on the sky. The cumulonimbus storm clouds explode from expanding moisture and pressure. One minute the sky is calm and happy with puffy picnic clouds, and five minutes later we turn around and they've turned nasty and black and ominous. We have about two hours of safe hiking each day, the rest is risky. Lightning cracks all around us, and we are frequently pelted by hail. The trail is sometimes like a river of pouring water, with white balls of hail floating on the surface. Our boots get soaked, and the icy BBs sting our calves. If it gets really wicked, we hole up in a dense evergreen thicket. The llamas smell different when they're wet, like a wet wool sweater combined with the smell of rich earth. We find their odors pleasant, both wet and dry. Even their compact little droppings are not offensive. When their coats are wet, their compacted fleece lies flat against their bodies. This late in a summer's hike, their winter fat is gone. They are lean hiking machines.

Besides being good companions and marvelous work animals, the llamas have always been a source of entertainment, especially for the children. Sierra noticed that as they walk they look to the left and then to the right and then to the left and then to the right. There is a definite rhythm to their watching that lets them cover all directions so no wild animals can go by unnoticed. We learned years ago not to put much energy into searching the open areas for game ourselves but to watch the llamas instead. They always see animals long before we do.

They chew their cuds in a rhythm too. Two chews on one side and then two chews on the other. It's almost comical. All these idiosyncrasies increase our fondness for these creatures that are completely responsible for making our wilderness excursions possible.

It's no wonder we are filled with horror when two women with a boxer dog come down the trail behind us. "We're not sure what our dog will do to your llamas," they warn. In a matter of seconds the dog breaks its flimsy snap latch and makes a beeline for our boys. I manage to get the kids off my llamas in time and safely to the side, but Bob's two llamas and Todd's three are ready targets. First the snarling, barking dog goes for their legs, biting their exposed tendons. The poor llamas go crazy, running in circles around Todd and Bob. The owner screams profanities at the dog and tries to catch it. Both men try to kick the dog away, but they have the frantic llamas to deal with. The ropes get tangled around their bodies, and Todd's pack frame keeps getting caught in the lead rope. Then the dog begins leaping in the air, aiming for the llamas' necks. It latches onto one of Bob's llamas and hangs on. The woman is screaming at the dog and finally grabs it and throws it onto the ground. She lays her full body weight on top, but it struggles to get back to its victims. Todd throws himself on top too, and they both manage to still it. No sooner does Todd tie the leash to its collar then the woman jumps up, and they both go running down the trail away from us with the dog. In a flash it's over, as quickly as it began, and we are left staring with our mouths open wide.

Bob's injured llama is standing by himself across the creek looking traumatized. His name is Bryce, after our son, for he was born while we were visiting Bob a few years ago. This is his first pack trip.

We descend to Weminuche Meadow to camp for the night and take stock of the situation. The dog evidently didn't penetrate the llama's skin, since his wool is so thick. But he's jumpy, and he flips out when he sees Beth's backpack with its rain cover on because he can't identify it. (Bob later reports that he's never gotten back to normal.)

Weminuche Meadow is directly on the pass, and it is so broad and flat that it's impossible to determine the route of the divide just by looking at it. This gentle mile-wide pass was a favorite crossing for the Weminuche Indians, a subtribe of the Utes. There were many well-established Indian trails here in the 1870s when the first European settlers arrived. But the pioneers and mineral discoveries pushed all the Utes out of their beautiful homeland onto reservations and then even farther into Utah.

The grasses in the meadow are long and luxurious. They nearly make us seasick swaying in the wind. We stake the llamas out in the great undulating waves of green, and it calms us all.

A few days after Weminuche Pass, we climb to Piedra Pass, where researchers recently discovered the remains of an ancient Anasazi settlement. The artifacts unearthed here date back to 5,900 B.C. The San Juan Mountains are some of the oldest in the state, dated to more than one billion years ago. Their high summits have eroded into grassy meadows with stunning lakes, our favorite places to camp. Tonight at Archuleta Lake we sit and look out over the mountains and watch the sun go down. We can see New Mexico from here. Tomorrow both Bob and Beth go home, and we are left with one small stretch to hike through the Southern San Juan Wilderness.

IN THIS beautiful setting I look at my tent, my home for these past weeks, and I think that this is all I need. All that "stuff" back home in my house—the papers, the clutter, the things to put away, to deal with, to clean—is all so complicated. It is so difficult to keep my focus on what's important and not get caught up in the minutiae of that life once we go home. I need to return again and again to the wilderness to help me remember how to focus.

This is why Beth keeps returning. Back home in Michigan, she has a high-powered job as a statistical analyst conducting surveys and gathering data from all over the world. She comes out here to settle down, to center herself, to be reminded of what she loves and what is important: mountains and the wilderness. She leaves behind a husband and a daughter (who is Bryce's age). In these mountains, she feels she's home.

I also need an annual pilgrimage to the mountains. Our goal of hiking the entire Continental Divide Trail has created a concrete reason to come out here summer after summer. I can look at it as a job, for without covering the miles and achieving the goal, I have no book to write. But for me as for Beth, it has also become my salvation, and I'm concerned about how I'll cope when it is indeed finally done and I'm left without a practical reason to return.

I ask Bob what he will do when this hike is over, when he needs an adventure and a fix of our company. He pops onto the trail to join us whenever he wants to hike, often a few times a summer. Pennsylvania is a long way from Colorado, and we don't expect to come west anytime soon after we finish this marathon journey. It's a lonely trail when you're going solo compared with our lively company. I can't imagine not seeing him and sharing an adventure every summer. When I tell him these feelings, he brushes me off with the flip answer, "Oh, we'll see each other," not suggesting how.

I realize that some people come into your life to serve a definite purpose, and once that is accomplished they fade back into your memory. Bob is too important to me to allow that to happen, and it makes me sad to think of him missing from my life.

It's disturbing to think of the end. The CDT has been our life-motivating force for six years. Although 650 miles of cycling through New Mexico remain, the hiking section will soon be over.

One thing that is bound to improve once we return home is our sex life. Sex simply isn't fun in our cramped tent, and it rarely occurs. The kids are too big and take up much more room than they did as toddlers. Their bodies are inches from ours. We have to freeze about three or four times and stare at children moving in their sleep to see if their eyes open. Bryce often rolls over into the "arena." Sierra throws an arm across us or turns and shoves her butt into our bodies. Todd and I certainly can't engage in any acrobatics. We can't let out a peep, let alone a moan. I'm not ready to explain the facts of life in detail should the kids catch us in a strange position or doing something that makes no sense to them. This has been one of Todd's very basic needs, like my hunger for affection and emotional connection, and it has been severely neglected on these hikes. My mother taught me that if a couple has a good sex life, they can overcome most obstacles and ignore most differences. But without it a man simply cannot be truly happy. I have to say Mom was pretty right on. I've found that all things in life, in marriage, run smoother with good and frequent sex, even a long-distance llama hike down the Continental Divide Trail. Next trip we'll bring a separate tent for the kids!

The Southern San Juan Wilderness is quiet and remote and is a fine blend of Colorado mountains and New Mexico's mesas. It is indeed our transition into our next adventure. In the beginning the land is just as beautiful as the Weminuche with its high open country packed full of peaks and drainages. These mountains are considerably drier, however. Lakes and ponds are infrequent, and our water sources are much farther apart. Sheep graze in flocks of more than a thousand. They scare our llamas, even from afar, and the herding dogs do their job and make us walk wide arcs around them.

The sheep are something different to look at and deal with out here, but it's the wild animals that have always pulled at the kids. Sierra spots a pika, a cute little furry member of the rabbit family with wide ears. It squeaks and hides from her, but she answers it and coaxes it out of its home in the rocks with pieces of grass. Pikas are "hay makers." They bite off seedheads and stalks of grass and lay them on the rocks to dry, making hay that they store for the winter. She patiently sits by the pika's rocky home, talking to it in a squeaky voice and hoping for even a glimpse.

Bryce would often rather draw the animals, but he's especially fond of make-believe creatures. These last days of hiking, his drawings have centered on creatures eating all kinds of delicious-looking food. He says he's starving for real barbecued meat, which he says he'd rather have than candy, especially tonight. One thing we'll enjoy from the upcoming cycling section is the opportunity to hit stores where we can indulge in something other than trail mix and freeze-dried slop.

The closer we get to the New Mexico border and Cumbres Pass, the more the landscape changes. It opens up into broad mesas where we strain our eyes to see as far as possible, searching for rock cairns to guide us to the border. Coyotes call, reminding us that the desert lies ahead. The night before heading into town, we heat water in a pot to wash up. We all use my clean underwear as a wash-cloth and enjoy how luxurious the steaming wet cotton feels against our cheeks. When we finish, the kids take turns putting their dirty feet in the pot of water and cannot believe how wonderful it feels: very simple pleasures.

24

Cycling New Mexico
SEPTEMBER 6, 1998

The way I see it, if you want the rainbows, you gotta put up with the rain.
—DOLLY PARTON

"SHOULD WE GO FOR IT?" I ask Sierra, my stoker on the rear of my tandem bike. She bends around my body to size up the long ribbon of asphalt. Our hill descends for twenty straight miles from the top of the Continental Divide at Cumbres Pass into the village of Chama, New Mexico, our destination for the night. Not a bad way to start this new adventure—the longest downhill coast we've ever experienced. Todd and Bryce snap on helmets, pull on their bike gloves, and get ready to follow us down the mountain.

"Let's do it," she yells, and I slip my shoes into the toe baskets, murmur a prayer, and shove off. I keep a firm grip on the brakes and roll at a conservative speed. The eighty pounds in my bike trailer are pushing us downward along with our own weight, which totals two hundred pounds, plus the bulk of our bike. That's a lot of weight barreling down the mountainside, and Todd is afraid we'll burn out our brakes from the start. Still, it's going to take a little while before I can confidently balance and take hairpin turns at an aggressive speed.

Sierra excitedly yells back one-word instructions for Bryce. "Up!" means to rise off your seat because we're approaching a bump, such as a railroad track. The stokers in the rear can't see what hazards lie ahead. They need to be alerted to jolts that could surprise them and throw off their balance or just plain hurt their bottoms. Sierra turns around to see how far the boys are trailing and to warn me when a vehicle is following. Already we are a team. Todd and I will be chained to our children for the next few weeks and 650 miles. Who knows what lies in store for us?

We boarded our llamas at Wally White's ranch in Durango, Colorado, and traded the boys for bikes. On our traverse down the state, we'll be using the newly designated Great Divide Mountain Bike Trail that parallels the Divide, from Canada to Mexico, for 2,465 miles. It often uses the Divide as a guide, sticking as close to it as possible while attempting to stay on public lands.

Our experience crossing the Great Divide Basin in Wyoming convinced us that this leg of the journey is no place for animals or small children. With water sources up to forty miles apart (that's four days of walking for this group) and the greatest part of the unbuilt "trail" being on roads, two-wheel travel seemed the only way possible. We figure that as long as it's self-propelled travel it's fair.

This longest off-pavement cycling route in the world was designed for "bike packers," long-distance riders who tote the gear they need to stay out for extended periods. It was never meant to be a hard-core mountain bike trail. Roughly 80 percent of the route is on dirt and gravel roads, with 10 percent single-track trails and 10 percent pavement.

We fly down the mountain and arrive in "camp" on the outskirts of Chama in what seems like minutes. We enjoy an ice cream Blizzard at Dairy Queen and quickly conclude, "We like this bike riding stuff!"

But as breezy as the first day is, day two is steeped in misery. The hills kill me—especially the hills we confront between 11:00 A.M. and 2:00 P.M., when the blazing sun is highest in the sky. Although it's September, it's unseasonably hot in New Mexico. I shift my gears lower and lower until I announce to my stoker, "That's it." First gear. Everything after this is sheer muscle power. My legs burn, feeling as if I'd spent the summer lounging on a sofa watching TV instead of climbing the Rocky Mountains. When I can no longer push, I make the second announcement: "I'm getting off."

Todd and I are now forced to push our rigs up the hill, making all of us walk in the sun. We tell the kids to take off their helmets, for the heat inside has built up to dizzying temperatures, and put up their colorful kiddie umbrellas in an attempt at shade. This infuriates Sierra.

"You're a wimp, Mom. You didn't even try. I wish I was on Dad's bike."

I respond the same way, "Well, you're not pushing. I'm doing most of the work myself."

The children don't *have* to power the bikes. They do have to peddle, however, for the chain connects both sets of pedals and their feet spin in the same rhythm as ours. Todd's bike has a rear "stoker set" that lifts Bryce's entire crankcase up so his short legs can peddle in unison. Sierra's pedals have metal blocks adding the few inches she needs to reach the pedals, allowing her feet to spin with mine. When we're on a tough hill, we can use all the help we can get. Although Sierra isn't interested in straining her muscles, mine give out pretty quickly.

Bryce is next to voice his opinion. "I'm so hot," he complains. "I hate this. I wish I was in school."

Todd gives me a look that communicates, "Rather be in school? That's pretty bad. Are we biting off too much here?" Still, after all these miles, we continue to ask that question.

I search the road ahead for a large sagebush or a tree that rises above the rest and casts a long shadow. But this vast sandy land is merely spotted with shrubs—mesquite, rabbitbrush, sage—nothing very tall or dense. The sky is so big, and there are very few places to hide from it. Trying to get cooler, we cram ourselves under, or rather into, a bush, with sticks and leaves in our hair. Even the meager shade from a speed-limit sign is welcome. The kids huddle together and contort their bodies to the shape of a triangle or a rectangle or a circle, depending on the sign, moving every few minutes as the sun travels across the sky.

Some sort of highway marker or metal sign to lean our bikes against is also a prerequisite before we can take a break, since our bikes have no kickstands. I lean my rig against the metal stake, and then Todd leans his against mine. Even if there were kickstands, they couldn't hold up all this weight.

Todd is pulling a one-wheeled B.O.B. (Beast of Burden) trailer behind his bike. It tracks great compared with my Burley two-wheeler, but he must balance his tandem perfectly upright when walking and pushing or else the weight of the trailer will pull his whole rig over. Of course both our trailers are packed way beyond the manufacturers' recommended weights, but we have four people's gear to cart, even though we've pared down considerably since the llamas carried our gear.

By 10:00 A.M. the sun is ferocious. I smear SPF 50 sunscreen on all exposed skin. Bryce scrunches up his face so it doesn't get in his eyes. "You're making me look like a vampire!"

"Eat something," I tell both children as I dump out the contents of our lunch bag in the dirt. But no one feels like eating. Just drinking. The water in our bottles is hot.

"I'm not drinking anymore," Bryce announces.

"You have to. You'll die."

In the midday hours, we're in hell. We fantasize about downhills, shade, small stores with cold sodas, and salty snacks. Ice would be more than a person could ask for.

After forty miles and eight hours in the saddle, I convince Todd to call it a day. Although the sun is still high with plenty of hours left to ride, we're spent. With the help of the kids pushing from behind, we plow through the roadside ditch and the scrubby desert to an out-of-sight shade patch. At first glance the bright land looks fairly flat, but it's laced with ditches and shallow ravines, providing our camping spot with a bit of privacy. Off come boots, socks, tight black cycling shorts. Our resilient children, already recovered, lounge on their foam pads, drawing and reading in T-shirts and bare butts. I open cans of chili and chunk chicken, dividing even the broth into fourths. No hot food for us. I ease back in my chair, face stiff with salty dried sweat and layers of suntan lotion, and say to my husband—Trail Boss turned Road Boss—"I want you to find the quickest, smoothest route to Mexico. Blacktop is my preference." This isn't an environment we want to linger in.

In the tent, the kids take turns sleeping next to me. They like a mother's hugs and kisses and back rubs. After reading a bit of *My Teacher Is an Alien* aloud, Bryce leans over to kiss me goodnight.

"I love this mama," he says to me.

"I love this son," I say in return.

Sierra is becoming a night owl like her mother and stays up with me to read.

I light a candle and begin to write in my journal while Todd studies tomorrow's route. He learns that the Great Divide Mountain Bike Route sometimes offers alternatives, which are often on the blacktop—a less than desirable option for those on foot, but just the opposite on two wheels. A bonus is that these routes are closer to the actual Divide, which has always been our focus. I feel relieved. In my journal I quote Helen Keller: "Life is either a daring adventure or nothing." Just because it isn't easy doesn't mean we can't find something of value out here. We've come so far from Canada, with its glaciers and grizzlies. I'm not going home now.

AFTER SIERRA and I have our little spat over our dissatisfaction with each other's performance on the bike, we quickly realize that neither of us can make it without the other. We need to be supportive and work together. Now when we see a hill on the horizon, we size it up and decide aloud whether we think can make it. We evaluate the downhill that precedes it to determine whether cranking into twenty-first gear will pull us up. Once we begin to climb, I announce the gears as I go through them and then tell her when we need to pump like well-oiled pistons. I tell her when she must give it all she's got for that last burning push and when she can relax.

Every time we gain a summit without getting off to walk, we collectively feel we've won a small victory.

Todd and I know how to take care of our kids' needs, but communicating with them as tandem partners is an all new skill. Anything that is second nature and done without thinking while riding alone on a single bike must be planned and announced while on a tandem. For instance, you should say when you need to stop pedaling to get a drink from your bottle or to stand up on the pedals and get the weight off your bottom for a few seconds. Any sudden jerkiness can cause a wreck. We also work together to get off and on the bikes. I straddle the bike while Sierra hops on. If I'm not ready and my feet aren't spread far apart, she rips the skin off my legs as she spins her pedals into position. Sometimes I kick her when I mount if she's not paying attention and I'm not careful. Sierra holds the bike steady for me when I stop to take a picture and can even hold it on a hill for a short time if she applies the brakes. I like this role where I am much more than a mom. I can see how my daughter, through this unique partnership, helps shape who I am and helps me to become a better person. (Todd sees things differently, he tells me jokingly. He does not see them as partners back there. He sees them as dead weight and thinks we're just hauling their butts around.)

After heading directly south from the Colorado border, our route leaves the town of Cuba and angles west across Navajo land, through the tiny reservation towns of Torreon, Pueblo Pintada, and White Horse. In the three days and one hundred or so miles it will take to cross reservation land, we will indeed be visitors in another nation. The Navajos have a sovereign government with their own laws. We are concerned about the laws on trespassing. This open country does not allow us to inconspicuously get off the road and set up camp. In Cuba's post office, however, Navajos Barbara and Wayne approach us and invite us to their home. The bikes are a source of conversation, and we look very nonthreatening—a family with young children on heavily loaded tandems. We're eager to get to know Native Americans. This is one of the joys of traveling by bike as opposed to hiking in the wilderness. The pace allows us to meet local people and get a better feel of the country we are traveling through.

We find Barbara and most of her eight children sitting on an old sofa outside a modular home, under the shade of a tin-roofed shelter. Barbara has long dark hair and wears designer eyeglasses and an oversized T-shirt. Her children have large dark eyes; there's dried snot under their noses, and they walk around in the dirt barefoot or in stocking feet. They watch us intently and smile shyly when we catch them watching. An American flag has been put up to welcome us. I tell her that the New Mexico sun is hard on us, and she laughs when I push up my wide silver bracelet to show how pale my skin is underneath.

After we unload our gear, our children run off to play hide-and-seek with the five young children—a universal game regardless of the language barrier. Although Navajo children learn English once they go to school, Navajo is the preferred language among all ages. Here on their native soil, they speak Navajo just as their ancestors have for hundreds of years, and English is a second language. The Navajo language is complex, learned through extensive exposure and training. Used as a code by the Marines during World War II, it stymied even the skilled Japanese code breakers. By 1945 there were up to 450 Navajos serving in the Marines, trained Navajo code talkers. They could orally decode a three-line message in twenty seconds, whereas a state-of-the-art machine needed thirty minutes. Even though Major Howard Connor, Fifth Marine Division signal officer, reported that "were it not for the Navajos, the Marines would never have taken Iwo Jima," it was not until recently that they gained recognition from the United States government and the public. The ancient Navajos said the Diné (the Navajo word for the tribe) would one day save the world. It is ironic that the same language that the Bureau of Indian Affairs tried to stop them from speaking many years ago helped the United States win a war.

This is the same language I listen to as I tell my kids to watch out for the barbed-wire clothesline that hangs dangerously at eye level. In the kitchen, Barbara shows me how to make fry bread. I watch as she mixes the dough and shapes the circles of bread with her hands, then pokes the air bubbles in the bread as it browns in the bubbling fat. While she works, she tells me that many Navajos still practice the old ways, despite religious groups who have come in to establish churches and teach them "a better way." Some still live in hogans, take sweat baths, and hold dances for the sick, and there are medicine women who still practice. I peel a ten-pound bag of potatoes while I listen, not sure if this and fry bread are all that's on the menu. I steal glances around the house and feel sheepish seeing the broken screens and doors, duct-taped windows, and Scotch-taped countertops. We must appear incredibly wealthy to them.

Streams of relatives stop in and eat in front of the TV. Old women wear huge turquoise necklaces and full cotton skirts. They pretend I'm not here. I'm not sure why, but I respect their space. The men who can speak English sit outside with Todd, telling stories of the land and their people. Although we feel welcome, we are visitors in this land. The older girls take our tandems and peddle the dirt roads of the neighborhood, giving smaller children rides on the second seat.

As the sun goes down, Barbara takes me on a walk to her favorite lookout point. We pass her relatives' broken-down trailers and modular homes. She recalls matter-of-factly a brother who abandoned his family, a sister-in-law who is in jail, a young boy who's just been murdered in a fight. Poverty, alcoholism, and unemployment define their lives. Then she proudly points out sacred peaks, sandstone cliffs, pastel bluffs, all radiating beautiful color in this evening light.

As we load up our bikes the next day, Barbara sorts through her children's things for presents to send us off with: a too-large blouse for Sierra, a broken toy for Bryce. Our whole family is quiet after this impoverished potlatch, for we're feeling so many emotions and trying to make sense of them. Even though our material things have been pared down to the basic essentials on this bike trip, we feel tremendously wealthy next to our new friends. Yet at the same time, with our high-tech gear and equipment, we feel indulged and ashamed. We all have a new reference point of wealth, even my six-year-old, as we head out across the reservation road.

WE REALIZE we have left the reservation when we see a truck driven by a redheaded, bearded man with a milk-colored face who doesn't wave! Nearly every Navajo we passed in these past two days waved at us. We immediately miss their handsome dark faces and slick black hair. Their friendliness.

We find the town of Ambrosia Lake, our first point of reference after leaving the reservation, to be far from friendly too. "Surely it must have at least a soda machine at a gas station," our Road Boss tells us after studying the map. But we find only two boarded-up houses and a dried-up settling pond for heavy metals from a nearby mine. I flag down a car to ask directions and inquire about our chances for refreshments.

"There's a bar five miles down the road."

"Will they have cheeseburgers?" Bryce asks me. "I'm dying for one."

"Absolutely. Beer drinkers get hungry too."

The kids crank their pedals into high gear as we search the road ahead for the mileage signs, announcing that we've ticked off one more mile and are that much closer to filling our stomachs. It always amazes me how quickly the bike rolls along when our children decide to really push. Otherwise their feet just spin, and sometimes Bryce takes his feet completely out of the pedals.

Our rush is in vain, however, for at the bar we find only jerky (no thanks, too much like trail food) and tiny bags of chips. We buy close to a dozen. Since the kids can't sit at the bar, we stand, shoving our thumbs and index fingers deep into the corners of the bags for the last crumbs and licking our fingers for the salt. Some mining executives are here for an after-work beer and find us amusing.

"Don't any of you guys have a half-eaten lunch in your truck cab?" I ask. We have enough food to get by, but after weeks on the trail and road, dry energy bars taste an awful lot like sawdust. And at this point in our journey, all our body fat is gone and we fight constant hunger.

"I have a cucumber from my garden," one man announces (a prize, for in this arid country all gardens must be heavily irrigated).

"I'll take it!"

Carl, the gardener, is also a cyclist and understands our hunger. He tells us of a good spot to camp nearby, on Bureau of Land Management land.

After we set up camp, I put water on for instant potatoes and begin to cut up the cucumber. The kids are drawing—Bryce, mountains of cheeseburgers. I turn at the sound of a four-wheel drive truck moving slowly across the desert toward our camp. Carl hops out and says, "Let's go to town for dinner. I know a place that makes great cheeseburgers."

Bryce's mouth drops open. "Mom, I created my own reality! I wanted a cheeseburger and now I'm going to get one!" Carl lives in the nearby town of Grants, our next resupply. He invites us to use his home when we get there, for his family is out of town visiting relatives and he was wondering how he was going to pass the time.

I tell the kids that this is the nature of an adventure. You never know what is going to happen, who you are going to meet, where you will end up. You have the tough parts, but you also have these great surprises. "Live an unpredictable life." This is the kind of stuff I love most about this lifestyle.

When we enter the post office in Grants the next day, the postmistress, Michele Ray, greets us like long-lost friends. "You must be Cindy, and you must be Todd, and these must be the children. We're been waiting for you for *years*! I would have died if I'd missed you."

She tries to talk us into coming to her house tonight, since her extended family is having a cookout, but we don't want to ride the extra miles to get out of town, and we already told Carl we'd come. She gives the kids DumDum lollipops and then tells them to take the whole bag—of a hundred! We hate to turn down all her offers, because she sure makes us feel welcome.

In the town park we meet two other "travelers," two old Navajo code talkers from the war. They ask if we have any money to buy food, and we happily pull out our lunch bag and load them up with our healthful fat-free blueberry bars, which we bought in excess. Trail mix, nuts—we try to give it all to them, remembering how the boys in the bar shared with us and feeling happy to have the opportunity to share with someone even more needy than we are. But it quickly becomes clear that they are not excited about our food. They take just a few bars and suggest we leave the rest at the St. Vincent de Paul food bank across the road. I suppose they were really hoping for some cash for a bottle of wine.

Carl completely opens his home to us: shower, laundry, VCR kiddie tapes. We take him out to dinner the next night and spend a very enjoyable evening talking hunting and photography and sharing our love of the mountains. While I look at Carl's kind face— tanned skin, a bit balding—the kids stare at the large wolf tattoo on his calf, which is now visible since he's wearing shorts. He flexes his muscle for them and the tattoo moves, looking as if it has come to life.

"My wife will never believe this," he admits. "I'm really a shy, quiet guy, and I've never done anything like this before, but I've had a great time." We invite him to our home if he's ever out that way or just wants to visit Pennsylvania. Rarely does someone like this take you up on your invitation, but you extend it anyway. Mostly these people are there for us in the moment and it's enough for them. Reciprocating is not what it's all about, at least not "direct" reciprocation. Todd and I will continue the flow of goodwill and take some other needy stranger home farther on down the line, perhaps from the nearby Appalachian Trail. We'll repay the kindness indirectly and complete the circle.

I PAUSE to wait for the boys after I cross a highway bridge outside Grants, New Mexico. Todd steers his long rig around the corner, and from this distance it doesn't even look like a bike. It seems like some other kind of machine. With fourteen feet of bike and connected trailer, you have to take wide turns like a tractor-trailer. The narrow silhouette when viewed from the front belies the actual size of this parade float. No wonder people look at us as we roll by and remember us. They don't see what's coming at them right away: first a person on a bike, then another person attached, then a trailer. In a few minutes another similar contraption cruises by carrying the opposite sex, and they probably wait a few moments expecting a red caboose. People wave a lot. I think they see us on consecutive days as they travel back and forth to work. People travel long distances here, and it takes us considerably longer to cover the same ground on a bike. I often tip my helmet back on downhills to get the wind moving through my sweaty hair. Folks driving the opposite direction think I'm gesturing hello. As friendly as I am, I don't take my hands off those handlebars to say hello every time a vehicle passes.

A little south of Grants, in the northwest quadrant of the state, we enter El Malpais National Monument. *El malpaís* means "the badlands" or "the bad country" in Spanish, and Todd would have to agree. It's here that he experiences his worst day of this section of the trip (although it's my best). For forty miles our route takes us along the base of five-hundred-foot, golden sandstone bluffs. The wind and weather have carved hollows and caves in the smooth rock. This is the first time we really feel the land close to us. It was always out there—across wide, windswept expanses—and I didn't realize how much I craved that contact and intimacy. Contrasting with this smoothness is a sharp black lava flow on our other side, which poured out of nearby McCarty's Cone two to three thousand years ago. When we come to a stretch of road that is lined with brilliant yellow black-eyed Susans, I feel I must take a picture. As I ask Todd to turn around for various shots, he grows more and more vexed. His trailer is loaded with thirty extra pounds of water for our dry camp tonight, totaling well over a hundred pounds. Making a sharp turn with his cumbersome load is like trying to get a small herd of cows to execute a graceful arabesque. If he gets off to walk, his single-wheel trailer wants to pull his entire bike over. It's a struggle, but these are probably my best shots of the entire state.

When we pull over at La Ventana Natural Arch to hike the short side trail, Road Boss stays behind, craving some time alone, something he rarely gets. La Ventana is the largest of New Mexico's readily reached natural arches. From its vantage point we can view the country as seen by the ancient Anasazi, whose artifacts lie scattered throughout this culturally rich land. The Anasazi used this area to gather herbs and medicines, renew ties, and pay respects, traditions that continue today with their descendants the Acoma, Zuni, and Laguna. We camp at the Narrows, where lava flowed very close to the cliffs. The children scramble up rocks to check out a cliff dwelling and thrill to see an obsidian arrowhead and a painted pottery shard lying in the sand. We sit in the sandy dirt of the dwelling and gaze out over the unchanging New Mexico landscape. We no longer feel like strangers here. We fit our fingertips into the thousand-year-old Anasazi prints, pressed into the hardened clay around the rocks of their home. We run our hands along the cracks in the stone. We try to feel something real, something true, try to make a tactile connection. Our fingers fit the prints perfectly, snug and comfortable.

AFTER ALL these years on the Continental Divide, on this final section of our journey I am catching a glimpse of how our children have grown and matured. Tandem cycling is showing us that they can contribute much more than just their loving presence. I *need* my daughter's strength to help me make it to the Mexican border. This changes the entire dynamics of our relationship. It makes us interdependent. It's the first glimpse of our going beyond the mother-daughter roles. And I can tell she appreciates the new level of respect I am giving her.

My stoker is also showing me how to have more fun. When we pause at the top of a long hill and see the road stretch over the land, mesas backlit with light, wind blowing, feeling so excited about the long roll, she reminds me how to scream with delight. We hear a scream answer us, and when we turn back to look at the mesa top, two boys thrust their arms in the air with the thumbs-up sign. They know the joy we're feeling.

I sometimes forget that one of a child's "needs" is having fun. The children aren't motivated by the long-term goal but live in the moment. They have battles by shooting rubber bands off their water bottles. They find a lizard and carry it around in a shirt, singing to it. They call it Cranberry Small because it's small and they're eating dried cranberries when they find it. They discover a long line of ants, trace them to their hole in the earth, and feed them breadcrumbs. But it's on our afternoon at the "swimming pool" that they really make do with what they find and have a blast.

"There's a stock tank a few miles from here," Todd announces. "If the windmill is working and the cows haven't polluted it, we may be able to go for a swim."

"Yippee!" the kids scream. Our fearless leader pores over the maps at every break, looking for tiny settlements that may support a soda machine or for windmills marked on the map. He usually waits until the last possible moment to announce their existence so we don't build up false expectations or, worse yet, use him as a scapegoat for our disappointment. Sure enough, no cattle are in sight, and the twenty-foot-wide, concrete-lined circular tank is full of water—brilliant blue reflecting the huge New Mexico sky like a precious liquid stone. I stick my hand in the tank to feel the water and it's cool. We rip off our clothing. Todd takes some coaxing, but I win because I'm quick to point out that we haven't seen a vehicle on this dirt road all day. Who would care anyway? The kids jump in and find an old board to use as a toy. They push it across the tank, having races. They splash and giggle with so much pleasure that it does my heart good. Long green plants are growing on the bottom of the tank, and the kids pull them out with their feet, pretending they're monsters. The damp organic smell pricks our nostrils and makes us aware that we haven't smelled anything fresh and wet in many days.

Every now and then a breeze turns the long galvanized blades of the windmill and startles us as the screeching piston clanks up and down, spewing cold water from the pipe. Todd and I sit in the scant shade cast by the windmill's arms. The breeze is blowing on my naked body. It feels so good to have those horrid tight cycling shorts off. We snack on fabulous tasting sour cream waffle chips and I lick the salt off my lips. Right now, I feel very happy.

Our next resupply after Grants is Pie Town, a tiny town famous for its home-baked pies. Grants and Pie Town are only a few days apart (eighty-two miles), but when Todd planned our resupplys, he didn't want to make us carry a lot of food and pull unnecessary weight. At this point we're about three hundred miles from the Mexican border, a little more than halfway into our ride, and nine days on the road.

Pie Town's pies have been the topic of conversation for many days of cycling. "Which kind are you eating first? Second? Before dinner or after? With ice cream or without? Warmed up or cold?" It helps keep our minds occupied, because this stretch is challenging, with ups and downs on sandy roads. The sand is deep in the low stretches and makes us lose control of steering. Our tires stop dead. Sierra and I fall over more than once.

When we pull into town, we discover that the restaurant closed down just yesterday! It was also the grocery store where we had planned to resupply for the next stretch. No food anywhere. To top it off, it's raining like crazy and the dirt roads we are riding on are now impassable with deep mud. We resort to hanging out in a dismal park pavilion, eating stale trail mix.

"I wish someone would take me home and feed me dinner," I whine.

Soon the rain stops, a brilliant double rainbow appears, and a truck pulls up. The driver says, "Why don't you folks come to our house for dinner? My wife just put a pork roast in the oven." He gives us directions to his house and tells us to look for the toasters in the trees. We don't know what he's talking about, but it's evident when we reach the right house. A dozen shiny toasters hang in the two trees that mark the entrance to their front yard, like ornaments on strings.

When we walk in the door, the comforting smell of food buoys our sullen spirits. A woman greets us wearing a T-shirt that says "No rain. No rainbows." Sierra's eyes widen. She gets it. You can't have one without the other. Like Bryce's cheeseburgers, if you want something badly enough, you can sometimes will it into happening.

WHEN I LIE in my sleeping bag at night, I run my hands over my body and feel my muscles changing. My midriff, shoulders, back, and arms are all getting tighter. You think you are in good shape until you change to a new sport. Then you discover muscles you didn't even know existed.

We were afraid our butt muscles would rebel since we couldn't train while we were hiking, but we haven't experienced even five minutes of discomfort. Between the wide gel seats that we special-ordered, the springs under our seats, and the fact that we walk a few miles every day, we may never get saddle sore.

Our hands, however, absolutely kill us. I constantly move mine into different positions on my handlebars and rotate and twist them and shake them out while I ride to try to relieve some of the ache. The jarring from rough gravel roads is the worst.

My toes feel tingly during the day from not being able to move them in my toe baskets. I usually take my shoes off a few times a day to improve my circulation, but if I skip doing it, my toe tips turn an alarming waxy white from lack of blood.

Despite these discomforts, we are feeling exceptionally fit. We all have our moments; mornings are Sierra's worst time. She often doesn't "feel" like biking, but this is a job that must be completed every day; the miles must get covered. There is some flexibility in our schedule, but given the unpredictability of weather, road conditions, and mechanical and physical problems, we don't have the luxury of taking unplanned days off. She takes out her frustrations on me, since this is "Mom's job." She jerks the pedals around fast because she "wants to get it over with so she can do something fun." She shakes the bike when she gets angry with me, which is extremely dangerous. It's interesting to be "chained together" during an argument. We can't walk away. We have to work it out. I try to talk, she snaps, then I refuse to communicate until she's ready to change her foul mood.

Then she announces she's hungry. She barely ate anything at breakfast because she's not a morning eater. *Now* her poor mood makes sense, so I yell back to the boys that we're taking a break. Todd doesn't like to stop so soon after we shove off, but you must have fuel in the tank before you can perform. Functioning with a low blood-sugar level while trying to pull a steep hill is a good reason for a deteriorated mood.

We work hard out here to ferret out each others' problems. It's tough to be in this close contact and expect to work together if there isn't harmony much of the time. In our other life we can send a kid to his room or go out for a walk to get away from a disagreeable spouse. It's more obvious that "stuff" doesn't go away out here. We don't have the opportunity to avoid it or bury it. We must deal with things or we'll never get to Mexico. And getting to Mexico happily is even more of a challenge.

My worst day comes when Todd announces we are going to take a shortcut. From my experience of following him as he bushwhacks over a mountain to save a mile a two, I've become a firm believer in the philosophy that the shortest distance between two points is always *on the trail*. But being the "good wife" of the Road Boss that I am, I consent, albeit warily. The children and I have our hearts set on a motel in the town of Reserve, and he promises he will have us there sooner.

Within the first half mile, I am miserable. When I begin to complain, Todd asks in an exasperated tone, "Do you want to turn around?"

As unhappy as I am with this decision, I don't like to go against Todd's decisions because I know he has put a lot of thought into them, and he usually makes good choices. In our marriage he often lets me have my way because he is so easygoing. The tables are turned on the trail, however, and I usually defer to his decisions. This time I'm not doing it very graciously.

I tell the kids this probably kills our chances of reaching the motel tonight, and we stage a mutiny. Three against one.

The dirt road is so steep and rocky that I begin to have serious doubts about whether I can do it. The kids try to help push the trailer, but I tell them to save their strength. My eyes fill with tears. Todd sarcastically asks if I think he should hook my entire rig to his; he'll pull them both up. I am grateful I have sunglasses on so I can cry and not let him see.

Once we reach the summit, I have to concentrate hard to aim my front tire as I weave around rocks and avoid ditches and ruts. It's hard to determine how much to brake on downhills before I lose control. It's hard enough to know how much to brake under ideal conditions, and this road is closer to a cheese grater than a thoroughfare. Sierra and I dump the bike three times—that's how rough it is. One time the trailer flips first and then throws the bike over, but lucky for us we're not hurt. Some hills are so steep I can't risk riding, then it's another challenge to hold all that weight *back* so it doesn't take off down the mountain without me. My hands are killing me from trying to balance the bike and keeping a death grip on the brakes. I'm so upset I can't even look at Todd. Another famous shortcut! We are exchanging a five-mile uphill on blacktop for four hours of rocky dirt road.

Just before we join up with the blacktop, Sierra announces that she left her shirt back at the last break. Todd offers to go back to find it, which is a long way. After he leaves, she finds it in a stuff sack, and we yell across the canyon for him to come back. We think he'll be fuming once he returns, but actually he enjoys the time away from the three of us. We feel as if he's done penance for subjecting us to this horrendous shortcut.

Somehow we make it to the motel. As I'm lying in bed, massaging my thigh muscles, Road Boss comments, "Your muscles are *still* getting sore? I'm shocked! That must mean your muscles are still developing. Mine stopped developing a long time ago." I regard him with a mixture of disgust and amusement and say, "I don't want to have this conversation."

WE'VE NOW covered the greater part of this challenging state and are heading into southern New Mexico. We'll soon be in Silver City, our last resupply, and from there it's only a few hot days to the border and the very end of this five-year journey. Every day seems to grow hotter. Sweat stings my eyes, and I constantly swab my brow with the back of my cotton-crocheted gloves. Our bread sits on top of everything in the trailer, just underneath the plastic cover. We make grilled cheese sandwiches without firing up the stove; the cheese melts on its own. Todd takes me by surprise and squirts my back with water. It makes me scream. Against my cool, perspiring skin, it feels scalding. Even racing down mountains, the air is not refreshing. It's more like blasts from a furnace.

The creatures we encounter are getting more hostile. At one lunch break, the biting red ants are so vicious that if we want to sit down we have to watch for them on our shoes and constantly stamp them off. We can't even sit in the middle of the gravel road, for it's infested too, so we end up walking in circles while we eat.

We've also had some really challenging rides on dirt roads lately. One stretch is being graded *while* we ride. We plow right through loose sandy soil that makes our tires behave as if we're on a runaway truck ramp. On one steep downhill, I feel my trailer fishtailing only to discover that one of the tires has lost air. Times like this remind me how easy it would be to wipe out. Sierra and I could experience a lot more than road rash if this big rig went down on a fast incline. Todd has plowed into me more than once too, nearly causing them to wreck. He follows awfully close sometimes, perhaps subconsciously prodding me along. If he goes first, whether on a foot trail or on a bike, his pace is so much faster that he soon leaves us in the dust, forgotten. Unfortunately for him, his place in line has always been behind his lovely wife or we would no longer be together as a family—even perhaps in the long-term sense! We haven't quite mastered hand signals, so after a few collisions he asks me to announce when I am going to stop.

Our calves and shins are covered with black chain grease from saving our bikes from toppling. We spit on our skin trying to wash it away, but we just end up smearing it around and rubbing it deeper into our pores.

It's a different kind of life out here on the road than on the trail. I have more freedom to look when I'm a passenger in a vehicle than when I'm piloting this tandem. On a hill, you get into a kind of meditation—concentrating, helping yourself get up it. It's work. If you're hiking you can pause to breathe, look around, take in the view. You can't hop off this bike easily. There are toe baskets to negotiate, a child to balance, weight to hold back on the inclines. It must be even more tedious for the stoker, never knowing what's in front. Since Sierra spends most of her days staring at my back, I suppose I should at least let her pick out my shirts.

Taking photographs is an extreme challenge. Even on downhills I must think about not losing control of the bike. I must *always* be careful not to lose control of that bike. On roads, I look for holes, ditches, and debris. I notice cans, bottles, and trash, bits of glass, and even sharp stones. I watch the shoulder, paying attention to where I can get over if a vehicle squeezes us. Todd spends much of his time looking in his rearview mirror to alert me to what is coming from behind. If an approaching vehicle will pass at the exact moment another is coming from behind, Todd yells "Squeeze!," which means I am to get myself onto the shoulder, no matter what shape it's in. It seems to be an unconscious trait in drivers everywhere that whenever two motorists are approaching a cyclist from opposite directions, the cars will slow down or speed up so both pass the bicycle at the same time, thus squeezing it off the road. Ask any bike rider. There are very few times we can lose ourselves in the countryside. We take glances sometimes. We never forget about the road.

We spend a lot of time in the ditches, taking breaks along with trash and car parts. We're either in town, leaving town, heading for town, or looking for that store. These are the activities that occupy us.

For those in love with the machine that the bicycle is or those who are attempting to cover ground quickly, particularly over land that proves less than friendly, as we are, two-wheeled travel is the way to go. But I miss my connection with the land. I miss hiking.

We're looking fried from the sun, heat, wind, and road dirt as we roll into Silver City, New Mexico. We're looking for a motel, a good meal, and a long shower. But our family on wheels is just the spark a couple from New Zealand have been looking for. They've ridden their bikes from Portland, Oregon, to Montana, then hopped on the Great Divide Mountain Bike Trail and covered over two thousand miles to arrive at this point in Silver City. But when they meet us they've just made the decision to pack it in. It's been too hard, they say, and rumor has it the last few days from Silver City to the Mexican border are the worst of all. But we've just restored their hope. When they see our family with little children roll into town, they decide they can make it too.

We feel proud. Sometimes we wonder if we're just too soft, if perhaps things aren't as difficult as we're making them out to be. This state, more than any other on this long journey, is showing us that it might not always be easy, but it is always worthwhile. Mexico, here we come!

25

The Last Days
SEPTEMBER 22, 1998

What they had done, what they had seen, heard, felt, feared—the places, the sounds, the colors, the cold, the darkness, the emptiness, the bleakness, the beauty. Till they died this stream of memory would set them apart, if imperceptibly to anyone but themselves, from everyone else. For they had crossed the continent and come back, the first of all.
                                            —BERNARD DE VOTO

THE LAST 125 miles from Silver City to the Mexican border cross the Chihuahuan Desert, highest and largest of the North American deserts. We see roadrunners zipping across the road, big black, hairy tarantulas creeping slowly, and more varieties of cactus growing than an easterner could imagine existed. We see dust devils: wind swirling the sand into miniature tornadoes across the open land. Giant grasshoppers (three inches long) lie dead along the road. Others are sucking the juices from the dead ones. Giant hares (Bryce thought they were baby deer) run into the brush, with ears so large, pink, and translucent that we can see sunlight shining through them. Road-killed rabbits last mere hours before the buzzards pick their bones clean. The birds fly across the sun, making large dark shadows on the ground. Goathead thorns are everywhere, flattening our tires in seconds. Thorns grow on every kind of vegetation. But the land and the climate are less daunting to me now. The end is in sight. The last leg of a journey is often characterized by confidence and gratitude.

One trick to make this day more bearable was packing all our water bottles with ice cubes from the motel ice machine. We also filled our water bladder with ice, pushing cube after cube into the small hole before topping everything off with water. Todd put them all in a box in the trailer and wrapped them with plastic as insulation. We felt pretty silly making close to a dozen trips to the ice machine, which sat right next to the main desk. The owner waved every time but, thank goodness, never asked why we were cleaning out the machine.

Because we are doing longer days to get to the border, the hours spent in the saddle are harder than usual. Todd and I zone out as we ride, but the kids need creative ways to entertain themselves. Bryce is now into tongue twisters. Sometimes he does "circus acts" on the bike—riding with his feet on the seat and his butt pushed in the air or straddling his seat while his butt sits on the pannier rack. (Todd has great patience, and balance!)

Bob Riley is planning to meet us with his motor home on our last day, to celebrate our completion and drive us back up to our truck, trailer, and llamas in Colorado. It'll take him two days to drive from his Colorado home pulling his stock trailer—not for our llamas, but for our long bikes. We tried to get him to join us in this new sport, but he swore he'd never get his butt on a bike. "But Bob," we moaned, "how can we finish this huge goal without you? You, more than anyone, have helped us make it a reality." He was easily persuaded to meet us for the grand finale and solve the problem of how to get back once we got to that remote border.

The kids spend a lot of energy thinking about exactly when we will see him, where we will be, what we'll be doing, what we'll do afterward. They love to speculate and dream, and they have whiled away many miles out here by thinking about the future in great detail. Sierra loves to talk about the pygmy goat she'd love to get, but she's far from persuading her parents. She plans all the details—his shed, his name, where she'll take him for walks, the jobs she'll do to support him. She goes on and on planning the details of her next Halloween costume or a birthday party she'd like to have or Brownie Scout outings. These topics get stretched for days and sometimes *weeks* of discussion. It's fatiguing, especially if I'm trying to steer or climb a hill or attempt to look out at the land zipping by. Sierra loves to be entertained, and it's sometimes a great chore to do it for her. But we all love to talk about seeing Bob.

Sierra is having an exceptionally hard day today. The heat is oppressive; she wants to take a break *now*, and I want to wait for shade. She doesn't want to walk up hills. When she goes to relieve herself, she manages to get a sharp thorn in her hand. She comes crying to Bryce and me as we sit on break with our boots off.

Suddenly we hear an unfamiliar sound, a motor on this remote dirt road that's been devoid of traffic all day. Our tandems are propped against the cattle guard, one on each side, and will not allow any vehicle to pass. I hobble over to move them, but I'm shocked when I see a motor home creeping down the narrow road. This is a four-wheel-drive road with loose sand that stops bicycle tires in their tracks. And wait, there's a trailer being pulled behind it! Why, it's Bob, two days early! We all run to him, screaming so loud we're hoarse. I pick up barefoot Bryce and swing him across the cattle guard. He decided to rescue us early and will accompany us these last days to the border. He is our savior, our angel, as he's been so many times before on this journey.

Now it feels as if it's over. Now we know we'll make it. We jabber on excitedly about the trip, laughing about our difficulties. He comments on the heat and we say, "You haven't felt anything yet!"

As we talk, he pours us glasses of orange juice—*with ice!*—while we unhook the trailers, unload the panniers, and throw it all into the motor home. From now on we're rolling free. No more weight, all the way to the border. We say good-bye and instruct him to stop every ten miles to meet us for a break.

We are immediately amazed at how easy it is to roll over the land with unladen bikes. We speed effortlessly without the weight. "I like this bike riding stuff!" I announce, and everyone agrees. We haven't felt this free since that twenty-mile downhill on our very first day. In a matter of seconds my mind starts to review other cycling adventures we might pursue. This is a natural result of an adventure's conclusion—planning the next, making sure there will be a next.

The land miraculously looks more inviting than we've ever seen it. What is really happening is that my vision is becoming clearer. It's not fogged over with daily discomfort. I am finally seeing this country for what it truly is—unique and beautiful in its own right. There are high mountains in the distance, but they are bare of any vegetation, even shrubs. There are only rocks and dirt. They are a dreamy light blue, the color of air. Yuccas stand tall and pale, and green grass covers the desert floor. Prickly pear cacti reach the size of small trees down here and are covered with oblong magenta fruits. We peel them carefully to avoid getting their prickers in our fingers and enjoy their tangy sour pear flavor.

But Bob does even better than this in the refreshment line. On one stretch he has Popsicles waiting for us. On another stretch he pops a Sara Lee coffeecake into his motor home's oven while we ride and Bryce comments, "Bob is a helluva cook!"

Todd and I are shocked by his language, but we say nothing. After all, he's out here pulling his weight like an adult through this desert land.

Bob's large motor home provides shade when the sun's shadows are long in the early part of the day. When the sun is blazing overhead, we go into the air-conditioned, carpeted living room, stretch out on the floor, and sip iced drinks. As we ride, we stare ahead for the boxy white shape on the horizon, for that's the sign that it's break time! The kids are in heaven. They say, once again, that we created our own reality. We wanted him to come, so he came.

Outside the tiny town of Hachita, New Mexico, there's a highway sign telling how far it is to the border of Mexico—forty-five miles. But it also tells how long it takes to get there. If you can't make it by 4:00 P.M. when the border police go home, don't bother coming. This stretch of New Mexico highway *really* gets deserted, because there is nothing between here and there. The folks in Hachita live at the end of the line. Tomorrow is our last day on the Continental Divide. But before we make history, we are spending the night in this interesting town of seventy-eight people to rest up for the big day.

The center of life here is a restaurant called the Egg Nest. Besides making hamburgers, the owners have a business creating all kinds of things out of blown-out birds' eggs, from tiny to huge. Most of them have three-dimensional miniature scenes inside, and the larger ostrich eggs even have tiny pumps to create waterfalls and fountains. There are hundreds inside the restaurant's adjoining showroom, and they ship them around the country, for the population of Hachita certainly can't support them. A few crafters work here, all huge of body. One woman has cut long slits in her white anklets so they can expand around her wide ankles. The white cotton hangs down in flaps around her shoes. In our guidebook this establishment is listed as offering groceries. When we ask if there's anything besides the bags of chips and sodas that we see at the cash register, the owner invites us to come behind the scenes into the kitchen. "Anything on the shelves or in the fridge is for sale."

There is a cat sitting in a wicker basket by the door, but when the kids bend down to pet it they discover it's made of stuffed rabbit fur. On a porch is a large box with a screen wired over it that has "Baby Rattlers" written on the outside. The kids creep over to peer at the contents, which are none other than plastic baby rattles. The toilet paper roll in the bathroom *sings* when you unroll it to get a few squares. We, especially Sierra and Bryce, find this place fascinating.

The couple from New Zealand are here, and the owners kindly grant all of us permission to camp in the scrub grass off to the side of their driveway. Todd has noticed there are an exceptional number of goathead thorns in this area, and he warns the New Zealanders as they begin to roll their bikes off the gravel. The bottoms of our rubber-soled sandals are riddled with the sharp thorns just from walking around their property. We've learned that we can't take our bikes even six inches off the blacktop for fear of getting a flat. But before Todd can even get the words out, Brian's tires go as flat as pancakes. When he examines them, he discovers more than three dozen thorns. The owners say they hope to make their establishment more attractive to folks doing the Continental Divide Trail. They're looking for ideas, for ways to cater to our traveling needs. We tell them they could make a killing here. With their healthy abundance of goathead thorns, they could retire on sales of bicycle tubes alone.

Bryce comes to me in the restaurant, his beautiful blue eyes spilling over with tears, his face distraught. He whispers that he was pulling his water bottle nozzle up with his teeth and it loosened his front tooth so badly that it's just hanging there. It hurts him, and he doesn't know how he can eat his ice cream cone. How is the Tooth Fairy going to find him in a place like Hachita? We write the fairy a note on a toilet paper square, wrap the tooth up, and place it under his pillow, made of a stuff sack full of clothes. Of all times to lose his first tooth—the last night of the Continental Divide Trail.

"THE LAST last day on the Continental Divide Trail," Todd announces as we suit up in our early morning windbreakers, helmets, and bike gloves. In only a few short weeks, this ritual has come to feel so comfortable, so normal.

There is quite a bit of fighting going on between the kids today. There's no traffic, so Todd and I ride side by side to talk about this momentous day. But the children are bored and resentful that we have an adult conversation that doesn't include them. They harass each other to win our attention and entertain themselves. Bryce makes up irritating stories about his sister and says them aloud. In them she might puke, or get eaten by a monster, or poo. She makes faces at him, they stick out their tongues, yell, and begin spitting at each other.

The wind is phenomenal. We are riding on flat ground, but the wind is hitting us head-on with such force that I can't get out of second gear. Todd leaves Sierra and me behind. I yell ahead and ask him to slow down and let me tailgate so he can block the wind and make it easier on me. After only a few miles, I'm exhausted.

On a break, Todd takes his bike three inches off the blacktop and gets a flat. While he's changing it, a Schwann's Frozen Food truck approaches us from the opposite direction—Mexico. He pulls up alongside, turns off the motor right in the lane of "traffic," hops out, and asks what kind of ice cream novelty we'd like. We examine the pictures on the side of his truck and soon find ourselves eating frozen desserts in the desert sun, wondering at our good fortune.

We hop back on our bikes and soon come to a sign stating, "Continental Divide—3,490 feet." We look around for even a hint of an elevation change, but there isn't the slightest rise in the land, only flat desert everywhere. But this is the highest land in this low desert of southern New Mexico, so it still divides the country's waters.

We notice signs warning of flooded roads, and this makes us laugh, for although we know there are moments when it rains out here and the gullies quickly fill with racing torrents, there's no indication that these signs are anything more than a joke.

The cacti are serious. We shiver to think of falling into the long spikes when we hide behind them to relieve ourselves. The folks who inhabited this part of the world evidently were serious in their everyday lives as well. As we move closer to the border, we roll through a wide gap between the Big Hatchet Mountains, so named because a cowboy insulted the cook for making bad coffee back in the 1800s. The cook expressed his displeasure by whacking the cowboy over the head with his hatchet and killing him.

The most fascinating part of our day is watching the mileage markers. When we reach 10, the countdown is on. We're all feeling so proud. These kids have been with us since the very beginning on the Colorado Trail. For five years we've weathered the storms, forded the rivers, crossed the deserts—together. Not for one second did we want to leave them behind. We are finally reaching the border because of *their* perseverance and hard work, not just ours, and because of their continued sense of joy even in the worst conditions. Todd and I could not have arrived here without their help. The highway markers go down: 5, 4, 3, 2, 1! Our chests swell and our eyes fill. Our stokers' arms are raised high in the air as we race to the border while their parents provide steering and balance.

Epilogue

APRIL 2002

FOUR YEARS have passed since we completed the Continental Divide Trail. Sierra is twelve now and Bryce is ten, and I wonder how much they now remember of that journey. They say they miss the big mountains: topping passes, camping out night after night. Todd and I know the journey affected them in a positive way, and that is enough. They are happy in the moment, and we try to ensure that they continue to be stimulated and fulfilled by adventures.

Todd and I felt tired after all that pushing, and we weren't interested in a long expedition for a few years, but that stage is over. Since walking the Triple Crown—the Appalachian Trail, the Pacific Crest Trail, and now the Continental Divide Trail—we look at the whole world as one big outdoor playground to discover.

Recently we've discovered kayak and canoe camping, and get excited thinking about all the "water trails" to explore after so many years of being obsessed with hiking. Both children are strong paddlers and have their own kayaks for short trips. For longer distances, they still travel in tandem boats with their mom and dad.

Bicycling on rail-trails is fun, too, and we've done some nice bike rides on our tandems, like the two-hundred-and-fifty-mile Katy Trail across Missouri. Bob Riley even joined us for that. He swore in New Mexico that "we would never get his butt on a bike," but we proved him wrong. With no more CDT to hike, he had to bend a little or his adventures with the Llama Family would be over.

We've also visited Beth Ellen in Switzerland, where she lived with her husband and daughter for a while, and enjoyed a month-long hike in the Alps with her.

A month in Thailand, hiking in the northern hill-tribe country and paddling in the southern islands, proved to be one of our most memorable adventures and whetted the kids' appetites for world travel.

The llamas have been in semiretirement since we finished the CDT, reduced to pets. Berrick is still hanging in there at twenty years old, and every time we take him out for a day hike, he hums and moans as if we're asking him to scale James Peak again. Summers are hard on him, and he spends the hotter days hanging his head over the water bucket. Jerry and Chips are the only other llamas left; the rest were sold. We'll take those two out for a weeklong backpack this summer as a last hurrah.

This quest and love of the adventuring life has caused some minor problems in our children's school lives. They don't relish large groups of children, preferring small groups of mixed-age people, young to old. Anyone who values them for who they are and treats them as people, not just as kids, is the kind of person they want to be around. Having struggled over rough terrain with friends, found their way cross-country, held hands crossing deep streams, and watched sunsets over undulating mountain ranges in the company of people whom they came to love, they're ambivalent about superficial interactions. None of their classmates understands their lives or can relate to what they've experienced. Usually that's OK, although I worry that our unique lifestyle may cause some social problems further down the line. But I think our kids have the strength and confidence to deal with these, whatever they might be.

Although they are superior athletes, they have no desire to participate in team sports. They see the practices and strings of games as infringements on their spare time, and they wouldn't want to miss out on any adventures that their mother has planned.

The public school that the children attend has been very cooperative. Both kids are high-honor students, and the principal believes their excellent grades are enhanced by all the experiences they have outside the classroom. When we travel, we homeschool. The kids get a nice break and we all make great memories as a family.

They spend a good deal of their time making things and reading. Both children win awards for drawing, writing, photography, science fairs, etc. Sierra is leaning toward science in her future—wildlife or marine biology, or geology and anthropology. Bryce is obsessed with drawing and illustrating books that he writes, and works on his projects many hours each day. They are exceptionally happy children, a fact people often comment on, as if happy children were an oddity today.

Todd and I figure we may only have a few years left before Sierra will resist missing out on something back home (a boyfriend, a job, schoolwork), so we have the next few major family trips planned. But other adventuring families have told me teenagers don't mind making exotic trips with their families. After all, they tell me, how long will it be before Sierra and Bryce can afford to trek the Himalaya or hike the Annapurna Circuit Route with their friends? Until that day, they may as well do it with their family. Both our kids love traveling and really enjoy each other's company. Maybe with that, we can buy a little more time.

I can't help but see many of our children's marvelous attributes as results of their CDT experience. That's where the seeds were planted. Of course, Todd and I set an example by going after the dreams that make us happy, including the huge one of taking our children across the rooftop of the world, regardless of the difficulties. Our kids see that and want equally satisfying lives. They probably won't be long-distance hikers, nor do we care. We just want them to follow their hearts in pursuit of their dreams, as we have done. And it seems as if they're heading in the right direction.

The enormous energy that Todd and I had to put out year after year in order to meet our goal of reaching Mexico had the *potential* to undermine our marriage. Through it all, we learned the importance of paying *a lot* of attention to each other's needs. No couple can afford to get lazy in a marriage, not even while preoccupied with a shared dream. Our marriage is all the stronger for that realization.

Todd had to neglect his huge garden and orchard while we hiked every summer, and he longed to raise a few pigs. Now he spends his "spare time" around our homestead pruning fruit trees, tending to the garden, putting up food, cutting firewood, blacksmithing, and making furniture. He works a few days a week painting houses with a friend and doing some specialized timber framing for contractors. He sometimes feels torn between being a homesteader and a wanderer. I have only gotten more wanderlust in my soul in the passing years. I want to see everything, go everywhere, and do everything, and the kids feel the same. Todd is sometimes a tad reluctant at first, for his heart is quite happy at home. But once he is away from all the chores at the homestead, he is content. No one in the family wants to miss out.

I continue to write magazine articles on outdoor travel and have begun finding great satisfaction writing essays on the more meaningful things in life. An illustrated book on the Continental Divide Trail through Sierra's eyes is in the works. It will give me an opportunity to paint again, using the best from my thousands of slides. I have put together a multimedia presentation on our long journey, which I enjoy showing to groups and organizations. Todd and I also have a special program for schools—slides, our complete camping outfit, and even the llamas, if the show is within driving distance.

Still, we yearn for that adventure into wild country where we don't come out for a long time. Next year we're planning a trip to Alaska and the Northwest Territories, including a five-hundred-mile paddle down the Yukon River (with Timmy Lebling). The year after that, assuming the kids are strong enough to carry a full pack, we'll pick up the CDT at Waterton-Glacier International

Peace Park on the Montana-Alberta border and hike five or six hundred miles of the Canadian Continental Divide Trail, without llamas this time. Wherever we traipse, we hope to feel as at home as we did on the Great Divide, with our children by our sides, as long as we are blessed with their company.

Our greatest satisfaction—besides raising our wonderful children—is sharing the magic that we find out there in the big wild world.

Acknowledgments

I would like to thank some very important people and company sponsors that helped make this adventure and book possible. First off, B.O.B. (Beast of Burden) and Burley for our bike trailers; Buckhorn Llamas for llamas and llama gear; Cascade Designs for our water filter and Therm-a-Rest pads; Kelty for our sleeping bags; Charlie Hackbarth of Mount Sopris Llamas, and Ollie Llamas for llama pack gear; Santana for our tandem mountain bikes; Sierra Designs for a tent and rain gear; and Teva for sport sandals.

A big thank you to the Rocky Mountain Llama and Alpaca Association and to the Northern Rockies Llama Association for shuttling us up and down the entire Continental Divide and hosting us in their homes. We were complete strangers at first but felt like family afterward. Thank you for your trust.

My friends who edited my manuscript: Steve Peck, Nancy Smith, and Maryalice Yakutchik . . . you encouraged me to tell "the rest of the story" and made it shine. Your wisdom, skill, and insight made this book what it is.

Our friends and families, who sent us mail and care packages, offered up prayers and good thoughts for our well-being and safety . . . you were like angels all around us.

For Bob Riley, the most amazingly generous man I have ever met. Every year on the trail, every stretch was made not only "do-able" because of your support but became very special in our memory because of your fine company. No one could be blessed with a better friend. And a big thank-you to your wife Jo, for sharing you with us.

For our "speechless brothers," the llamas, who carried our gear and our children across the greatest trail. For our wanderlust friends who made time in their busy lives, even leaving spouses and children, to share the miles, and keep us company. The memories will last our lifetime.

And my family: Todd, Sierra, and Bryce, who persevered and followed that crest up and down ridges, across rivers and deserts, year after year, knowing we had to finish the trail "before Mom can write her book." You gave me a reason for being there and you are the best trail companions (and life companions) a person could ask for. I'd go anywhere with you.

To LEARN more about llamas and hiking with them, go to www. llamas.org.

You can contact me at 85 Red Mountain Lane, New Ringgold, PA, 17960.